Deployment Guide

SUSE Linux Enterprise Server 12 SP3

Deployment Guide

SUSE Linux Enterprise Server 12 SP3

Shows how to install single or multiple systems and how to exploit the product inherent capabilities for a deployment infrastructure. Choose from various approaches, ranging from a local installation or a network installation server to a mass deployment using a remote-controlled, highly-customized, and automated installation technique.

Publication Date: September 01, 2017

SUSE LLC
10 Canal Park Drive
Suite 200
Cambridge MA 02141
USA
https://www.suse.com/documentation ↗

Changes to original document: page numbers added to top right corner of book.

Contents

About This Guide

Installations of SUSE Linux Enterprise Server are possible in different ways. It is impossible to cover all combinations of boot, or installation server, automated installations or deploying images. This manual should help with selecting the appropriate method of deployment for your installation.

Part I, "Installation Preparation"

> The standard deployment instructions differ depending on the architecture used. For differences and requirements regarding the architecture, see this part.

Part II, "The Installation Workflow"

> Most tasks that are needed during installations are described here. This includes the manual setup of your computer and installation of additional software.

Part III, "Setting Up an Installation Server"

> SUSE® Linux Enterprise Server can be installed in different ways. Apart from the usual media installation, you can choose from various network-based approaches. This part describes setting up an installation server and how to prepare the boot of the target system for installation.

Part IV, "Remote Installation"

> This part introduces the most common installation scenarios for remote installations. While some still require user interaction or some degree of physical access to the target system, others are completely automated and hands-off. Learn which approach is best for your scenario.

Part V, "Initial System Configuration"

> Learn how to configure your system after installation. This part covers common tasks like setting up hardware components, installing or removing software, managing users, or changing settings with YaST.

Part VI, "Updating and Upgrading SUSE Linux Enterprise"

> This part will give you some background information on terminology, SUSE product lifecycles and Service Pack releases, and recommended upgrade policies.

1 Required Background

To keep the scope of these guidelines manageable, certain technical assumptions have been made:

- You have some computer experience and are familiar with common technical terms.

- You are familiar with the documentation for your system and the network on which it runs.

- You have a basic understanding of Linux systems.

2 Available Documentation

 Note: Online Documentation and Latest Updates

Documentation for our products is available at http://www.suse.com/documentation/ ↗, where you can also find the latest updates, and browse or download the documentation in various formats.

In addition, the product documentation is usually available in your installed system under `/usr/share/doc/manual`.

The following documentation is available for this product:

Article "Installation Quick Start"

Lists the system requirements and guides you step-by-step through the installation of SUSE Linux Enterprise Server from DVD, or from an ISO image.

Deployment Guide

Shows how to install single or multiple systems and how to exploit the product inherent capabilities for a deployment infrastructure. Choose from various approaches, ranging from a local installation or a network installation server to a mass deployment using a remote-controlled, highly-customized, and automated installation technique.

Book "Administration Guide"

Covers system administration tasks like maintaining, monitoring and customizing an initially installed system.

Book "Virtualization Guide"

Describes virtualization technology in general, and introduces libvirt—the unified interface to virtualization—and detailed information on specific hypervisors.

Book "Storage Administration Guide"

Provides information about how to manage storage devices on a SUSE Linux Enterprise Server.

Book "AutoYaST"

AutoYaST is a system for unattended mass deployment SUSE Linux Enterprise Server systems using an AutoYaST profile containing installation and configuration data. The manual guides you through the basic steps of auto-installation: preparation, installation, and configuration.

Book "Security Guide"

Introduces basic concepts of system security, covering both local and network security aspects. Shows how to use the product inherent security software like AppArmor or the auditing system that reliably collects information about any security-relevant events.

Book "Security and Hardening Guide"

Deals with the particulars of installing and setting up a secure SUSE Linux Enterprise Server, and additional post-installation processes required to further secure and harden that installation. Supports the administrator with security-related choices and decisions.

Book "System Analysis and Tuning Guide"

An administrator's guide for problem detection, resolution and optimization. Find how to inspect and optimize your system by means of monitoring tools and how to efficiently manage resources. Also contains an overview of common problems and solutions and of additional help and documentation resources.

Book "Subscription Management Tool for SLES 12 SP3"

An administrator's guide to Subscription Management Tool—a proxy system for SUSE Customer Center with repository and registration targets. Learn how to install and configure a local SMT server, mirror and manage repositories, manage client machines, and configure clients to use SMT.

Book "GNOME User Guide"

Introduces the GNOME desktop of SUSE Linux Enterprise Server. It guides you through using and configuring the desktop and helps you perform key tasks. It is intended mainly for end users who want to make efficient use of GNOME as their default desktop.

3 Feedback

Several feedback channels are available:

Bugs and Enhancement Requests

For services and support options available for your product, refer to http://www.suse.com/support/ ↗.

Help for openSUSE is provided by the community. Refer to https://en.opensuse.org/Portal:Support ↗ for more information.

To report bugs for a product component, go to https://scc.suse.com/support/requests ↗, log in, and click *Create New*.

User Comments

We want to hear your comments about and suggestions for this manual and the other documentation included with this product. Use the User Comments feature at the bottom of each page in the online documentation or go to http://www.suse.com/documentation/feedback.html ↗ and enter your comments there.

Mail

For feedback on the documentation of this product, you can also send a mail to doc-team@suse.com. Make sure to include the document title, the product version and the publication date of the documentation. To report errors or suggest enhancements, provide a concise description of the problem and refer to the respective section number and page (or URL).

4 Documentation Conventions

The following notices and typographical conventions are used in this documentation:

- `/etc/passwd`: directory names and file names

- *PLACEHOLDER*: replace *PLACEHOLDER* with the actual value

- `PATH`: the environment variable PATH

- `ls`, `--help`: commands, options, and parameters

- `user`: users or groups

- `package name` : name of a package

- `Alt`, `Alt`–`F1`: a key to press or a key combination; keys are shown in uppercase as on a keyboard

- *File, File > Save As*: menu items, buttons

- `x86_64` This paragraph is only relevant for the AMD64/Intel 64 architecture. The arrows mark the beginning and the end of the text block.
  `System z, POWER` This paragraph is only relevant for the architectures `z Systems` and `POWER`. The arrows mark the beginning and the end of the text block.

- *Dancing Penguins* (Chapter *Penguins*, ↑Another Manual): This is a reference to a chapter in another manual.

- Commands that must be run with `root` privileges. Often you can also prefix these commands with the **sudo** command to run them as non-privileged user.

```
root # command
tux > sudo command
```

- Commands that can be run by non-privileged users.

```
tux > command
```

- Notices

Warning: Warning Notice
Vital information you must be aware of before proceeding. Warns you about security issues, potential loss of data, damage to hardware, or physical hazards.

Important: Important Notice
Important information you should be aware of before proceeding.

Note: Note Notice
Additional information, for example about differences in software versions.

 Tip: Tip Notice

Helpful information, like a guideline or a piece of practical advice.

1 Planning for SUSE Linux Enterprise Server

1.1 Considerations for Deployment of a SUSE Linux Enterprise Server

The implementation of an operating system either in an existing IT environment or as a completely new rollout must be carefully prepared. At the beginning of the planning process, you should try to define the project goals and necessary features. This must always be done individually for each project, but the questions to answer should include the following:

- How many installations should be done? Depending on this, the best deployment methods differ.

- Will the system run as physical host or as a virtual machine?

- Will the system be in a hostile environment? Have a look at *Book "Security Guide", Chapter 1 "Security and Confidentiality"* to get an overview of consequences.

- How will you get regular updates? All patches are provided online for registered users. Find the registration and patch support database at http://download.suse.com/ ↗.

- Do you need help for your local installation? SUSE provides training, support, and consulting for all topics pertaining to SUSE Linux Enterprise Server. Find more information about this at https://www.suse.com/products/server/ ↗.

- Do you need third-party products? Make sure that the required product is also supported on the desired platform. SUSE can provide help to support software on different platforms when needed.

1.2 Deployment of SUSE Linux Enterprise Server

To make sure that your system will run flawlessly, always try to use certified hardware. The hardware certification process is an ongoing process and the database of certified hardware is updated regularly. Find the search form for certified hardware at http://www.suse.com/yessearch/Search.jsp ↗.

Depending on the number of desired installations, it is beneficial to use installation servers or even completely automatic installations. When using Xen or KVM virtualization technologies, network root file systems or network storage solutions like iSCSI should be considered.

SUSE Linux Enterprise Server provides you with a broad variety of services. Find an overview of the documentation in this book in *Book "Administration Guide", Preface "About This Guide"*. Most of the needed configurations can be made with YaST, the SUSE configuration utility. In addition, many manual configurations are described in the corresponding chapters.

In addition to the plain software installation, you should consider training the end users of the systems and help desk staff.

1.3   Running SUSE Linux Enterprise Server

The SUSE Linux Enterprise Server operating system is a well-tested and stable system. Unfortunately, this does not prevent hardware failures or other causes for downtime or data loss. For any serious computing task where data loss could occur, a regular backup should be done.

For optimal security and data safety, you should make regular updates of all the operated machines. If you have a mission critical server, you should run a second identical (pre-production) machine that you can use to test all changes. This also gives you the possibility of switching machines in the case of hardware failure.

I Installation Preparation

2 Installation on AMD64 and Intel 64

This chapter describes the steps necessary to prepare for the installation of SUSE Linux Enterprise Server on AMD64 and Intel 64 computers. It introduces the steps required to prepare for various installation methods. The list of hardware requirements provides an overview of systems supported by SUSE Linux Enterprise Server. Find information about available installation methods and several common known problems. Also learn how to control the installation, provide installation media, and boot with regular methods.

2.1 System Requirements for Operating Linux

The SUSE® Linux Enterprise Server operating system can be deployed on a wide range of hardware. It is impossible to list all the different combinations of hardware SUSE Linux Enterprise Server supports. However, to provide you with a guide to help you during the planning phase, the minimum requirements are presented here.

If you want to be sure that a given computer configuration will work, find out which platforms have been certified by SUSE. Find a list at https://www.suse.com/yessearch/ ↗.

2.1.1 Hardware for Intel 64 and AMD64

The Intel 64 and AMD64 architectures support the simple migration of x86 software to 64 bits. Like the x86 architecture, they constitute a value-for-money alternative.

CPU

All CPUs available on the market to date are supported.

Maximum Number of CPUs

The maximum number of CPUs supported by software design is 8192 for Intel 64 and AMD64. If you plan to use such a large system, verify with our hardware system certification Web page for supported devices, see https://www.suse.com/yessearch/ ↗.

Memory Requirements

A minimum of 512 MB of memory is required for a minimal installation. However, the minimum recommended is 1024 MB or 512 MB per CPU on multiprocessor computers. Add 150 MB for a remote installation via HTTP or FTP. Note that these values are only valid for the installation of the operating system—the actual memory requirement in production depends on the system's workload.

Hard Disk Requirements

The disk requirements depend largely on the installation selected and how you use your machine. Minimum requirements for different selections are:

System	Hard Disk Requirements
Minimal System	800 MB - 1GB
Minimal X Window System	1.4 GB
GNOME Desktop	3.5 GB
All patterns	8.5 GB
Using snapshots for virtualization	min. 8 GB

Boot Methods

The computer can be booted from a CD or a network. A special boot server is required to boot over the network. This can be set up with SUSE Linux Enterprise Server.

2.2 Installation Considerations

This section encompasses many factors that need to be considered before installing SUSE Linux Enterprise Server on AMD64 and Intel 64 hardware.

2.2.1 Installation Type

SUSE Linux Enterprise Server is normally installed as an independent operating system. With the introduction of Virtualization, it is also possible to run multiple instances of SUSE Linux Enterprise Server on the same hardware. However, the installation of the VM Host Server is performed like a typical installation with some additional packages. The installation of virtual guests is described in *Book "Virtualization Guide", Chapter 9 "Guest Installation"*.

2.2.2 Boot Methods

Depending on the hardware used, the following boot methods are available for the first boot procedure (prior to the installation of SUSE Linux Enterprise Server).

TABLE 2.1: BOOT OPTIONS

Boot Option	Use
CD or DVD drive	The simplest booting method. The system requires a locally-available CD-ROM or DVD-ROM drive for this.
Flash disks	Find the images required for creating boot disks on the first CD or DVD in the `/boot` directory. See also the `README` in the same directory. Booting from a USB memory stick is only possible if the BIOS of the machine supports this method.
PXE or bootp	Must be supported by the BIOS or by the firmware of the system used. This option requires a boot server in the network. This task can be handled by a separate SUSE Linux Enterprise Server.
Hard disk	SUSE Linux Enterprise Server can also be booted from hard disk. For this, copy the kernel (`linux`) and the installation system

Boot Option	Use
	(`initrd`) from the `/boot/loader` directory of the first CD or DVD onto the hard disk and add an appropriate entry to the boot loader.

2.2.3 Installation Source

When installing SUSE Linux Enterprise Server, the actual installation data must be available in the network, on a hard disk partition, or on a local DVD. To install from the network, you need an installation server. To make the installation data available, set up any computer in a Unix or Linux environment as an NFS, HTTP, SMB, or FTP server. To make the installation data available from a Windows computer, release the data with SMB.

The installation source is particularly easy to select if you configure an *SLP server* in the local network. For more information, see *Chapter 7, Setting Up the Server Holding the Installation Sources*.

2.2.4 Installation Target

Most installations are to a local hard disk. Therefore, it is necessary for the hard disk controllers to be available to the installation system. If a special controller (like a RAID controller) needs an extra kernel module, provide a kernel module update disk to the installation system.

Other installation targets may be various types of block devices that provide sufficient disk space and speed to run an operating system. This includes network block devices like `iSCSI` or `SAN`. It is also possible to install on network file systems that offer the standard Unix permissions. However, it may be problematic to boot these, because they must be supported by the `initramfs` before the actual system can start. Such installations can be useful when you need to start the same system in different locations or you plan to use virtualization features like domain migration.

2.2.5 Different Installation Methods

SUSE Linux Enterprise Server offers several methods for controlling installation:

* Installation on the console
* Installation via serial console

- Installation with AutoYaST

- Installation with KIWI images

- Installation via SSH

- Installation with VNC

By default, the graphical console is used. If you have many similar computers to install, it is advisable to create an AutoYaST configuration file or a KIWI preload image and make this available to the installation process. See also the documentation for AutoYaST at https://www.suse.com/documentation/sles-12/book_autoyast/data/book_autoyast.html ↗ and **KIWI** at http://doc.opensuse.org/projects/kiwi/doc/ ↗ .

2.3 Boot and Installation Media

When installing the system, the media for booting and for installing the system may be different. All combinations of supported media for booting and installing may be used.

2.3.1 Boot Media

Booting a computer depends on the capabilities of the hardware used and the availability of media for the respective boot option.

Booting from DVD

This is the most common possibility of booting a system. It is straightforward for most computer users, but requires a lot of interaction for every installation process.

Booting from a USB Hard Disk

Depending on the hardware used, it is possible to boot from a USB hard disk. The respective media must be created as described in *Section 6.2.2, "PC (AMD64/Intel 64/ARM AArch64): System Start-up"*.

Booting from the Network

You can only boot a computer directly from the network if this is supported by the computer's firmware or BIOS. This booting method requires a boot server that provides the needed boot images over the network. The exact protocol depends on your hardware. Commonly you need several services, such as TFTP and DHCP or PXE boot. If you need a boot server, also read *Section 9.1.3, "Remote Installation via VNC—PXE Boot and Wake on LAN"*.

2.3.2 Installation Media

The installation media contain all the necessary packages and meta information that is necessary to install a SUSE Linux Enterprise Server. These must be available to the installation system after booting for installation. Several possibilities for providing the installation media to the system are available with SUSE Linux Enterprise Server.

Installation from DVD

All necessary data is delivered on the boot media. Depending on the selected installation, a network connection or add-on media may be necessary.

Networked Installation

If you plan to install several systems, providing the installation media over the network makes things a lot easier. It is possible to install from many common protocols, such as NFS, HTTP, FTP, or SMB. For more information on how to run such an installation, refer to *Chapter 9, Remote Installation*.

2.4 Installation Procedure

This section offers an overview of the steps required for the complete installation of SUSE® Linux Enterprise Server in the required mode. *Part II, "The Installation Workflow"* contains a full description of how to install and configure the system with YaST.

2.4.1 Booting from a Local Interchangeable Drive

DVD-ROM and USB storage devices can be used for installation purposes. Adjust your computer to your needs:

1. Make sure that the drive is entered as a bootable drive in the BIOS.

2. Insert the boot medium in the drive and start the boot procedure.

3. The installation boot menu of SUSE Linux Enterprise Server allows transferring different parameters to the installation system. See also *Section 9.2.2, "Using Custom Boot Options"*. If the installation should be performed over the network, specify the installation source here.

4. If unexpected problems arise during installation, use safe settings to boot.

2.4.2 Installing over the Network

An installation server is required to perform the installation by using a network source. The procedure for installing this server is outlined in *Chapter 7, Setting Up the Server Holding the Installation Sources*.

If you have an SLP server, select SLP as the installation source in the first boot screen. During the boot procedure, select which of the available installation sources to use.

If the DVD is available on the network, use it as an installation source. In this case, specify the parameter `install=<URL>` with suitable values at the boot prompt. Find a more detailed description of this parameter in *Section 9.2.2, "Using Custom Boot Options"*.

2.5 Controlling the Installation

Control the installation in one of several ways. The method most frequently used is to install SUSE® Linux Enterprise Server from the computer console. Other options are available for different situations.

2.5.1 Installation on the Computer Console

The simplest way to install SUSE Linux Enterprise Server is using the computer console. With this method, a graphical installation program guides you through the installation. This installation method is discussed in detail in *Chapter 6, Installation with YaST*.

You can still perform the installation on the console without a working graphics mode. The text-based installation program offers the same functionality as the graphical version. Find some hints about navigation in this mode in *Book "Administration Guide", Chapter 5 "YaST in Text Mode", Section 5.1 "Navigation in Modules"*.

2.5.2 Installation Using a Serial Console

For this installation method, you need a second computer that is connected by a *null modem* cable to the computer on which to install SUSE Linux Enterprise Server. Depending on the hardware, even the firmware or BIOS of the computer may already be accessible to the serial console. If this is possible, you can carry out the entire installation using this method. To activate the serial console installation, specify the additional `console=ttyS0` parameter at the boot prompt. This should be done after the boot process has completed and before the installation system starts.

On most computers, there are two serial interfaces, *ttyS0* and *ttyS1*. For the installation, you need a terminal program like minicom or screen. To initiate the serial connection, launch the screen program in a local console by entering the following command:

```
screen /dev/ttyS0 9600
```

This means that screen listens to the first serial port with a baud rate of 9600. From this point on, the installation proceeds similarly to the text-based installation over this terminal.

2.5.3   Installation with SSH

If you do not have direct access to the machine and the installation initiated from a management console, you can control the entire installation process over the network. To do this, enter the parameters `ssh=1` and `ssh.password=SECRET` at the boot prompt. An SSH daemon is then launched in the system and you can log in as user `root` with the password *SECRET* .

To connect, use **ssh -X**. X-Forwarding over SSH is supported, if you have a local X server available. Otherwise, YaST provides a text interface over ncurses. YaST then guides you through the installation. This procedure is described in detail in *Section 9.1.5, "Simple Remote Installation via SSH—Dynamic Network Configuration".*

If you do not have a DHCP server available in your local network, manually assign an IP address to the installation system. Do this by entering the option `HostIP=IPADDR` at the boot prompt.

2.5.4   Installation over VNC

If you do not have direct access to the system, but want a graphical installation, install SUSE Linux Enterprise Server over VNC. This method is described in detail in *Section 9.3.1, "VNC Installation".*

As suitable VNC clients are also available for other operating systems, such as Microsoft Windows and mac OS, the installation can also be controlled from computers running those operating systems.

2.5.5 Installation with AutoYaST

If you need to install SUSE Linux Enterprise Server on several computers with similar hardware, it is recommended you perform the installations using AutoYaST. In this case, start by installing one SUSE Linux Enterprise Server and use this to create the necessary AutoYaST configuration files.

2.6 Dealing with Boot and Installation Problems

Prior to delivery, SUSE® Linux Enterprise Server is subjected to an extensive test program. Despite this, problems occasionally occur during boot or installation.

2.6.1 Problems Booting

Boot problems may prevent the YaST installer from starting on your system. Another symptom is when your system does not boot after the installation has been completed.

Installed System Boots, Not Media

> Change your computer's firmware or BIOS so that the boot sequence is correct. To do this, consult the manual for your hardware.

The Computer Hangs

> Change the console on your computer so that the kernel outputs are visible. Be sure to check the last outputs. This is normally done by pressing `Ctrl`–`Alt`–`F10`. If you cannot resolve the problem, consult the SUSE Linux Enterprise Server support staff. To log all system messages at boot time, use a serial connection as described in *Section 2.5, "Controlling the Installation".*

Boot Disk

> The boot disk is a useful interim solution if you have difficulties setting the other configurations or if you want to postpone the decision regarding the final boot mechanism. For more details on creating boot disks, see *Book "Administration Guide", Chapter 12 "The Boot Loader GRUB 2" grub2-mkrescue.*

Virus Warning after Installation

There are BIOS variants that check the structure of the boot sector (MBR) and erroneously display a virus warning after the installation of GRUB 2. Solve this problem by entering the BIOS and looking for corresponding adjustable settings. For example, switch off *virus protection*. You can switch this option back on again later. It is unnecessary, however, if Linux is the only operating system you use.

2.6.2   Problems Installing

If an unexpected problem occurs during installation, information is needed to determine the cause of the problem. Use the following directions to help with troubleshooting:

- Check the outputs on the various consoles. You can switch consoles with the key combination Ctrl – Alt – Fn . For example, obtain a shell in which to execute various commands by pressing Ctrl – Alt – F2 .

- Try launching the installation with "Safe Settings" (press F5 on the installation screen and choose *Safe Settings*). If the installation works without problems in this case, there is an incompatibility that causes either ACPI or APIC to fail. In some cases, a BIOS or firmware update fixes this problem.

- Check the system messages on a console in the installation system by entering the command `dmesg -T`.

2.6.3   Redirecting the Boot Source to the Boot DVD

To simplify the installation process and avoid accidental installations, the default setting on the installation DVD for SUSE Linux Enterprise Server is that your system is booted from the first hard disk. At this point, an installed boot loader normally takes over control of the system. This means that the boot DVD can stay in the drive during an installation. To start the installation, choose one of the installation possibilities in the boot menu of the media.

3 Installation on IBM POWER

This chapter describes the procedure for preparing the installation of SUSE® Linux Enterprise Server on IBM POWER systems.

3.1 Requirements

A standard installation requires at least 512 MB of RAM. The installation of a standard system with the GNOME desktop requires at least 3.5 GB of free hard disk space; a complete installation requires approximately 8.5 GB.

3.1.1 Hardware Requirements

The SUSE® Linux Enterprise Server operating system can be operated on IBM POWER8 servers. To provide you with a guide to help you during the planning phase, the minimum requirements are presented here.

If you want to be sure that a given computer configuration will work, check the database of hardware certified by SUSE. Find a list of certified hardware at http://www.suse.com/yessearch/Search.jsp ↗.

SUSE Linux Enterprise Server may support additional IBM POWER systems not listed below. For the latest information, see the IBM Information Center for Linux at http://www.ibm.com/support/knowledgecenter/linuxonibm/liaam/liaamdistros.htm ↗.

Find up-to-date firmware at IBM FixCentral (http://www.ibm.com/support/fixcentral/ ↗). Select your system from the Product Group list. Additional software is available from the IBM Power-Linux Tools Repository. The IBM Tools Repository is also called the Yum Repository. For more information about using the IBM PowerLinux Tools Repository, see https://ibm.biz/Bdxn3N ↗.

3.1.1.1 IBM POWER8 Processor-Based Servers

All POWER8 servers are supported that are PowerKVM-capable.

- 8247-21L (IBM Power® System S120L)
- 8247-22L (IBM Power System S220L)
- 8284-22A (IBM Power System S2200)

- 8286-41A (IBM Power System S1400)

- 8286-42A (IBM Power System S2400)

3.2 Preparation

This section describes the preparatory steps that must be taken before the actual installation of SUSE Linux Enterprise Server. The installation procedure depends on the system used. The following methods are supported:

- *Installation on Servers with IBM PowerKVM using Kimchi*

- *Installation on Servers with IBM PowerKVM using* `virt-install`

- *Installation in a Partition Using IVM*

- *Installation on Servers with no Open Power Abstraction Layer*

If SUSE® Linux Enterprise Server needs to be installed on several systems or partitions, it is recommended you create a network installation source. The same source can also be used for the concurrent installation on several partitions or several systems. The configuration of a network installation source is described in *Section 7.1, "Setting Up an Installation Server Using YaST"*.

3.2.1 Installation on Servers with IBM PowerKVM using Kimchi

This section covers the preparatory steps for installing on IBM PowerLinux systems with PowerKVM. It explains the installation from an ISO image with the Kimchi Web interface. Kimchi is a tool for administrating IBM PowerKVM.

This section assumes you have PowerKVM running on your IBM PowerLinux server. If PowerKVM is not preinstalled see "Configuring IBM PowerKVM on Power Systems" at http://www.ibm.com/support/knowledgecenter/linuxonibm/liabp/liabpkickoff.htm ↗ for installing and setting up PowerKVM.

3.2.1.1 Creating a SUSE Linux Enterprise Server Template with Kimchi

Templates are the installation source for PowerKVM guests. You can create a template, edit an existing template, or clone a template. To clone a template from an existing guest, that guest must be deactivated.

1. In the Web browser, enter the URL of the PowerLinux server where PowerKVM is running, for example `https://POWERLINUX_IP:8001` (replace *POWERLINUX_IP* with the IP address of your system).

2. Click the *Templates* tab to activate the *Templates* page.

3. Click the green plus sign (+) to create the SUSE Linux Enterprise Server template.

4. On the *Add Template* dialog, select from the following options:

   Local ISO Image

   > Select to scan storage pools for installation ISO images available on the system.

   Local Image File

   > Select to specify a path to a local image file.

   Remote ISO file

   > Select to specify a remote location for an installation ISO image.

5. Select the ISO file that you want to use to create a guest and click *Create Templates from Selected ISO*.

6. To configure the newly created template, click *Actions › Edit*, and change the default values as required by your workload.

For more information, see "Setting up a template using Kimchi" at http://www.ibm.com/support/knowledgecenter/linuxonibm/liabp/liabpkimchitemplate.htm↗.

3.2.1.2   Installing SUSE Linux Enterprise Server as a Guest with Kimchi

1. In the Web browser, enter the URL of the PowerLinux server where PowerKVM is running, for example `https://POWERLINUX_IP:8001` (replace `POWERLINUX_IP` with the IP address of your system).

2. Click the *Guests* tab to activate the *Guests* page.

3. Click the green plus sign (+) to create the SUSE Linux Enterprise Server guest.

4. Enter a *Virtual Machine Name* for the SUSE Linux Enterprise Server guest.
   Choose the SUSE Linux Enterprise Server template created in *Section 3.2.1.1, "Creating a SUSE Linux Enterprise Server Template with Kimchi"* and click *Create*.

5. After the guest is created, it is ready to be started. Click the red power button to start the SUSE Linux Enterprise Server guest. Alternatively, select *Actions > Start*.

6. Click *Actions > Connect*, and connect your VNC viewer to the installation process as outlined in *Section 9.3.1.2, "Connecting to the Installation Program"*.

 Tip: Creating Multiple Guests

To create multiple guests of a similar type, select *Clone* from the *Actions* menu of an existing guest.

Now you can continue with the default installation via VNC as described in *Section 6.3, "Steps of the Installation"*.

3.2.2 Installation on Servers with IBM PowerKVM using `virt-install`

Alternatively to installing with Kimchi, use the **`virt-install`** command line tool to install on servers with IBM PowerKVM. This is especially useful you need to install multiple virtual machines on IBM PowerLinux Server systems. **`virt-install`** allows many installation scenarios; in the following a remote installation scenario via VNC and PXE boot is outlined. For more information about **`virt-install`**, see Book *"Virtualization Guide", Chapter 9 "Guest Installation", Section 9.2 "Installing from the Command Line with* **`virt-install`***"*.

Prepare a repository with the installation sources and PXE boot enabled target system as described in *Section 9.1.3, "Remote Installation via VNC—PXE Boot and Wake on LAN"*.

On the command line, enter something similar as follows (adjust the options according to your needs and matching your hardware):

```
virt-install --name server_sle12 --memory 4096 --vcpus=2 --pxe \
--graphics vnc --os-variant sles11 \
--disk pool=default,size=3000,format=qcow2,allocation=1G,bus=virtio \
-w mac=MAC_ADDRESS,model=spapr-vlan
```

It will use VNC graphics, and it will automatically launch the graphical client. Complete the installation as described in *Section 6.3, "Steps of the Installation"*.

3.2.3 Installation in a Partition Using IVM

This guide helps you install SUSE Linux Enterprise Server on a Power Systems server partition using the Integrated Virtualization Manager (IVM) Web interface. Before starting the installation, make sure the following requirements are met:

- the Linux on Power system is powered on

- the Virtual I/O server is installed

- the IVM is initially configured

PROCEDURE 3.2: LOG IN TO THE IVM WEB INTERFACE

1. Open a Web browser window, and connect using the HTTP or HTTPS protocol to the IP address that was assigned to the IVM during the installation process (for example, https://*IP_ADDRESS*). The Welcome window is displayed.

2. Log in as the user `padmin`, providing the password that you defined during the installation process. The IVM interface is displayed.

3. Select *View/Modify Virtual Ethernet.*

4. Click *Initialize Virtual Ethernet* to provide Ethernet connectivity among the partitions.

5. When the Virtual Ethernet is initialized, click Apply.

6. If your installation requires external networking, create a virtual Ethernet bridge.

    a. Select the *Virtual Ethernet Bridge* tab.

    b. Select the physical adapter to bridge and proceed with *Apply*.

Next, create a partition, following these steps:

PROCEDURE 3.3: CREATE A PARTITION

1. In the IVM Web interface, click *View/Modify Partition* › *Create Partition.*

2. Enter a name for the partition. To advance to the next step, click *Next* on this and the following steps.

3. Specify memory for your partition. If you have created a shared memory pool, your partitions can share memory. Otherwise, select *Dedicated.*

4. Specify the number of processors and the processing mode for the partition.

5. Specify a virtual Ethernet for the partition. If you do not want to configure an adapter, select *none* for the virtual Ethernet.

6. Create a new virtual disk or assign existing virtual disks and physical volumes that are not currently assigned to a partition.

7. Verify the *Virtual disk name* and *Storage pool name* for your disk and specify a *Virtual disk size.*

8. Configure optical devices for your partition by expanding the *Physical Optical Devices* and *Virtual Optical Devices* and select the device(s) you want to assign to the partition.

9. Verify your partition configuration settings and click *Finish.* The partition is created and available from the *View/Modify Partitions* list.

Now activate the partition you have created:

1. In the IVM Web interface, click *View/Modify Partition* and select the box next to the partition you would like to activate.

2. Select *More Tasks*.

3. Select *Open a terminal window*.

4. Click *Activate* next to the partition.

5. In the terminal window, enter 1 to start the system management services (SMS).

The machine is set up now and you can boot into the installation:

PROCEDURE 3.5: BOOT THE LINUX INSTALLATION

1. At the *Boot selection* window, enter 1 to select the *SMS Menu*. Enter 1 before the firmware boot screen is completely shown on the display, because it will disappear when complete. If you miss the screen, reboot the system.

2. At this time, you can insert the Virtual I/O Server (VIOS) media disk into the disk drive.

3. Enter 2 to continue to the password entry on the *Language selection* menu. Enter the password for the admin ID.

4. On the main SMS menu, enter 5 to choose *Select Boot Options*.

5. Enter 1 to select *Install/Boot Device*.

6. Enter 7 to view all of the available boot devices.

7. Enter the number corresponding to the device you want to use. If your device is not listed, enter N to display more.

8. Enter 2 to perform a *Normal Mode Boot*.

9. Enter 1 to leave the SMS menu and to start the boot process.

10. At the boot prompt from the installer, type

```
install vnc=1
```

```
vncpassword=VNC_PASSWORD
```

Replace *VNC_PASSWORD* with a password of your choice (minimum length is eight characters) and press `Enter` to start the installation of SUSE Linux Enterprise Server. The kernel will begin loading.

After the kernel has started to load, the installer needs some information from the system in order to set up a VNC session. You must have a valid TCP/IP stack in order to use VNC. Either use DHCP or manually define your networking information using directions provided by the installer.

PROCEDURE 3.6: START THE VNC SESSION

1. On the *Network device* window, select *eth0* as your network device. Select *OK* and press `Enter`.

2. Test the installation media. Alternatively, proceed without the test by selecting *Skip*.

3. After the system has started the VNC server, you will see a message to connect your VNC client followed by an IP address. Take note of this IP address.

4. Start a VNC client on your laptop or PC. Enter the IP address from the previous step followed by `:1`, for example 192.168.2.103:1.

5. Complete the installation as described in *Section 6.3, "Steps of the Installation"*.

3.2.4 Installation on Servers with no Open Power Abstraction Layer

Use this information to install Linux using a serial console or using a monitor and keyboard on a Power Systems server. This installation assumes an unmanaged (stand-alone) system that is ready to boot.

1. Power on your system by selecting *Power On* from the *Power On/Off System* menu. When asked if you want to continue using the console, enter `0` to continue doing so.

2. Insert the SUSE Linux Enterprise Server installation media into the disk drive.

3. From the *Select Language* window, enter `2` to continue to booting.

4. Enter `1` to accept the license agreement.

5. At the *Boot selection* window, enter ⌐1⌐ to select the *SMS Menu*. Enter ⌐1⌐ before the firmware boot screen is completely shown on the display, because it will disappear when complete. If you miss the screen, reboot the system.

6. Enter ⌐2⌐ to continue to the password entry on the *Language selection* menu. Enter the password for the admin ID.

7. On the main SMS menu, enter ⌐5⌐ to choose *Select Boot Options*.

8. Enter ⌐7⌐ to view all of the available boot devices.

9. Enter the number corresponding to the device you want to use. If your device is not listed, enter ⌐N⌐ to display more.

10. Enter ⌐2⌐ to perform a *Normal Mode Boot*.

11. Enter ⌐1⌐ to leave the SMS menu and to start the boot process.

12. At the boot prompt from the installer, type

```
install vnc=1
vncpassword=VNC_PASSWORD
```

Replace VNC_PASSWORD with a password of your choice (minimum length is eight characters) and press ⌐Enter⌐ to start the installation of SUSE Linux Enterprise Server. The kernel will begin loading.

After the kernel has started to load, the installer needs some information from the system in order to set up a VNC session. You must have a valid TCP/IP stack in order to use VNC. Either use DHCP or manually define your networking information using directions provided by the installer.

PROCEDURE 3.7: START THE VNC SESSION

1. On the *Network device* window, select *eth0* as your network device. Select *OK* and press ⌐Enter⌐.

2. Test the installation media. Alternatively, proceed without the test by selecting *Skip*.

3. After the system has started the VNC server, you will see a message to connect your VNC client followed by an IP address. Take note of this IP address.

4. Start a VNC client on your laptop or PC. Enter the IP address from the previous step followed by :1, for example 192.168.2.103:1.

5. Complete the installation as described in *Section 6.3, "Steps of the Installation"*.

3.3 For More Information

More information on IBM PowerLinux is available from SUSE and IBM:

- The SUSE Support Knowledge Base at https://www.suse.com/support/kb/ ⌐ is an effective help tool for assisting customers in solving problems. Search the knowledge base on SUSE Linux Enterprise Server using keywords like POWER or PowerKVM.

- Find security alerts at https://www.suse.com/support/security/ ⌐. SUSE also maintains two security-related mailing lists to which anyone may subscribe.

  - `suse-security` — General discussion of security regarding Linux and SUSE. All security alerts for SUSE Linux Enterprise Server are sent to this list.

  - `suse-security-announce` — The SUSE mailing list exclusively for security alerts.

- In case of hardware errors, check the control panel for any codes that might be displayed. You can look up any codes that are displayed at the IBM Power Systems Hardware Information Center at https://ibm.biz/Bdxn3T ⌐.

- For troubleshooting tips, see the IBM PowerLinux FAQ topic in the Information Center at https://ibm.biz/Bdxn35 ⌐.

- To participate in the linuxppc-dev mailing list, register using the forms at http://lists.ozlabs.org/listinfo/linuxppc-dev/ ⌐.

4 Installation on IBM z Systems

This chapter describes the procedure for preparing the installation of SUSE® Linux Enterprise Server on IBM z Systems. It provides all information needed to prepare the installation on the LPAR and z/VM side.

4.1 General Information and Requirements

This section gives basic information about the system requirements (like supported hardware), level of MicroCode, and software. It also covers the different installation types and how to do an IPL for the first installation. For detailed technical information about IBM z Systems on SUSE Linux Enterprise Server refer to http://www.ibm.com/developerworks/linux/linux390/documentation_suse.html ↗.

4.1.1 System Requirements

This section provides a list of hardware for IBM z Systems supported by SUSE Linux Enterprise Server. Next, the level of the MicroCode (MCL) used in your IBM z Systems system, which is very important for the installation, is covered. Additional software to install and use for installation is mentioned at the end of this section.

4.1.1.1 Hardware

SUSE Linux Enterprise Server has run successfully on the following platforms:

- IBM zEnterprise System z196 (2817)

- IBM zEnterprise System z114 (2818)

- IBM zEnterprise EC12 (zEC12) (2827)

- IBM zEnterprise BC12 (zBC12) (2828)

- IBM z Systems z13 (2964)

- IBM z Systems z13s (2965)

- IBM LinuxONE Emperor (2964)

- IBM LinuxONE Rockhopper (2965)

4.1.1.1.1   Memory Requirements

Different installation methods have different memory requirements during installation. After installation is completed, the system administrator may reduce memory to the desired size. SUSE recommends using:

1 GB	For installation under z/VM.
1 GB	For installation under LPAR.
1 GB	For installation under KVM.

 Note: Memory Requirements with Remote Installation Sources

> For installation from NFS, FTP, or SMB installation sources or whenever VNC is used, 512MB of memory is required as a minimum. Otherwise, the installation attempt is likely to fail. Further note that the number of devices visible to the z/VM guest or LPAR image affects memory requirements. Installation with literally hundreds of accessible devices (even if unused for the installation) may require more memory.

4.1.1.1.2   Disk Space Requirements

The disk requirements depend largely on the installation. Commonly, you need more space than the installation software itself needs to have a system that works properly. Minimal requirements for different selections are:

800 MB	Minimal Installation
1.4 GB	Minimal Installation + Base System
2.6 GB	Default Installation
3.6 GB+	Recommended (this is with graphical desktop, development packages and Java).

A network connection is needed to communicate with your SUSE Linux Enterprise Server system. This can be one or more of the following connections or network cards:

- OSA Express Ethernet (including Fast and Gigabit Ethernet)

- HiperSockets or Guest LAN

- 10 GBE, VSWITCH

- RoCE (RDMA over Converged Ethernet)

The following interfaces are still included, but no longer supported:

- CTC (or virtual CTC)

- ESCON

- IP network interface for IUCV

For installations under KVM make sure the following requirements are met to enable the VM Guest to access the network transparently:

- The virtual network interface is connected to a host network interface.

- The host network interface is connected to a network in which the virtual server will participate.

- If the host is configured to have a redundant network connection by grouping two independent OSA network ports into a bonded network interface, the identifier for the bonded network interface is bond0 (or, if more than one bonded interface exists, bond1, bond2, ...). See http://www.ibm.com/support/knowledgecenter/SSNW54_1.1.0/ com.ibm.kvm.v110.admin/toc.htm ↗ for further information about how to configure network bonding.

- If the host network connection has *not* been set up redundantly, the identifier of the single network interface needs to be used. It has the form enccw0.0.*NNNN*, where *NNNN* is the device number of the desired network interface.

4.1.1.2 MicroCode Level, APARs, and Fixes

Documentation about restrictions and requirements for this release of SUSE Linux Enterprise Server be found on IBM developerWorks at http://www.ibm.com/developerworks/linux/linux390/documentation_suse.html↗. It is recommended always to use the highest service level available. Contact your IBM support for minimum requirements.

4.1.1.2.1 z/VM

- z/VM 5.4

- z/VM 6.2

- z/VM 6.3, we strongly suggest installing the APAR VM65419 (or higher) to improve the output of qclib.

Negotiate the order of installation with your IBM support, because it might be necessary to activate the VM APARs before installing the new MicroCode levels.

4.1.1.3 Software

When installing SUSE Linux Enterprise Server via non-Linux–based NFS or FTP, you might experience problems with NFS or FTP server software. The Windows* standard FTP server can cause errors, so installing via SMB on these machines is generally recommended.

To connect to the SUSE Linux Enterprise Server installation system, one of the following methods is required (SSH or VNC are recommended):

SSH with Terminal Emulation (xterm compatible)

> SSH is a standard Unix tool that should be present on any Unix or Linux system. For Windows, there is an SSH client called Putty. It is free to use and is available from http://www.chiark.greenend.org.uk/~sgtatham/putty/↗.

VNC Client

> For Linux, a VNC client called vncviewer is included in SUSE Linux Enterprise Server as part of the `tightvnc` package. For Windows, TightVNC is also available. Download it from http://www.tightvnc.com/↗.

X Server

> Find a suitable X server implementation on any Linux or Unix workstation. There are many commercial X Window System environments for Windows and macOS*. Some can be downloaded as free trial versions. A trial version of the Mocha X Server from MochaSoft can be obtained at http://www.mochasoft.dk/freeware/x11.htm ↗.

 Tip: Additional Information

> Consult the README file located in the root directory of DVD 1 of your SUSE Linux Enterprise Server before installing SUSE Linux Enterprise Server on IBM z Systems. This file complements this documentation.

4.1.2 Installation Types

This section gives an overview of the different types of installation possible with SUSE Linux Enterprise Server for IBM z Systems:

LPAR

> Installation of SUSE Linux Enterprise Server using a logical partition (LPAR).

z/VM

> Installation of SUSE Linux Enterprise Server as a guest operating system within z/VM.

KVM

> Installation of SUSE Linux Enterprise Server as a guest operating system within KVM.

Depending on the mode of installation (LPAR or z/VM), there are different possibilities for starting the installation process and IPLing the installed system.

4.1.2.1 LPAR

If you install SUSE Linux Enterprise Server for IBM z Systems into a logical partition (LPAR), assign memory and processors to the instance. Installing into LPAR is recommended for highly loaded production machines. Running in LPAR also makes higher security standards available. Networking between LPARs is possible over external interfaces or Hipersockets. In case you plan to use your installation for virtualization with KVM, installing into LPAR is highly recommended.

4.1.2.2   z/VM

Running SUSE Linux Enterprise Server for IBM z Systems in z/VM means that SUSE Linux Enterprise Server is a guest system within z/VM. An advantage of this mode is that you have full control over SUSE Linux Enterprise Server from z/VM. This is very helpful for kernel development or kernel-based debugging. It is also very easy to add or remove hardware to and from Linux guests. Creating additional SUSE Linux Enterprise Server guests is simple and you can run hundreds of Linux instances simultaneously.

4.1.2.3   KVM Guest

Being able to install SUSE Linux Enterprise Server for IBM z Systems as a KVM guest requires a KVM host server instance installed into LPAR. For details on the guest installation, refer to *Procedure 4.3, "Overview of a KVM Guest Installation"*.

4.1.3   IPL Options

This section provides the information needed to do an IPL for the first installation. Depending on the type of installation, different options need to be used. The VM reader, load from CD-ROM or server and load from an SCSI-attached DVD-ROM options are discussed. Installing the software packages, which is done over the network, does not require the IPL medium.

4.1.3.1   VM Reader

To IPL from a VM reader, transfer the necessary files into the reader first. For convenience of administration, it is recommended to create a user linuxmnt that owns a minidisk with the files and scripts needed for IPL. This minidisk is then accessed read-only by the Linux guests.

4.1.3.2   Load from Removable Media or Server

For IPLing into an LPAR, it is possible to either load the kernel image directly from the SE's or the HMC's CD/DVD-ROM device or from any remote system accessible through FTP. This function can be performed from the HMC. The installation process requires a file with a mapping of the location of the installation data in the file system and the memory locations where the data is to be copied.

For SUSE Linux Enterprise Server, there are two such files. Both are located in the root directory of the file system of DVD 1:

- `suse.ins`, for which to work you need to set up network access in Linuxrc before starting the installation.

- `susehmc.ins` which allows installing without network access.

In the left navigation pane of the HMC expand *Systems Management* › *Systems* and select the mainframe system you want to work with. Choose the LPAR where you want to boot SUSE Linux Enterprise Server from the table of LPARs and select *Load from Removable Media or Server*.

Now either choose *Hardware Management Console CD-ROM/DVD* or *FTP Source*. If having chosen the latter option, provide the servers address or name and your credentials. If the appropriate `.ins` file is not located in the root directory of the server, provide the path to this file. Continue to the *Select the software to load* menu and select the appropriate `.ins` entry. Start the installation with *OK*.

4.1.3.3 Load from SCSI-Attached DVD

To IPL from an SCSI DVD, you need access to an FCP adapter connected to a DVD drive. You need the values for WWPN and LUN from the SCSI drive. For details, see *Section 4.2.4.1.2, "IPL from FCP-Attached SCSI DVD"*.

4.1.3.4 Load from the Network with zPXE

IPLing from the Network with zPXE requires a Cobbler server providing the kernel, RAM disk and a parmfile. It is initiated by running the ZPXE EXEC script. See *Section 4.2.1.3, "Using a Cobbler Server for zPXE"* for details. zPXE is only available on z/VM.

4.2 Preparing for Installation

Learn how to make the data accessible for installation, install SUSE Linux Enterprise Server using different methods, and prepare and use the IPL of the SUSE Linux Enterprise Server installation system. Also find out about network configuration and network installation.

4.2.1   Making the Installation Data Available

This section provides detailed information about making the SUSE Linux Enterprise Server IBM z Systems installation data accessible for installation. Depending on your computer and system environment, choose between NFS or FTP installation. If you are running Microsoft Windows workstations in your environment, you can use the Windows network (including the SMB protocol) to install SUSE Linux Enterprise Server on your IBM z Systems system.

 Tip: IPL from DVD

Starting with Service Pack 1 of SUSE Linux Enterprise Server Version 10, it is possible to IPL from DVD and use the DVD as the installation medium. This is very convenient if you have restrictions setting up an installation server providing installation media over your network. The prerequisite is an FCP-attached SCSI DVD Drive.

 Note: No Installation "From Hard Disk"

It is not possible to install from hard disk by putting the content of the DVD to a partition on a DASD.

4.2.1.1   Using a Linux Workstation or SUSE Linux Enterprise Server DVD

If you have a Linux workstation running in your computer environment, use the workstation to provide the installation data to the IBM z Systems installation process by NFS or FTP. If the Linux workstation runs under SUSE Linux Enterprise Server, you can set up an installation server (NFS or FTP) using the YaST *Installation Server* module as described in *Section 7.1, "Setting Up an Installation Server Using YaST"*.

4.2.1.1.1   Over NFS

Use NFS (network file system) to make the installation media available.

Important: Exporting Mounted Devices with NFS

Exporting the file system root (/) does not imply the export of mounted devices, such as DVD. Explicitly name the mount point in `/etc/exports`:

```
/media/dvd  *(ro)
```

After changing this file, restart the NFS server with the command **sudo systemctl restart nfsserver**.

4.2.1.1.2   Over FTP

Setting up an FTP server on a Linux system involves the installation and configuration of the server software like `pure-ftpd` or `vsftpd`. If you are using SUSE Linux Enterprise Server, refer to *Book "Administration Guide", Chapter 32 "Setting Up an FTP Server with YaST"* for installation instructions. Downloading the installation data via anonymous login is not supported, therefore you need to configure the FTP server to support user authentication.

4.2.1.1.3   SUSE Linux Enterprise Server on DVD

DVD1 of the SUSE Linux Enterprise Server for IBM z Systems contains a bootable Linux image for Intel-based workstations and an image for z Systems.

For Intel-based workstations, boot from this DVD, answer the questions regarding your language and keyboard layout, and select *Start rescue system*. You need at least 64 MB RAM for this. No disk space is needed because the entire rescue system resides in the workstation's RAM. This approach takes some Linux and networking experience, because you need to set up the networking of the workstation manually.

For z Systems, IPL your LPAR/VM guest from this DVD as described in *Section 4.2.4.1.2, "IPL from FCP-Attached SCSI DVD"*. After entering your network parameters, the installation system treats the DVD as the source of installation data. Because z Systems cannot have an X11-capable terminal attached directly, choose between VNC or SSH installation. SSH also provides a graphical installation by tunneling the X connection through SSH with **ssh -X**.

4.2.1.2   Using a Microsoft Windows Workstation

If there is a Microsoft Windows workstation available in your network, use this computer to make the installation media available. The easiest way to do this is to use the SMB protocol, already included in the Windows operating system. Be sure to activate *SMB over TCP/IP* as this enables the encapsulation of SMB packages into TCP/IP packages. Find details in the Windows online help or other Windows-related documentation that covers networking. Another option is to use FTP. This also requires some third-party software for Windows.

4.2.1.2.1   With SMB

To make the installation media available with SMB, insert the SUSE Linux Enterprise Server DVD 1 into the DVD drive of the Windows workstation. Then create a new share using the DVD-ROM drive's letter and make it available for everyone in the network.

The installation path in YaST can be:

```
smb://DOMAIN;USER:PW@SERVERNAME/SHAREPATH
```

Where the placeholders mean:

DOMAIN

>   Optional workgroup or active directory domain.

USER,

PW

>   Optional user name and password of a user who can access this server and its share.

SERVERNAME

>   The name of the server that hosts the share(s).

SHAREPATH

>   The path to the share(s).

4.2.1.2.2   With NFS

Refer to the documentation provided with the third party product that enables NFS server services for your Windows workstation. The DVD-ROM drive containing the SUSE Linux Enterprise Server DVDs must be in the available NFS path.

4.2.1.2.3   With FTP

Refer to the documentation provided with the third party product that is enabling FTP server services on your Windows workstation. The DVD-ROM drive containing the SUSE Linux Enterprise Server DVDs must be in the available FTP path.

The FTP server that is bundled with some Microsoft Windows releases implements only a subset of the FTP commands, and it is not suitable for providing the installation data. If this applies to your Windows workstation, use a third party FTP server providing the required features.

4.2.1.2.4   Using an FCP-Attached SCSI DVD Drive

After you IPLed from the SCSI DVD as described in *Section 4.1.3.3, "Load from SCSI-Attached DVD"*, the installation system uses the DVD as the installation medium. In that case, you do not need the installation media on an FTP, NFS, or SMB server. However, you need the network configuration data for your SUSE Linux Enterprise Server, because you must set up the network during the installation to perform a graphical installation by VNC or by X.

4.2.1.3   Using a Cobbler Server for zPXE

IPLing from the network requires a Cobbler server, to provide the kernel, initrd, and the installation data. Preparing the Cobbler server requires four steps:

- Importing the Installation Data
- Adding a Distribution
- Adding Profiles
- Adding Systems

4.2.1.3.1   Importing the Installation Data

Importing the media requires the installation source to be available on the Cobbler server—either from DVD or from a network source. Run the following command to import the data:

```
cobbler import --path=PATH❶ --name=IDENTIFIER❷ --arch=s390x
```

❶   Mount point of the installation data.

② A string identifying the imported product, for example "sles12_s390x". This string is used as the name for the subdirectory where the installation data is copied to. On a Cobbler server running on SUSE Linux Enterprise this is `/srv/www/cobbler/ks_mirror/IDENTIFIER`. This path may be different if Cobbler runs on another operating system.

4.2.1.3.2   Adding a Distribution

By adding a distribution, you tell Cobbler to provide the kernel and the initrd required to IPL via zPXE. Run the following command on the Cobbler server to add SUSE Linux Enterprise Server for IBM z Systems:

```
cobbler distro add --arch=s390 --breed=suse --name="IDENTIFIER" ① \
  --os-version=sles12② \
  --initrd=/srv/www/cobbler/ks_mirror/IDENTIFIER/boot/s390x/initrd③ \
  --kernel=/srv/www/cobbler/ks_mirror/IDENTIFIER/boot/s390x/linux④ \
  --kopts="install=http://cobbler.example.com/cobbler/ks_mirror/IDENTIFIER" ⑤
```

① Custom identifier for the distribution, for example "SLES 12 SP3 z Systems". Must be unique.

② Operating system identifier. Use `sles12`.

③ Path to the initrd. The first part of the path (`/srv/www/cobbler/ks_mirror/IDEN-TIFIER/`) depends on the location where Cobbler imported the data and the subdirectory name you chose when importing the installation data.

④ Path to the kernel. The first part of the path (`/srv/www/cobbler/ks_mirror/IDEN-TIFIER/`) depends on the location where Cobbler imported the data and the subdirectory name you chose when importing the installation data.

⑤ URl to the installation directory on the Cobbler server.

4.2.1.3.3   Adjusting the Profile

When adding a distribution (see *Section 4.2.1.3.2, "Adding a Distribution"*) a profile with the corresponding `IDENTIFIER` is automatically generated. Use the following command to make a few required adjustments:

```
cobbler distro edit \
--name=IDENTIFIER① --os-version=sles10② --ksmeta=""③
--kopts="install=http://cobbler.example.com/cobbler/ks_mirror/IDENTIFIER" ④
```

① Identifier for the profile. Use the same string as specified when having added the distribution.

② Operating system version. Distribution to which the profile should apply. You must use the string specified with `--name=IDENTIFIER` in the importing step here.

③ Option needed for templating kickstart files. Not used for SUSE, so set to an empty value as specified in the example.

④ Space-separated list of kernel parameters. Should include at least the `install` parameter as shown in the example.

4.2.1.3.4   Adding Systems

The last step that is required is to add systems to the Cobbler server. A system addition needs to be done for every z Systems guest that should boot via zPXE. Guests are identified via their z/VM user ID (in the following example, an ID called "linux01" is assumed). Note that this ID needs to be a lowercase string. To add a system, run the following command:

```
cobbler system add --name=linux01 --hostname=linux01.example.com \
--profile=IDENTIFIER --interface=qdio \
--ip-address=192.168.2.103 --subnet=192.168.2.255 --netmask=255.255.255.0 \
--name-servers=192.168.1.116 --name-servers-search=example.com \
--gateway=192.168.2.1 --kopts="KERNEL_OPTIONS"
```

With the `--kopts` option you can specify the kernel and installation parameters you would normally specify in the parmfile. The parameters are entered as a space-separated list in the form of *PARAMETER1=VALUE1 PARAMETER2=VALUE2*. The installer will prompt you for missing parameters. For a completely automated installation you need to specify all parameters for networking, DASDs and provide an AutoYaST file. The following shows an example for a guest equipped with an OSA interface using the same network parameters as above.

```
--kopts=" \
AutoYaST=http://192.168.0.5/autoinst.xml \
Hostname=linux01.example.com \
Domain=example.com \
HostIP=192.168.2.103 \
Gateway=192.168.2.1 \
Nameserver=192.168.1.116 \
Searchdns=example.com \
InstNetDev=osa; \
Netmask=255.255.255.0 \
Broadcast=192.168.2.255 \
```

```
OsaInterface=qdio \
Layer2=0 \
PortNo=0 \
ReadChannel=0.0.0700 \
WriteChannel=0.0.0701 \
DataChannel=0.0.0702 \
DASD=600"
```

4.2.1.4 Installing from DVD or Flash Disk of the HMC

To install SUSE Linux Enterprise Server on IBM z Systems servers, usually a network installation source is needed. However, in certain environments, it could occur that this requirement cannot be fulfilled. With SUSE Linux Enterprise Server, you can use the existing DVD or the flash disk of the Hardware Management Console (HMC) as an installation source for installation on an LPAR.

To install from the media in the DVD or the flash disk of the HMC, proceed as follows:

- Add

  `install=hmc:/`

  to the `parmfile` (see *Section 4.3, "The parmfile—Automating the System Configuration"*) or kernel options.

- Alternatively, in manual mode, in `linuxrc`, choose:

  Start Installation, then

  Installation, then

  Hardware Management Console.

  The installation medium must be inserted in the HMC.

> **Important: Configure Network**
>
> Do not forget to configure the network in `linuxrc` before starting the installation. There is no way to pass on boot parameters later in time, and it is very likely that you will need network access. In `linuxrc`, go to *Start Installation*, then choose *Network Setup*.

Important: Linux System Must Boot First

Before granting access to the media in the DVD or the flash disk of the HMC, wait until the Linux system is booting. IPLing can disrupt the connection between the HMC and the LPAR. If the first attempt to use the described method fails, you can grant the access and retry the option HMC.

 Note: Installation Repository

Because of the transitory nature of the assignment, the DVD or the flash disk files will not be kept as a repository for installation. If you need an installation repository, register and use the online repository.

4.2.2 Installation Types

This section provides information about which steps must be performed to install SUSE Linux Enterprise Server for each of the installation modes and where to find the appropriate information. When the preparation steps described in the previous chapters have been completed, follow the installation overview of the desired installation mode to install SUSE Linux Enterprise Server on your system.

As described in *Section 4.2.1, "Making the Installation Data Available"*, there are three different installation modes for Linux on IBM z Systems:

- LPAR installation

- z/VM installation

- KVM guest installation

PROCEDURE 4.1: OVERVIEW OF AN LPAR INSTALLATION

1. Prepare the devices needed for installation. See *Section 4.2.3.1, "Preparing the IPL of an LPAR Installation"*.

2. IPL the installation system. See *Section 4.2.4.1, "IPLing an LPAR Installation"*.

3. Configure the network. See *Section 4.2.5, "Network Configuration"*.

4. Connect to the SUSE Linux Enterprise Server installation system. See *Section 4.2.6, "Connecting to the SUSE Linux Enterprise Server Installation System"*.

5. Start the installation using YaST and IPL the installed system. See *Chapter 6, Installation with YaST*.

PROCEDURE 4.2: INSTALLATION OVERVIEW OF Z/VM INSTALLATION

1. Prepare the devices needed for installation. See *Section 4.2.3.2, "Preparing the IPL of a z/VM Installation"*.

2. IPL the installation system. See *Section 4.2.4.2, "IPLing a z/VM Installation"*.

3. Configure the network. See *Section 4.2.5, "Network Configuration"*.

4. Connect to the SUSE Linux Enterprise Server installation system. See *Section 4.2.6, "Connecting to the SUSE Linux Enterprise Server Installation System"*.

5. Start the installation using YaST and IPL the installed system. See *Chapter 6, Installation with YaST*.

PROCEDURE 4.3: OVERVIEW OF A KVM GUEST INSTALLATION

1. Create a virtual disk image and write a domain XML file. See *Section 4.2.3.3, "Preparing the IPL of a KVM Guest Installation"*.

2. Prepare the installation target and IPL the VM Guest. See *Section 4.2.4.3, "IPLing a KVM Guest Installation"*.

3. *Section 4.2.5.3, "Set Up the Network and Select the Installation Source"*.

4. Connect to the SUSE Linux Enterprise Server installation system. See *Section 4.2.6, "Connecting to the SUSE Linux Enterprise Server Installation System"*.

5. Start the installation using YaST and IPL the installed system. See *Chapter 6, Installation with YaST*.

4.2.3 Preparing the IPL of the SUSE Linux Enterprise Server Installation System

4.2.3.1 Preparing the IPL of an LPAR Installation

Configure your IBM z Systems system to start in ESA/S390 or Linux-only mode with an appropriate activation profile and IOCDS. Consult IBM documentation for more on how to achieve this. Proceed with *Section 4.2.4.1, "IPLing an LPAR Installation"*.

4.2.3.2 Preparing the IPL of a z/VM Installation

4.2.3.2.1 Adding a Linux Guest

The first step is to attach and format one or multiple DASDs in the system to be used by the Linux guest in z/VM. Next, create a new user in z/VM. The example shows the directory for a user LINUX1 with the password LINPWD, 1 GB of memory (extendable up to 2 GB), 32 MB of expanded RAM (XSTORE), several minidisks (MDISK), two CPUs, and an OSA QDIO device.

 Tip: Assigning Memory to z/VM guests

When assigning memory to a z/VM guest, make sure that the memory size suits the needs of your preferred installation type. See *Section 4.1.1.1.1, "Memory Requirements"*. To set the memory size to 1 GB, use the command **CP DEFINE STORAGE 1G**. After the installation has finished, reset the memory size to the desired value.

EXAMPLE 4.1: CONFIGURATION OF A Z/VM DIRECTORY

```
USER LINUX1 LINPWD 1024M 2048M G
* _____
* LINUX1
* _____
* This VM Linux guest has two CPUs defined.

CPU 01 CPUID 111111
CPU 02 CPUID 111222
IPL CMS PARM AUTOCR
IUCV ANY
IUCV ALLOW
MACH ESA 10
OPTION MAINTCCW RMCHINFO
SHARE RELATIVE 2000
CONSOLE 01C0 3270 A
SPOOL 000C 2540 READER *
SPOOL 000D 2540 PUNCH A
SPOOL 000E 3203 A
* OSA QDIO DEVICE DEFINITIONS
DEDICATE 9A0 9A0
DEDICATE 9A1 9A1
DEDICATE 9A2 9A2
*
LINK MAINT 0190 0190 RR
```

```
LINK MAINT 019E 019E RR
LINK MAINT 019D 019D RR
* MINIDISK DEFINITIONS
MDISK 201 3390 0001 0050 DASD40 MR ONE4ME TWO4ME THR4ME
MDISK 150 3390 0052 0200 DASD40 MR ONE4ME TWO4ME THR4ME
MDISK 151 3390 0253 2800 DASD40 MR ONE4ME TWO4ME THR4ME
```

This example uses minidisk 201 as the guest's home disk. Minidisk 150 with 200 cylinders is the Linux swap device. Disk 151 with 2800 cylinders holds the Linux installation.

Now add (as the user `MAINT`) the guest to the user directory with **DIRM FOR LINUX1 ADD**. Enter the name of the guest (`LINUX1`) and press `F5`. Set up the environment of the user with:

```
DIRM DIRECT
DIRM USER WITHPASS
```

The last command returns a reader file number. This number is needed for the next command:

```
RECEIVE <number> USER DIRECT A (REPL)
```

You can now log in on the guest as user `LINUX1`.

If you do not have the `dirmaint` option available, refer to the IBM documentation to set up this user.

Proceed with *Section 4.2.4.2, "IPLing a z/VM Installation"*.

4.2.3.3 Preparing the IPL of a KVM Guest Installation

A KVM guest installation requires a domain XML file defining the virtual machine and at least one virtual disk image for the installation.

4.2.3.3.1 Create a Virtual Disk Image

By default libvirt searches for disk images in `/var/lib/libvirt/images/` on the VM Host Server. Although images can also be stored anywhere on the file system, it is recommended to store all images in a single location for easier maintainability. The following example creates a qcow2 image with a size of 10 GB in `/var/lib/libvirt/images/`. For more information refer to *Book "Virtualization Guide", Chapter 28 "Guest Installation", Section 28.2 "Managing Disk Images with* **qemu-img**".

1. Log in to the KVM host server.

2. Run the following command to create the image:

```
qemu-img create -f qcow2 /var/lib/libvirt/images/s12lin_qcow2.img 10G
```

4.2.3.3.2 Write a Domain XML File

A domain XML file is used to define the VM Guest. To create the domain XML file open an empty file s12-1.xml with an editor and create a file like in the following example.

EXAMPLE 4.2: EXAMPLE DOMAIN XML FILE

The following example creates a VM Guest with a single CPU, 1 GB RAM, and the virtual disk image created in the previous section (*Section 4.2.3.3.1, "Create a Virtual Disk Image"*). It assumes that the host network interface to which the virtual server is attached is bond0. Change the source devices element to match your network setup.

```xml
<domain type="kvm">
 <name>s12-1</name>
 <description>Guest-System SUSE Sles12</description>
 <memory>1048576</memory>
 <vcpu>1</vcpu>
 <os>
  <type arch="s390x" machine="s390-ccw-virtio">hvm</type>
  <!-- Boot kernel - remove 3 lines after successfull installation -->
  <kernel>/var/lib/libvirt/images/s12-kernel.boot</kernel>
  <initrd>/var/lib/libvirt/images/s12-initrd.boot</initrd>
  <cmdline>linuxrcstderr=/dev/console</cmdline>
 </os>
 <iothreads>1</iothreads>
 <on_poweroff>destroy</on_poweroff>
 <on_reboot>restart</on_reboot>
 <on_crash>preserve</on_crash>
 <devices>
  <emulator>/usr/bin/qemu-system-s390x</emulator>
  <disk type="file" device="disk">
   <driver name="qemu" type="qcow2" cache="none" iothread="1" io="native"/>
   <source file="/var/lib/libvirt/images/s12lin_qcow2.img"/>
   <target dev="vda" bus="virtio"/>
  </disk>
  <interface type="direct">
   <source dev="bond0" mode="bridge"/>
   <model type="virtio"/>
  </interface>
  <console type="pty">
   <target type="sclp"/>
```

```
    </console>
  </devices>
</domain>
```

4.2.4   IPLing the SUSE Linux Enterprise Server Installation System

4.2.4.1   IPLing an LPAR Installation

There are different ways to IPL SUSE Linux Enterprise Server into an LPAR. The preferred way is to use the *Load from CD-ROM or server* feature of the SE or HMC.

4.2.4.1.1   IPL from DVD-ROM

Mark the LPAR to install and select *Load from CD-ROM or server*. Leave the field for the file location blank or enter the path to the root directory of the first DVD-ROM and select continue. In the list of options that appears, select the default selection. *Operating system messages* should now show the kernel boot messages.

4.2.4.1.2   IPL from FCP-Attached SCSI DVD

You can use the *Load* procedure by selecting *SCSI* as *Load type* to IPL from SCSI. Enter the WWPN (Worldwide port name) and LUN Logical unit number) provided by your SCSI bridge or storage (16 digits—do not omit the trailing 0s). The boot program selector must be 2. Use your FCP adapter as *Load address* and perform an IPL.

4.2.4.2   IPLing a z/VM Installation

This section is about IPLing the installation system to install SUSE Linux Enterprise Server for IBM z Systems on a z/VM system.

4.2.4.2.1   IPL from the z/VM Reader

You need a working TCP/IP connection and an FTP client program within your newly defined z/VM guest to transfer the installation system via FTP. Setting up TCP/IP for z/VM is beyond the scope of this manual. Refer to the appropriate IBM documentation.

Log in as the z/VM Linux guest to IPL. Make the content of the directory /boot/s390x on DVD 1 of the SUSE Linux Enterprise Server for IBM z Systems available via FTP within your network. From this directory, get the files linux, initrd, parmfile, and sles12.exec. Transfer the files with a fixed block size of 80 characters. Specify it with the FTP command **locsite fix 80**. It is important to copy linux (the Linux kernel) and initrd (the installation image) as binary files, so use the binary transfer mode. parmfile and sles12.exec need to be transferred in ASCII mode.

The example shows the steps necessary. In this example, the required files are accessible from an FTP server at the IP address 192.168.0.3 and the login is lininst. It may differ for your network.

EXAMPLE 4.3: TRANSFERRING THE BINARIES VIA FTP

```
FTP 192.168.0.3
VM TCP/IP FTP Level 530
Connecting to 192.168.0.3, port 21
220 ftpserver FTP server (Version wu-2.4.2-academ[BETA-18](1)
Thu Feb 11 16:09:02 GMT 2010) ready.
USER
lininst
331 Password required for lininst
PASS
******
230 User lininst logged in.
Command:
binary
200 Type set to I
Command:
locsite fix 80
Command:
get /media/dvd1/boot/s390x/linux sles12.linux
200 PORT Command successful
150 Opening BINARY mode data connection for /media/dvd1/boot/s390x/linux
(10664192 bytes)
226 Transfer complete.
10664192 bytes transferred in 13.91 seconds.
Transfer rate 766.70 Kbytes/sec.
Command:
get /media/dvd1/boot/s390x/initrd sles12.initrd
200 PORT Command successful
150 Opening BINARY mode data connection for /media/dvd1/boot/s390x/initrd
(21403276 bytes)
226 Transfer complete.
21403276 bytes transferred in 27.916 seconds.
```

```
Transfer rate 766.70 Kbytes/sec.
Command:
ascii
200 Type set to A
Command:
get /media/dvd1/boot/s390x/parmfile sles12.parmfile
150 Opening ASCII mode data connection for /media/dvd1/boot/s390x/parmfile
(5 bytes)
226 Transfer complete.
5 bytes transferred in 0.092 seconds.
Transfer rate 0.05 Kbytes/sec.
Command:
get /media/dvd1/boot/s390x/sles12.exec sles12.exec
150 Opening ASCII mode data connection for /media/dvd1/boot/s390x/sles12.exec
(891 bytes)
226 Transfer complete.
891 bytes transferred in 0.097 seconds.
Transfer rate 0.89 Kbytes/sec.
Command:
quit
```

Use the REXX script sles12.exec you downloaded to IPL the Linux installation system. This script loads the kernel, parmfile, and the initial RAM disk into the reader for IPL.

EXAMPLE 4.4: SLES12 EXEC

```
/* REXX LOAD EXEC FOR SUSE LINUX S/390 VM GUESTS      */
/* LOADS SUSE LINUX S/390 FILES INTO READER           */
SAY ''
SAY 'LOADING SLES12 FILES INTO READER...'
'CP CLOSE RDR'
'PURGE RDR ALL'
'SPOOL PUNCH * RDR'
'PUNCH SLES12 LINUX A (NOH'
'PUNCH SLES12 PARMFILE A (NOH'
'PUNCH SLES12 INITRD A (NOH'
'IPL 00C'
```

With this script you can IPL the SUSE Linux Enterprise Server installation system with the command **sles12**. The Linux kernel then starts and prints its boot messages.

To continue the installation, proceed to *Section 4.2.5, "Network Configuration"*.

4.2.4.2.2   IPL from FCP-Attached SCSI DVD

To IPL in z/VM, prepare the SCSI IPL process by using the SET LOADDEV parameter:

```
SET LOADDEV PORTNAME 200400E8 00D74E00 LUN 00020000 00000000 BOOT 2
```

After setting the LOADDEV parameter with the appropriate values, IPL your FCP adapter, for example:

```
IPL FC00
```

To continue the installation, proceed with *Section 4.2.5, "Network Configuration"*.

4.2.4.2.3   IPL from a Cobbler Server with zPXE

To IPL from a Cobbler server with zPXE you need to transfer the zpxe.rexx script via FTP from the Cobbler server to your z/VM guest. The z/VM guest needs a working TCP/IP connection and an FTP client program.

Log in as the z/VM Linux guest to IPL and transfer the script with a fixed size of 80 characters in ASCII mode (see *Example 4.3, "Transferring the Binaries via FTP"* for an example). The zpxe.rexx script is available on the Cobbler server at /usr/share/doc/packages/s390-tools/.

zpxe.rexx is supposed to replace the PROFILE EXEC of your guest. Make a backup copy of the existing PROFILE EXEC and rename ZPXE REXX to PROFILE EXEC. Alternatively call ZPXE REXX from the existing PROFILE EXEC by using a new line with the following content: 'ZPXE REXX'.

The last step is to create a configuration file, ZPXE CONF, telling ZPXE REXX which Cobbler server to contact and which disk to IPL. Run **xedit zpxe conf a** and create ZPXE CONF with the following content (replace the example data accordingly):

```
HOST cobbler.example.com
IPLDISK 600
```

On the next login to your z/VM guest, the Cobbler server will be connected. If an installation is scheduled on the Cobbler server, it will be executed. To schedule the installation, run the following command on the Cobbler server:

```
cobbler system edit --name ID❶ --netboot-enabled 1❷ --profile PROFILENAME❸
```

❶   z/VM user ID.

❷   Enable IPLing from the network.

❸ Name of an existing profile, see *Section 4.2.1.3.3, "Adjusting the Profile"*.

4.2.4.3 IPLing a KVM Guest Installation

To start the guest installation, you first need to start the VM Guest defined in *Section 4.2.3.3.1, "Create a Virtual Disk Image"*. A prerequisite for this is to first make the kernel and initrd required for IPLing available.

4.2.4.3.1 Preparing the installation source

Kernel and initrd of the installation system need to be copied to the VM Host Server to be able to IPL the VM Guest into the installation system.

1. Log in to the KVM host and make sure you can connect to the remote host or device serving the installation source.

2. Copy the following two files from the installation source to `/var/lib/libvirt/images/`. If the data is served from a remote host, use **ftp**, **sftp**, or **scp** to transfer the files:

   `/boot/s390x/initrd`
   `/boot/s390x/cd.ikr`

3. Rename the files on the KVM host:

   ```
   cd /var/lib/libvirt/images/
   mv initrd s12-initrd.boot
    mv cd.ikr s12-kernel.boot
   ```

4.2.4.3.2 IPL the VM Guest

To IPL the VM Guest, log in to the KVM host and run the following command:

```
virsh  create s12-1.xml --console
```

After the start-up of the VM Guest has completed, the installation system starts and you will see the following message:

```
Domain s12-1 started
Connected to domain s12-1
Escape character is ^]
Initializing cgroup subsys cpuset
```

```
Initializing cgroup subsys cpu
Initializing
cgroup subsys cpuacct
.
.
.
Please make sure your installation medium is available.
Retry?
0) <-- Back <--
1) Yes
2) No
```

Answer *2) No* and choose *Installation* on the next step. Proceed as described in *Section 4.2.5.3, "Set Up the Network and Select the Installation Source"*.

4.2.5   Network Configuration

Wait until the kernel has completed its start-up routines. If you are installing in basic mode or in an LPAR, open the *Operating System Messages* on the HMC or SE.

First, choose *Start Installation* in the linuxrc main menu then *Start Installation or Update* to start the installation process. Select *Network* as your installation medium then select the type of network protocol you will be using for the installation. *Section 4.2.1, "Making the Installation Data Available"* describes how to make the installation data available for the various types of network connections. Currently, *FTP*, *HTTP*, *NFS*, and *SMB/CIFS* (Windows file sharing) are supported.

Now choose an OSA or HiperSockets network device over which to receive the installation data from the list of available devices. The list may also contain CTC, ESCON, or IUCV devices, but they are no longer supported on SUSE Linux Enterprise Server.

4.2.5.1   Configure a HiperSockets Interface

Select a Hipersocket device from the list of network devices. Then enter the numbers for the read, write and data channels:

EXAMPLE 4.5: SUPPORTED NETWORK CONNECTION TYPES AND DRIVER PARAMETERS

```
Choose the network device.

 1) IBM parallel CTC Adapter (0.0.0600)
 2) IBM parallel CTC Adapter (0.0.0601)
 3) IBM parallel CTC Adapter (0.0.0602)
 4) IBM Hipersocket (0.0.0800)
 5) IBM Hipersocket (0.0.0801)
```

```
 6) IBM Hipersocket (0.0.0802)
 7) IBM OSA Express Network card (0.0.0700)
 8) IBM OSA Express Network card (0.0.0701)
 9) IBM OSA Express Network card (0.0.0702)
10) IBM OSA Express Network card (0.0.f400)
11) IBM OSA Express Network card (0.0.f401)
12) IBM OSA Express Network card (0.0.f402)
13) IBM IUCV

> 4

Device address for read channel. (Enter '+++' to abort).
[0.0.800]> 0.0.800

Device address for write channel. (Enter '+++' to abort).
[0.0.801]> 0.0.801

Device address for data channel. (Enter '+++' to abort).
[0.0.802]> 0.0.802
```

4.2.5.2 Configure an OSA Express Device

Select an OSA Express device from the list of network devices and provide a port number. Then enter the numbers for the read, write and data channels and the port name, if applicable. Choose whether to enable OSI Layer 2 support.

The port number was added to support the new 2 port OSA Express 3 Network devices. If you are not using an OSA Express 3 device, enter 0. OSA Express cards also have the option of running in an "OSI layer 2 support" mode or using the older more common "layer 3" mode. The card mode affects all systems that share the device including systems on other LPARs. If in doubt, specify 2 for compatibility with the default mode used by other operating systems such as z/VM and z/OS. Consult with your hardware administrator for further information on these options.

EXAMPLE 4.6: NETWORK DEVICE DRIVER PARAMETERS

```
Choose the network device.

 1) IBM parallel CTC Adapter (0.0.0600)
 2) IBM parallel CTC Adapter (0.0.0601)
 3) IBM parallel CTC Adapter (0.0.0602)
 4) IBM Hipersocket (0.0.0800)
 5) IBM Hipersocket (0.0.0801)
 6) IBM Hipersocket (0.0.0802)
 7) IBM OSA Express Network card (0.0.0700)
 8) IBM OSA Express Network card (0.0.0701)
```

```
  9) IBM OSA Express Network card (0.0.0702)
 10) IBM OSA Express Network card (0.0.f400)
 11) IBM OSA Express Network card (0.0.f401)
 12) IBM OSA Express Network card (0.0.f402)
 13) IBM IUCV

 > 7

 Enter the relative port number. (Enter '+++' to abort).
 > 0

 Device address for read channel. (Enter '+++' to abort).
 [0.0.0700]> 0.0.0700

 Device address for write channel. (Enter '+++' to abort).
 [0.0.0701]> 0.0.0701

 Device address for data channel. (Enter '+++' to abort).
 [0.0.0702]> 0.0.0702

 Enable OSI Layer 2 support?

 0) <-- Back <--
 1) Yes
 2) No

 > 1

 MAC address. (Enter '+++' to abort).
 > +++
```

4.2.5.3   Set Up the Network and Select the Installation Source

When all network device parameters have been entered, the respective driver is installed and you see the corresponding kernel messages.

Next, decide whether to use DHCP autoconfiguration for setting up the network interface parameters. Because DHCP only works on a few devices and requires special hardware configuration settings, you probably want to say *NO* here. When you do so, you are prompted for the following networking parameters:

- The IP address of the system to install

- The corresponding netmask (if not having been specified with the IP address)

- The IP address of a gateway to reach the server

- A list of search domains covered by the domain name server (DNS)

- The IP address of your domain name server

EXAMPLE 4.7: NETWORKING PARAMETERS

```
Automatic configuration via DHCP?

0) <-- Back <--
1) Yes
2) No

> 2

Enter your IP address with network prefix.

You can enter more than one, separated by space, if necessary.
Leave empty for autoconfig.

Examples: 192.168.5.77/24 2001:db8:75:fff::3/64. (Enter '+++' to abort).
> 192.168.0.20/24

Enter your name server IP address.

You can enter more than one, separated by space, if necessary.
Leave empty if you don't need one.

Examples: 192.168.5.77 2001:db8:75:fff::3. (Enter '+++' to abort).
> 192.168.0.1

Enter your search domains, separated by a space:. (Enter '+++' to abort).
> example.com

Enter the IP address of your name server. Leave empty if you do not need one. (En
ter '+++' to abort).
> 192.168.0.1
```

Finally, you are prompted for details on the installation server, such as the IP address, the directory containing the installation data, and login credentials. Once all required data is entered, the installation system loads.

4.2.6 Connecting to the SUSE Linux Enterprise Server Installation System

After having loaded the installation system, linuxrc wants to know what type of display you want to use to control the installation procedure. Possible choices are X11 (X Window System), VNC (Virtual Network Computing protocol), SSH (text mode or X11 installation via Secure Shell), or ASCII Console. Selecting VNC or SSH is recommended.

When selecting the latter (ASCII Console), YaST will be started in text mode and you can perform the installation directly within your terminal. See *Book "Administration Guide", Chapter 5 "YaST in Text Mode"* for instructions on how to use YaST in text mode. Using the ASCII Console is only useful when installing into LPAR.

 Note: Terminal Emulation for ASCII Console

To be able to work with YaST in text mode, it needs to run in a terminal with VT220/Linux emulation (also called ASCII console). You cannot use YaST in a 3270 terminal, for example.

4.2.6.1 Initiating the Installation for VNC

1. After the installation option VNC has been chosen, the VNC server starts. A short note displayed in the console provides information about which IP address and display number is needed for a connection with vncviewer.

2. Start a VNC client application on your client system.

3. Enter the IP address and the display number of the SUSE Linux Enterprise Server installation system when prompted to do so.

4. After the connection has been established, start installing SUSE Linux Enterprise Server with YaST.

4.2.6.2   Initiating the Installation for the X Window System

 Important: X Authentication Mechanism

The direct installation with the X Window System relies on a primitive authentication mechanism based on host names. This mechanism is disabled on current SUSE Linux Enterprise Server versions. Installation with SSH or VNC is preferred.

1. Make sure that the X server allows the client (the system that is installed) to connect. Set the variable **DISPLAYMANAGER_XSERVER_TCP_PORT_6000_OPEN="yes"** in the file `/etc/sysconfig/displaymanager`. Then restart the X server and allow client binding to the server using **xhost <client IP address>**.

2. When prompted at the installation system, enter the IP address of the machine running the X server.

3. Wait until YaST opens then start the installation.

4.2.6.3   Initiating the Installation for SSH

To connect to an installation system with the name `earth` using SSH, execute **ssh -X earth**. If your workstation runs on Microsoft Windows, use the SSH and telnet client and terminal emulator Putty which is available from http://www.chiark.greenend.org.uk/~sgtatham/putty/↗. Set *Enable X11 forwarding* in Putty under *Connection > SSH > X11*. If you use another operating system, execute **ssh -X earth** to connect to an installation system with the name `earth`. X-Forwarding over SSH is supported if you have a local X server available. Otherwise, YaST provides a text interface over ncurses.

A login prompt appears. Enter `root` and log in with your password. Enter **yast.ssh** to start YaST. YaST then guides you through the installation.

Proceed with the detailed description of the installation procedure that can be found in *Chapter 6, Installation with YaST*.

4.2.7   The SUSE Linux Enterprise Server Boot Procedure on IBM z Systems

The boot process for SLES 10 and 11 followed the scheme provided below. For in-depth information refer to the documentation provided at http://www.ibm.com/developerworks/linux/linux390/documentation_suse.html ↗.

1. Provide the kernel.

2. Provide or create an initrd for the given kernel.

3. Provide the correct paths for the initrd and the kernel in `/etc/zipl.conf`.

4. Install the configuration provided by `/etc/zipl.conf` to the system.

With SLES 12 the way SUSE Linux Enterprise Server is booted on IBM z Systems has changed. Several reasons led to this change:

- Alignment with other architectures: From an administrative point of view SLES systems should behave the same on all architectures.

- Btrfs: The zipl boot loader is technically incompatible with Btrfs, the new default root file system for SLES (see *Book "Storage Administration Guide", Chapter 1 "Overview of File Systems in Linux", Section 1.2 "Btrfs"* for details).

- Support for system rollbacks with Snapper: Snapper, in combination with Btrfs, provides bootable system snapshots which can be used for system rollbacks (see *Book "Administration Guide", Chapter 7 "System Recovery and Snapshot Management with Snapper"* for details).

For those reasons, starting with SLES 12, GRUB 2 replaces zipl on IBM SUSE Linux Enterprise Server for z Systems. GRUB 2 on the AMD64/Intel 64 architecture includes device drivers on the firmware level to access the file system. On the mainframe there is no firmware and adding `ccw` to GRUB 2 would not only be a major undertaking, but would also require a reimplementation of zipl in GRUB 2. Therefore SUSE Linux Enterprise Server uses a two-stage approach:

Stage One:

> A separate partition containing the kernel and an initrd is mounted to `/boot/zipl` (somewhat similar to `/boot/efi` on UEFI platforms). This kernel and the initrd are loaded via zipl using the configuration from `/boot/zipl/config`.

This configuration adds the keyword `initgrub` to the kernel command line. When the kernel and initrd are loaded, the initrd activates the devices required to mount the root file system (see `/boot/zipl/active_devices.txt`). Afterward a GRUB 2 user space program is started, which reads `/boot/grub2/grub.cfg`.

Stage Two:

The kernel and the initrd specified in `/boot/grub2/grub.cfg` are started via **kexec**. All devices listed in `/boot/zipl/active_devices.txt` are activated, the root file system is mounted and the boot procedure continues like on the other architectures.

4.3 The parmfile—Automating the System Configuration

The installation process can be partly automated by specifying the crucial parameters in the `parmfile`. The `parmfile` contains all the data required for network setup and DASD configuration. In addition to that, it can be used to set up the connection method to the SUSE Linux Enterprise Server installation system and the YaST instance running there. User interaction is thus limited to the actual YaST installation controlled by YaST dialogs.

The following parameters can be passed to the installation routine, which takes them as default values for installation. All IP addresses, server names, and numerical values are examples. Replace these values with the ones needed in your installation scenario.

The number of lines in the parmfile is limited to 10. Specify more than one parameter on a line. Parameter names are not case-sensitive. Separate the parameters by spaces. You may specify the parameters in any order. Always keep the `PARAMETER=value` string together in one line. For example:

```
Hostname=s390zvm01.suse.de HostIP=10.11.134.65
```

 Tip: Using IPv6 during the Installation

By default you can only assign IPv4 network addresses to your machine. To enable IPv6 during installation, enter one of the following parameters at the boot prompt: `ipv6=1` (accept IPv4 and IPv6) or `ipv6only=1` (accept IPv6 only).

Some of the following parameters are required. If they are missing, the automatic process pauses and asks you to enter the value manually.

4.3.1 General Parameters

AutoYaST= <*URL*> Manual=0

The `AutoYaST` parameter specifies the location of the `autoinst.xml` control file for auto-matic installation. The `Manual` parameter controls if the other parameters are only default values that still must be acknowledged by the user. Set this parameter to `0` if all values should be accepted and no questions asked. Setting `AutoYaST` implies setting `Manual` to `0`.

Info= <*URL*>

Specifies a location for a file from which to read additional options. This helps to over-come the limitations of 10 lines (and 80 characters per line under z/VM) for the parmfile. More documentation on the Info file can be found in *Book "AutoYaST", Chapter 6 "The Auto-In-stallation Process", Section 6.3.3 "Combining the linuxrc `info` file with the AutoYaST control file"*. Since the Info file can typically only be accessed through the network on z Systems, you cannot use it to specify options required to set up the network (these options described in *Section 4.3.2, "Configuring the Network Interface"*). Also other linuxrc specific options such as for debugging need to be specified in the parmfile to be effective.

Upgrade=<0|1>

To upgrade your SUSE Linux Enterprise, specify **Upgrade=1**. Therefore, a custom parmfile is required for upgrading an existing installation of SUSE Linux Enterprise. Without this parameter, the installation provides no upgrade option.

 Tip: Creating a File with Autoinstallation Information

At the very end of the installation of a system you can check *Clone This System for Autoyast*. This creates a ready-to-use profile as `/root/autoinst.xml` that can be used to create clones of this particular installation. To create an autoinstallation file from scratch or to edit an existing one, use the YaST module *Autoinstallation*.

4.3.2 Configuring the Network Interface

 Important: Configuring the Network Interface

The settings discussed in this section apply only to the network interface used during installation. Configure additional network interfaces in the installed system by following the instructions given in *Book "Administration Guide", Chapter 16 "Basic Networking", Section 16.5 "Configuring a Network Connection Manually"*.

Hostname=zsystems.example.com

Enter the fully qualified host name.

Domain=example.com

Domain search path for DNS. Allows you to use short host names instead of fully qualified ones.

HostIP=192.168.1.2

Enter the IP address of the interface to configure.

Gateway=192.168.1.3

Specify the gateway to use.

Nameserver=192.168.1.4

Specify the DNS server in charge.

InstNetDev=osa

Enter the type of interface to configure. Possible values are osa, hsi, ctc, escon, and iucv (CTC, ESCON, and IUCV are no longer officially supported).

For the interfaces of type hsi and osa, specify an appropriate netmask and an optional broadcast address:

```
Netmask=255.255.255.0
Broadcast=192.168.255.255
```

For the interfaces of type ctc, escon, and iucv (CTC, ESCON, and IUCV are no longer officially supported), enter the IP address of the peer:

```
Pointopoint=192.168.55.20
```

OsaInterface=<lcs|qdio>

For osa network devices, specify the host interface (qdio or lcs).

Layer2=<0|1>

> For osa QDIO Ethernet and hsi devices, specify whether to enable (1) or disable (0) OSI Layer 2 support.

OSAHWAddr=02:00:65:00:01:09

> For Layer 2-enabled osa QDIO Ethernet devices. Either specify a MAC address manually or state OSAHWADDR= (with trailing white space) for the system default.

PortNo=<0|1>

> For osa network devices, specify the port number (provided the device supports this feature). The default value is 0.

Each of the interfaces requires certain setup options:

- Interfaces ctc and escon (CTC and ESCON are no longer officially supported):

```
ReadChannel=0.0.0600
WriteChannel=0.0.0601
```

ReadChannel specifies the READ channel to use. WriteChannel specifies the WRITE channel.

- For the ctc interface (no longer officially supported), specify the protocol that should be used for this interface:

```
CTCProtocol=<0/1/2>
```

Valid entries would be:

0	Compatibility mode, also for non-Linux peers other than OS/390 and z/OS (this is the default mode)
1	Extended mode
2	Compatibility mode with OS/390 and z/OS

- Network device type osa with interface lcs:

```
ReadChannel=0.0.0124
```

`ReadChannel` stands for the channel number used in this setup. A second port number can be derived from this by adding one to `ReadChannel`. `Portnumber` is used to specify the relative port.

- Interface `iucv`:

```
IUCVPeer=PEER
```

Enter the name of the peer machine.

- Network device type `osa` with interface `qdio` for OSA-Express Gigabit Ethernet:

```
ReadChannel=0.0.0700
WriteChannel=0.0.0701
DataChannel=0.0.0702
```

For `ReadChannel`, enter the number of the READ channel. For `WriteChannel`, enter the number of the WRITE channel. `DataChannel` specifies the DATA channel. Make sure that the READ channel carries an even device number.

- Interface `hsi` for HiperSockets and VM guest LANs:

```
ReadChannel=0.0.0800
WriteChannel=0.0.0801
DataChannel=0.0.0802
```

For `ReadChannel`, enter the appropriate number for the READ channel. For `WriteChannel` and `DataChannel`, enter the WRITE and DATA channel numbers.

4.3.3 Specifying the Installation Source and YaST Interface

`Install=nfs://server/directory/DVD1/`

Specify the location of the installation source to use. Possible protocols are `nfs`, `smb` (Samba/CIFS), `ftp`, `tftp` `http`, and `https`.

If an `ftp`, `tftp` or `smb` URL is given, specify the user name and password with the URL. These parameters are optional and anonymous or guest login is assumed if they are not given.

```
Install=ftp://USER:PASSWORD@SERVER/DIRECTORY/DVD1/
Install=tftp://USER:PASSWORD@SERVER/DIRECTORY/DVD1/
```

If you want to install over an encrypted connection, use an `https` URL. If the certificate cannot be verified, use the `sslcerts=0` boot option to disable certificate checking.

In case of a Samba or CIFS installation, you can also specify the domain that should be used:

```
Install=smb://WORKDOMAIN;USER:PASSWORD@SERVER/DIRECTORY/DVD1/
```

ssh=1 vnc=1 Display_IP=192.168.42.42

Depending on which parameter you give, a remote X server, SSH, or VNC will be used for installation. `ssh` enables SSH installation, `vnc` starts a VNC server on the installing machine, and `Display_IP` causes the installing system to try to connect to an X server at the given address. Only one of these parameters should be set at any time.

 Important: X Authentication Mechanism

The direct installation with the X Window System relies on a primitive authentication mechanism based on host names. This mechanism is disabled on current SUSE Linux Enterprise Server versions. Installation with SSH or VNC is preferred.

To allow a connection between YaST and the remote X server, run **xhost** `<IP address>` with the address of the installing machine on the remote machine.

For `VNC`, specify a password of six to eight characters to use for installation:

```
VNCPassword=<a password>
```

For `SSH`, specify a password of six to eight characters to use for installation:

```
ssh.password=<a password>
```

4.3.4   Example Parmfiles

The maximum capacity of a parmfile is 860 characters. As a rule of thumb, the parmfile should contain a maximum of 10 lines with no more than 79 characters. When reading a parmfile, all lines are concatenated without adding white spaces, therefore the last character (79) of each line needs to be a `Space`.

To receive potential error messages on the console, use

```
linuxrclog=/dev/console
```

EXAMPLE 4.8: PARMFILE FOR AN INSTALLATION FROM NFS WITH VNC AND AUTOYAST

```
ramdisk_size=131072 root=/dev/ram1 ro init=/linuxrc TERM=dumb
instnetdev=osa osainterface=qdio layer2=1 osahwaddr=
pointopoint=192.168.0.1
hostip=192.168.0.2
nameserver=192.168.0.3
install=nfs://192.168.0.4/SLES/SLES-12-Server/s390x/DVD1
autoyast=http://192.168.0.5/autoinst.xml
linuxrclog=/dev/console vnc=1
VNCPassword=testing
```

EXAMPLE 4.9: PARMFILE FOR INSTALLATION WITH NFS, SSH, AND HSI AND AUTOYAST WITH NFS

```
ramdisk_size=131072 root=/dev/ram1 ro init=/linuxrc TERM=dumb
AutoYast=nfs://192.168.1.1/autoinst/s390.xml
Hostname=zsystems.example.com HostIP=192.168.1.2
Gateway=192.168.1.3 Nameserver=192.168.1.4
InstNetDev=hsi layer2=0
Netmask=255.255.255.128 Broadcast=192.168.1.255
readchannel=0.0.702c writechannel=0.0.702d datachannel=0.0.702e
install=nfs://192.168.1.5/SLES-12-Server/s390x/DVD1/
ssh=1 ssh.password=testing linuxrclog=/dev/console
```

4.4 Using the vt220 Terminal Emulator

Recent MicroCode Levels allow the use of an integrated vt220 terminal emulator (ASCII terminal) in addition to the standard line mode terminal. The vt220 terminal is connected to /dev/ttysclp0. The line mode terminal is connected to /dev/ttysclp_line0. For LPAR installations, the vt220 terminal emulator is activated by default.

To start the ASCII console on HMC, log in to the HMC, and select *Systems Management › Systems › IMAGE_ID* . Select the radio button for the LPAR and select *Recovery › Integrated ASCII Console*.

To redirect the kernel messages at boot time from the system console to the vt220 terminal, add the following entries to the parameters line in /etc/zipl.conf:

```
console=ttysclp0 console=ttysclp_line0
```

The resulting parameters line would look like the following example:

```
parameters = "root=/dev/dasda2 TERM=dumb console=ttysclp0 console=ttysclp_line0"
```

Save the changes in `/etc/zipl.conf`, run **zipl**, and reboot the system.

4.5 Further In-Depth Information about IBM z Systems

Find additional in-depth technical documentation about IBM z Systems in the IBM Redbooks (https://www.redbooks.ibm.com/Redbooks.nsf/domains/zsystems ⏶) or at IBM developerWorks (https://www.ibm.com/developerworks/linux/linux390/ ⏶). SUSE Linux Enterprise Server-specific documentation is available from https://www.ibm.com/developerworks/linux/linux390/documentation_suse.html ⏶.

4.5.1 General Documents about Linux on IBM z Systems

A general coverage of Linux on IBM z Systems can be found in the following documents:

* Linux on IBM eServer zSeries and S/390: ISP and ASP Solutions (SG24-6299)

These documents might not reflect the current state of Linux, but the principles of Linux deployment outlined there remain accurate.

4.5.2 Technical Issues of Linux on IBM z Systems

Refer to the following documents to get in-depth technical information about the Linux kernel and application topics. Refer to the Internet for up-to-date versions of these documents for the most recent code drop (http://www.ibm.com/developerworks/linux/linux390/index.html ⏶).

* Linux on System z Device Drivers, Features, and Commands

* zSeries ELF Application Binary Interface Supplement

* Linux on System z Device Drivers, Using the Dump Tools

* IBM zEnterprise 196 Technical Guide

* IBM zEnterprise EC12 Technical Guide

* IBM z13 Technical Guide

There also is a Redbook for Linux application development at http://www.redbooks.ibm.com ↗:

- Linux on IBM eServer zSeries and S/390: Application Development (SG24-6807)

4.5.3 Advanced Configurations for Linux on IBM z Systems

Refer to the following Redbooks, Redpapers, and links for some more complex IBM z Systems scenarios:

- Linux on IBM eServer zSeries and S/390: Large Scale Deployment (SG24-6824)

- Linux on IBM eServer zSeries and S/390: Performance Measuring and Tuning (SG24-6926)

- Linux with zSeries and ESS: Essentials (SG24-7025)

- IBM TotalStorage Enterprise Storage Server Implementing ESS Copy Services with IBM eServer zSeries (SG24-5680)

- Linux on IBM zSeries and S/390: High Availability for z/VM and Linux (REDP-0220)

- Saved Segments Planning and Administration
  http://publibz.boulder.ibm.com/epubs/pdf/hcsg4a00.pdf ↗

- Linux on System z documentation for "Development stream"
  http://www.ibm.com/developerworks/linux/linux390/development_documentation.html ↗

4.5.4 Virtualization with KVM on IBM z Systems

Refer to the following documents at https://www.ibm.com/developerworks/linux/linux390/documentation_dev.html ↗ for more information on KVM on IBM z Systems:

- *Installing SUSE Linux Enterprise Server 12 as a KVM Guest* (SC34-2755-00)

- *KVM Virtual Server Quick Start* (SC34-2753-01)

- *KVM Virtual Server Management* (SC34-2752-01)

- *Device Drivers, Features, and Commands for Linux as a KVM Guest (Kernel 4.4)* (SC34-2754-01)

5 Installation on ARM AArch64

This chapter describes the steps necessary to prepare for the installation of SUSE Linux Enterprise Server on ARM AArch64 computers. It introduces the steps required to prepare for various installation methods. The list of hardware requirements provides an overview of systems supported by SUSE Linux Enterprise Server. Find information about available installation methods and several common known problems. Also learn how to control the installation, provide installation media, and boot with regular methods.

5.1 System Requirements for Operating Linux

The SUSE® Linux Enterprise Server operating system can be deployed on a wide range of hardware. It is impossible to list all the different combinations of hardware SUSE Linux Enterprise Server supports. However, to provide you with a guide to help you during the planning phase, the minimum requirements are presented here.

If you want to be sure that a given computer configuration will work, find out which platforms have been certified by SUSE. Find a list at https://www.suse.com/yessearch/ ↗.

5.1.1 Hardware for ARM AArch64

CPU

The minimum requirement is a CPU that supports the ARMv8-A instruction set architecture (ISA), for example, ARM Cortex-A53 or Cortex-A57. Refer to https://www.arm.com/products/processors/cortex-a/ ↗ for a list of available ARMv8-A processors.

CPUs with the ARMv8-R (realtime) and ARMv8-M (microcontroller) ISA are currently not supported.

Maximum Number of CPUs

The maximum number of CPUs supported by software design is 128. If you plan to use such a large system, check our hardware system certification Web page for supported devices, see https://www.suse.com/yessearch/ ↗.

Memory Requirements

A minimum of 1 GB of memory is required for a minimal installation. However, the minimum recommended is 1024 MB or 512 MB per CPU on multiprocessor computers. Add 150 MB for a remote installation via HTTP or FTP. Note that these values are only valid for the installation of the operating system—the actual memory requirement in production depends on the system's workload.

Hard Disk Requirements

The disk requirements depend largely on the installation selected and how you use your machine. Minimum requirements for different selections are:

System	Hard Disk Requirements
Minimal System	800 MB - 1GB
Minimal X Window System	1.4 GB
GNOME Desktop	3.5 GB
All patterns	8.5 GB
Using snapshots for virtualization	min. 8 GB

Boot Methods

The computer can be booted from a CD or a network. A special boot server is required to boot over the network. This can be set up with SUSE Linux Enterprise Server.

5.2   Installation Considerations

This section encompasses many factors that need to be considered before installing SUSE Linux Enterprise Server on ARM AArch64 hardware.

5.2.1 Installation Type

SUSE Linux Enterprise Server is normally installed as an independent operating system. With the introduction of Virtualization, it is also possible to run multiple instances of SUSE Linux Enterprise Server on the same hardware. However, the installation of the VM Host Server is performed like a typical installation with some additional packages. The installation of virtual guests is described in *Book "Virtualization Guide", Chapter 9 "Guest Installation".*

5.2.2 Boot Methods

Depending on the hardware used, the following boot methods are available for the first boot procedure (prior to the installation of SUSE Linux Enterprise Server).

TABLE 5.1: BOOT OPTIONS

Boot Option	Use
CD or DVD drive	The simplest booting method. The system requires a locally-available CD-ROM or DVD-ROM drive for this.
Flash disks	Find the images required for creating boot disks on the first CD or DVD in the `/boot` directory. See also the `README` in the same directory. Booting from a USB memory stick is only possible if the BIOS of the machine supports this method.
PXE or bootp	Must be supported by the firmware of the system used. This option requires a boot server in the network. This task can be handled by a separate SUSE Linux Enterprise Server.
Hard disk	SUSE Linux Enterprise Server can also be booted from hard disk. For this, copy the kernel (`linux`) and the installation system

Boot Option	Use
	(`initrd`) from the `/boot/loader` directory of the first CD or DVD onto the hard disk and add an appropriate entry to the boot loader.

5.2.3   Installation Source

When installing SUSE Linux Enterprise Server, the actual installation data must be available on the network, a hard disk partition, or a local DVD. To install from the network, you need an installation server. To make the installation data available, set up any computer in a Unix or Linux environment as an NFS, HTTP, SMB, or FTP server. To make the installation data available from a Windows computer, release the data with SMB.

The installation source is particularly easy to select if you configure an *SLP server* in the local network. For more information, see *Chapter 7, Setting Up the Server Holding the Installation Sources*.

5.2.4   Installation Target

Most installations are to a local hard disk. Therefore, it is necessary for the hard disk controllers to be available to the installation system. If a special controller (like a RAID controller) needs an extra kernel module, provide a kernel module update disk to the installation system.

Other installation targets may be various types of block devices that provide sufficient disk space and speed to run an operating system. This includes network block devices like `iSCSI` or `SAN`. It is also possible to install on network file systems that offer the standard Unix permissions. However, it may be problematic to boot these, because they must be supported by the `initramfs` before the actual system can start. Such installations are useful if there is a need to start the same system in different locations.

5.2.5   Different Installation Methods

SUSE Linux Enterprise Server offers several methods for controlling installation:

- Installation on the graphical console

- Installation via serial console

- Installation with AutoYaST
- Installation with KIWI images
- Installation via SSH
- Installation with VNC

By default, the graphical console is used. If you have many similar computers to install, it is advisable to create an AutoYaST configuration file or a KIWI preload image and make this available to the installation process. See also the documentation for AutoYaST at https://www.suse.com/documentation/sles-12/book_autoyast/data/book_autoyast.html and `KIWI` at http://doc.opensuse.org/projects/kiwi/doc/.

5.3 Boot and Installation Media

When installing the system, the media for booting and for installing the system may be different. All combinations of supported media for booting and installing may be used.

5.3.1 Boot Media

Booting a computer depends on the capabilities of the hardware used and the availability of media for the respective boot option.

Booting from DVD

This is the most common possibility of booting a system. It is straightforward for most computer users, but requires a lot of interaction for every installation process.

Booting from a USB Flash Drive

Depending on the hardware used, it is possible to boot from a USB hard disk. The respective media must be created as described in *Section 6.2.2, "PC (AMD64/Intel 64/ARM AArch64): System Start-up"*.

Booting from the Network

You can only boot a computer directly from the network if this is supported by the computer's firmware. This booting method requires a boot server that provides the needed boot images over the network. The exact protocol depends on your hardware. Commonly you need several services, such as TFTP and DHCP or PXE boot. If you need a boot server, also read *Section 9.1.3, "Remote Installation via VNC—PXE Boot and Wake on LAN"*.

5.3.2 Installation Media

The installation media contain all the necessary packages and meta information that is necessary to install a SUSE Linux Enterprise Server. These must be available to the installation system after booting for installation. Several possibilities for providing the installation media to the system are available with SUSE Linux Enterprise Server.

Installation from DVD

All necessary data is delivered on the boot media. Depending on the selected installation, a network connection or add-on media may be necessary.

Networked Installation

If you plan to install several systems, providing the installation media over the network makes things a lot easier. It is possible to install from many common protocols, such as NFS, HTTP, FTP, or SMB. For more information on how to run such an installation, refer to *Chapter 9, Remote Installation*.

5.4 Installation Procedure

This section offers an overview of the steps required for the complete installation of SUSE® Linux Enterprise Server in the required mode. *Part II, "The Installation Workflow"* contains a full description of how to install and configure the system with YaST.

5.4.1 Booting from a Local Interchangeable Drive

DVD-ROM and USB storage devices can be used for installation purposes. Adjust your computer to your needs:

1. Make sure that the drive is entered as a bootable drive in the firmware.

2. Insert the boot medium in the drive and start the boot procedure.

3. The installation boot menu of SUSE Linux Enterprise Server allows transferring different parameters to the installation system. See also *Section 9.2.2, "Using Custom Boot Options"*. If the installation should be performed over the network, specify the installation source here.

4. If unexpected problems arise during installation, use safe settings to boot.

5.4.2 Installing over the Network

An installation server is required to perform the installation by using a network source. The procedure for installing this server is outlined in *Chapter 7, Setting Up the Server Holding the Installation Sources*.

If you have an SLP server, select SLP as the installation source in the first boot screen. During the boot procedure, select which of the available installation sources to use.

If the DVD is available on the network, use it as an installation source. In this case, specify the parameter `install=<URL>` with suitable values at the boot prompt. Find a more detailed description of this parameter in *Section 9.2.2, "Using Custom Boot Options"*.

5.5 Controlling the Installation

Control the installation in one of several ways. The method most frequently used is to install SUSE® Linux Enterprise Server from the computer console. Other options are available for different situations.

5.5.1 Installation on the Computer Console

The simplest way to install SUSE Linux Enterprise Server is using the computer console. With this method, a graphical installation program guides you through the installation. This installation method is discussed in detail in *Chapter 6, Installation with YaST*.

You can still perform the installation on the console without a working graphics mode. The text-based installation program offers the same functionality as the graphical version. Find some hints about navigation in this mode in *Book "Administration Guide", Chapter 5 "YaST in Text Mode", Section 5.1 "Navigation in Modules"*.

5.5.2 Installation Using a Serial Console

For this installation method, you need a second computer connected by a *null modem* cable to the computer on which to install SUSE Linux Enterprise Server. Hardware and firmware of both machines need to support the serial console. Some firmware implementations are already configured to send the boot console output to a serial console (by providing a device tree with /chosen/stdout-path set appropriately). In this case no additional configuration is required.

If the firmware is not set up to use the serial console for the boot console output, you need to provide the following boot parameter at the boot prompt of the installation system (see *Book "Administration Guide", Chapter 12 "The Boot Loader GRUB 2", Section 12.2.5 "Editing Menu Entries during the Boot Procedure"* for details): `console=TTY,BAUDRATE`

`BAUDRATE` needs to be replaced by the baud rate for the interface. Valid values are 115200, 38400, or 9600. `TTY` needs to be replaced by the name of the interface. On most computers, there is one or more serial interfaces. Depending on the hardware, the names of the interfaces may vary:

- *ttyS0* for APM

- *ttyAMA0* for Server Base System Architecture (SBSA)

- *ttyPS0* for Xilinx

For the installation, you need a terminal program like minicom or screen. To initiate the serial connection, launch the screen program in a local console by entering the following command:

```
screen /dev/ttyUSB0 115200
```

This means that screen listens to the first serial port with a baud rate of 115200. From this point on, the installation proceeds similarly to the text-based installation over this terminal.

5.5.3   Installation with SSH

If you do not have direct access to the machine and the installation must be initiated from a management console, you can control the entire installation process over the network. To do this, enter the parameters `ssh=1` and `ssh.password=SECRET` at the boot prompt. An SSH daemon is then launched in the system and you can log in as user `root` with the password `SECRET`.

To connect, use **ssh -X**. X-Forwarding over SSH is supported, if you have a local X server available. Otherwise, YaST provides a text interface over ncurses. YaST then guides you through the installation. This procedure is described in detail in *Section 9.1.5, "Simple Remote Installation via SSH—Dynamic Network Configuration"*.

If you do not have a DHCP server available in your local network, manually assign an IP address to the installation system. Do this by entering the option `HostIP=IPADDR` at the boot prompt.

5.5.4   Installation over VNC

If you do not have direct access to the system, but want a graphical installation, install SUSE Linux Enterprise Server over VNC. This method is described in detail in *Section 9.3.1, "VNC Installation"*.

As suitable VNC clients are also available for other operating systems, such as Microsoft Windows and mac OS, the installation can also be controlled from computers running those operating systems.

5.5.5   Installation with AutoYaST

If you need to install SUSE Linux Enterprise Server on several computers with similar hardware, it is recommended you perform the installations with the aid of AutoYaST. In this case, start by installing one SUSE Linux Enterprise Server and use this to create the necessary AutoYaST configuration files.

5.6   Dealing with Boot and Installation Problems

Prior to delivery, SUSE® Linux Enterprise Server is subjected to an extensive test program. Despite this, problems occasionally occur during boot or installation.

5.6.1   Problems Booting

Boot problems may prevent the YaST installer from starting on your system. Another symptom is when your system does not boot after the installation has been completed.

Installed System Boots, Not Media

Change your computer's firmware so that the boot sequence is correct. To do this, consult the manual for your hardware.

The Computer Hangs

Change the console on your computer so that the kernel outputs are visible. Be sure to check the last outputs. This is normally done by pressing `Ctrl`-`Alt`-`F10`. If you cannot resolve the problem, consult the SUSE Linux Enterprise Server support staff. To log all system messages at boot time, use a serial connection as described in *Section 2.5, "Controlling the Installation"*.

Boot Disk

The boot disk is a useful interim solution if you have difficulties setting the other configurations or if you want to postpone the decision regarding the final boot mechanism. For more details on creating boot disks, see *Book "Administration Guide", Chapter 12 "The Boot Loader GRUB 2" grub2-mkrescue.*

5.6.2   Problems Installing

If an unexpected problem occurs during installation, information is needed to determine the cause of the problem. Use the following directions to help with troubleshooting:

- Check the outputs on the various consoles. You can switch consoles with the key combination `Ctrl`-`Alt`-`Fn`. For example, obtain a shell in which to execute various commands by pressing `Ctrl`-`Alt`-`F2`.

- Try launching the installation with "Safe Settings" (press `F5` on the installation screen and choose *Safe Settings*). If the installation works without problems in this case, there is an incompatibility that causes either `ACPI` or `APIC` to fail. In some cases, a firmware update fixes this problem.

- Check the system messages on a console in the installation system by entering the command `dmesg -T`.

5.6.3   Redirecting the Boot Source to the Boot DVD

To simplify the installation process and avoid accidental installations, the default setting on the installation DVD for SUSE Linux Enterprise Server is that your system is booted from the first hard disk. At this point, an installed boot loader normally takes over control of the system. This means that the boot DVD can stay in the drive during an installation. To start the installation, choose one of the installation possibilities in the boot menu of the media.

II The Installation Workflow

6 Installation with YaST

After your hardware has been prepared for the installation of SUSE® Linux Enterprise Server as described in *Part I, "Installation Preparation"* and after the connection with the installation system has been established, you are presented with the interface of SUSE Linux Enterprise Server's system assistant YaST. YaST guides you through the entire installation.

During the installation process, YaST analyzes both your current system settings and your hardware components. Based on this analysis your system will be set up with a basic configuration including networking (provided the system could be configured using DHCP). To fine-tune the system after the installation has finished, start YaST from the installed system.

6.1 Choosing the Installation Method

After having selected the installation medium, determine the suitable installation method and boot option that best matches your needs:

Installing from the SUSE Linux Enterprise Server Media (DVD, USB)

Choose this option if you want to perform a stand-alone installation and do not want to rely on a network to provide the installation data or the boot infrastructure. The installation proceeds exactly as outlined in *Section 6.3, "Steps of the Installation"*.

Installing from a Network Server

Choose this option if you have an installation server available in your network or want to use an external server as the source of your installation data. This setup can be configured to boot from physical media (flash disk, CD/DVD, or hard disk) or configured to boot via network using PXE/BOOTP. Refer to *Section 6.2, "System Start-up for Installation"* for details. The installation program configures the network connection with DHCP and retrieves the location of the network installation source from the OpenSLP server. If no DHCP is available, choose *F4 Source › Network Config › Manual* and enter the network data. On EFI systems modify the network boot parameters as described in *Section 6.2.2.2, "The Boot Screen on Machines Equipped with UEFI"*.

Installing from an SLP Server. If your network setup supports OpenSLP and your network installation source has been configured to announce itself via SLP (described in *Chapter 7, Setting Up the Server Holding the Installation Sources*), boot the system, press `F4` in the boot screen and select *SLP* from the menu. On EFI systems set the `install` parameter to `install=slp:/` as described in *Section 6.2.2.2, "The Boot Screen on Machines Equipped with UEFI"*.

Installing from a Network Source without SLP. If your network setup does not support OpenSLP for the retrieval of network installation sources, boot the system and press `F4` in the boot screen to select the desired network protocol (NFS, HTTP, FTP, or SMB/CIFS) and provide the server's address and the path to the installation media. On EFI systems modify the boot parameter `install=` as described in *Section 6.2.2.2, "The Boot Screen on Machines Equipped with UEFI"*.

6.2 System Start-up for Installation

The way the system is started for the installation depends on the architecture—system start-up is different for PC (AMD64/Intel 64) or mainframe, for example. If you install SUSE Linux Enterprise Server as a VM Guest on a KVM or Xen hypervisor, follow the instructions for the AMD64/Intel 64 architecture.

6.2.1 IBM z Systems: System Start-up

For IBM z Systems platforms, the system is booted (IPL, Initial Program Load) as described in *Section 4.2.4, "IPLing the SUSE Linux Enterprise Server Installation System"*. SUSE Linux Enterprise Server does not show a splash screen on these systems. During the installation, load the kernel, initrd, and parmfile manually. YaST starts with its installation screen when a connection has been established to the installation system via VNC, X, or SSH. Because there is no splash screen, kernel or boot parameters cannot be entered on screen, but must be specified in a parmfile (see *Section 4.3, "The parmfile—Automating the System Configuration"*).

6.2.2   PC (AMD64/Intel 64/ARM AArch64): System Start-up

SUSE Linux Enterprise Server supports several boot options from which you can choose, depending on the hardware available and on the installation scenario you prefer. Booting from the SUSE Linux Enterprise Server media is the most straightforward option, but special requirements might call for special setups:

TABLE 6.1: BOOT OPTIONS

Boot Option	Description
DVD	This is the easiest boot option. This option can be used if the system has a local DVD-ROM drive that is supported by Linux.
Flash Disks (USB Mass Storage Device)	In case your machine is not equipped with an optical drive, you can boot the installation image from a flash disk. To create a bootable flash disk, you need to copy either the DVD or the Mini CD ISO image to the device using the **dd** command (the flash disk must not be mounted, all data on the device will be erased): ```dd if=PATH_TO_ISO_IMAGE of=USB_STORAGE_DEVICE bs=4M``` **!** **Important: Compatibility** Note that booting from a USB Mass Storage Device is *not* supported on UEFI machines and on the POWER architecture.
PXE or BOOTP	Booting over the network must be supported by the system's BIOS or firmware, and a boot server must be available in the network. This task can also be handled by an-

Boot Option	Description
	other SUSE Linux Enterprise Server system. Refer to *Chapter 9, Remote Installation* for more information.
Hard Disk	SUSE Linux Enterprise Server installation can also be booted from the hard disk. To do this, copy the kernel (`linux`) and the installation system (`initrd`) from the directory `/boot/ARCHITECTURE/` on the installation media to the hard disk and add an appropriate entry to the existing boot loader of a previous SUSE Linux Enterprise Server installation.

Tip: Booting from DVD on UEFI Machines

DVD1 can be used as a boot medium for machines equipped with UEFI (Unified Extensible Firmware Interface). Refer to your vendor's documentation for specific information. If booting fails, try to enable CSM (Compatibility Support Module) in your firmware.

Note: Add-on Product Installation Media

Media for add-on products (extensions or third-party products) cannot be used as standalone installation media. They can either be embedded as additional installation sources during the installation process (see *Section 6.9, "Extension Selection"*) or be installed from the running system using the YaST Add-on Products module (see *Chapter 13, Installing Modules, Extensions, and Third Party Add-On Products* for details).

6.2.2.1 The Boot Screen on Machines Equipped with Traditional BIOS

The boot screen displays several options for the installation procedure. *Boot from Hard Disk* boots the installed system and is selected by default, because the CD is often left in the drive. Select one of the other options with the arrow keys and press ⌷Enter⌷ to boot it. The relevant options are:

Installation

The normal installation mode. All modern hardware functions are enabled. In case the installation fails, see ⌷F5⌷ *Kernel* for boot options that disable potentially problematic functions.

Upgrade

Perform a system upgrade. For more information refer to *Chapter 18, Upgrading SUSE Linux Enterprise.*

Rescue System

Starts a minimal Linux system without a graphical user interface. For more information, see *Book "Administration Guide", Chapter 40 "Common Problems and Their Solutions", Section 40.6.2 "Using the Rescue System".*

Check Installation Media

This option is only available when you install from media created from downloaded ISOs. In this case it is recommended to check the integrity of the installation medium. This option starts the installation system before automatically checking the media. In case the check was successful, the normal installation routine starts. If a corrupt media is detected, the installation routine aborts.

 Warning: Failure of Media Check

If the media check fails, your medium is damaged. Do not continue the installation because installation may fail or you may lose your data. Replace the broken medium and restart the installation process.

Memory Test

Tests your system RAM using repeated read and write cycles. Terminate the test by rebooting. For more information, see *Book "Administration Guide", Chapter 40 "Common Problems and Their Solutions", Section 40.2.4 "Fails to Boot".*

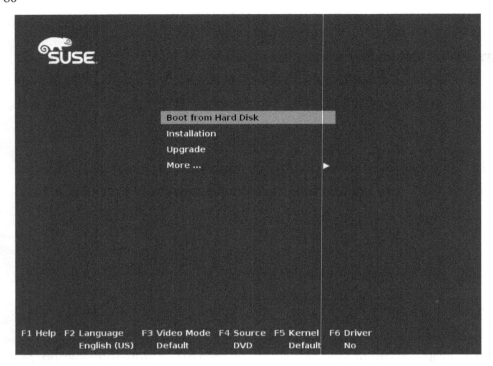

FIGURE 6.1: THE BOOT SCREEN ON MACHINES WITH A TRADITIONAL BIOS

Use the function keys shown at the bottom of the screen to change the language, screen resolution, installation source or to add an additional driver from your hardware vendor:

F1 *Help*

> Get context-sensitive help for the active element of the boot screen. Use the arrow keys to navigate, Enter to follow a link, and Esc to leave the help screen.

F2 *Language*

> Select the display language and a corresponding keyboard layout for the installation. The default language is English (US).

F3 *Video Mode*

> Select various graphical display modes for the installation. By *Default* the video resolution is automatically determined using KMS ("Kernel Mode Setting"). If this setting does not work on your system, choose *No KMS* and, optionally, specify `vga=ask` on the boot command line to get prompted for the video resolution. Choose *Text Mode* if the graphical installation causes problems.

F4 *Source*

Normally, the installation is performed from the inserted installation medium. Here, select other sources, like FTP or NFS servers. If the installation is deployed on a network with an SLP server, select an installation source available on the server with this option. Find information about setting up an installation server with SLP at *Chapter 7, Setting Up the Server Holding the Installation Sources*.

F5 *Kernel*

If you encounter problems with the regular installation, this menu offers to disable a few potentially problematic functions. If your hardware does not support ACPI (advanced configuration and power interface) select *No ACPI* to install without ACPI support. *No local APIC* disables support for APIC (Advanced Programmable Interrupt Controllers) which may cause problems with some hardware. *Safe Settings* boots the system with the DMA mode (for CD/DVD-ROM drives) and power management functions disabled.

If you are not sure, try the following options first: *Installation—ACPI Disabled* or *Installation—Safe Settings*. Experts can also use the command line (*Boot Options*) to enter or change kernel parameters.

F6 *Driver*

Press this key to notify the system that you have an optional driver update for SUSE Linux Enterprise Server. With *File* or *URL*, load drivers directly before the installation starts. If you select *Yes*, you are prompted to insert the update disk at the appropriate point in the installation process.

 Tip: Getting Driver Update Disks

Driver updates for SUSE Linux Enterprise are provided at http://drivers.suse.com/ ↗. These drivers have been created via the SUSE SolidDriver Program.

6.2.2.2 The Boot Screen on Machines Equipped with UEFI

UEFI (Unified Extensible Firmware Interface) is a new industry standard which replaces and extends the traditional BIOS. The latest UEFI implementations contain the "Secure Boot" extension, which prevents booting malicious code by only allowing signed boot loaders to be executed. See *Book "Administration Guide", Chapter 11 "UEFI (Unified Extensible Firmware Interface)"* for more information.

The boot manager GRUB 2, used to boot machines with a traditional BIOS, does not support UEFI, therefore GRUB 2 is replaced with GRUB 2 for EFI. If Secure Boot is enabled, YaST will automatically select GRUB 2 for EFI for installation. From an administrative and user perspective, both boot manager implementations behave the same and are called GRUB 2 in the following.

 Tip: UEFI and Secure Boot are Supported by Default

The installation routine of SUSE Linux Enterprise Server automatically detects if the machine is equipped with UEFI. All installation sources also support Secure Boot. If an EFI system partition already exists on dual boot machines (from a Microsoft Windows 8 installation, for example), it will automatically be detected and used. Partition tables will be written as GPT on UEFI systems.

 Warning: Using Non-Inbox Drivers with Secure Boot

There is no support for adding non-inbox drivers (that is, drivers that do not come with SLE) during installation with Secure Boot enabled. The signing key used for SolidDriver/PLDP is not trusted by default.

To solve this problem, it is necessary to either add the needed keys to the firmware database via firmware/system management tools before the installation or to use a bootable ISO that will enroll the needed keys in the MOK list at first boot. For more information, see *Book "Administration Guide", Chapter 11 "UEFI (Unified Extensible Firmware Interface)", Section 11.1 "Secure Boot"*.

The boot screen displays several options for the installation procedure. Change the selected option with the arrow keys and press Enter to boot it. The relevant options are:

Installation

The normal installation mode.

Upgrade

Perform a system upgrade. For more information refer to *Chapter 18, Upgrading SUSE Linux Enterprise*.

Rescue System

Starts a minimal Linux system without a graphical user interface. For more information, see *Book "Administration Guide", Chapter 40 "Common Problems and Their Solutions", Section 40.6.2 "Using the Rescue System"*.

Check Installation Media

> This option is only available when you install from media created from downloaded ISOs. In this case it is recommended to check the integrity of the installation medium. This option starts the installation system before automatically checking the media. In case the check was successful, the normal installation routine starts. If a corrupt media is detected, the installation routine aborts.

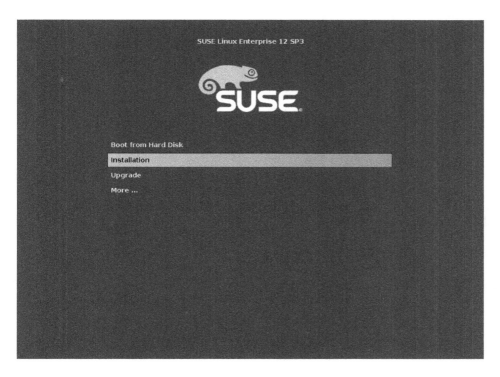

FIGURE 6.2: THE BOOT SCREEN ON MACHINES WITH UEFI

GRUB 2 for EFI on SUSE Linux Enterprise Server does not support a boot prompt or function keys for adding boot parameters. By default, the installation will be started with American English and the boot media as the installation source. A DHCP lookup will be performed to configure the network. To change these defaults or to add additional boot parameters you need to edit the respective boot entry. Highlight it using the arrow keys and press E . See the on-screen help for editing hints (note that only an English keyboard is available now). The *Installation* entry will look similar to the following:

```
setparams 'Installation'

    set gfxpayload=keep
    echo 'Loading kernel ...'
    linuxefi /boot/x86_64/loader/linux splash=silent
    echo 'Loading initial ramdisk ...'
```

```
initrdefi /boot/x86_64/loader/initrd
```

Add space-separated parameters to the end of the line starting with `linuxefi`. To boot the edited entry, press [F10]. If you access the machine via serial console, press [Esc]-[0]. A complete list of parameters is available at http://en.opensuse.org/Linuxrc↗. The most important ones are:

TABLE 6.2: INSTALLATION SOURCES

CD/DVD (default)	`install=cd:/`
Hard disk	`install=hd:/?device=sda/PATH_TO_ISO`
SLP	`install=slp:/`
FTP	`install=ftp://ftp.example.com/PATH_TO_ISO`
HTTP	`install=http://www.example.com/PATH_TO_ISO`
NFS	`install=nfs:/PATH_TO_ISO`
SMB / CIFS	`install=smb://PATH_TO_ISO`

TABLE 6.3: NETWORK CONFIGURATION

DHCP (default)	`netsetup = dhcp`
Prompt for Parameters	`netsetup=hostip,netmask,gateway,nameserver`
Host IP address	`hostip=192.168.2.100` `hostip=192.168.2.100/24`
Netmask	`netmask=255.255.255.0`
Gateway	`gateway=192.168.5.1`
Name Server	`nameserver=192.168.1.116` `nameserver=192.168.1.116,192.168.1.118`
Domain Search Path	`domain=example.com`

TABLE 6.4: MISCELLANEOUS

Driver Updates: Prompt	`dud=1`

Driver Updates: URL	dud=ftp://*ftp.example.com/PATH_TO_DRIVER* dud=http://*www.example.com/PATH_TO_DRIVER*
Installation Language	Language=*LANGUAGE* Supported values for *LANGUAGE* are, among others, `cs_CZ`, `de_DE`, `es_ES`, `fr_FR`, `ja_JP`, `pt_BR`, `pt_PT`, `ru_RU`, `zh_CN`, and `zh_TW`.
Kernel: No ACPI	acpi=off
Kernel: No Local APIC	noapic
Video: Disable KMS	nomodeset
Video: Start Installer in Text Mode	Textmode=1

6.2.3   Boot Parameters for Advanced Setups

To configure access to a local SMT or `supportconfig` server for the installation, you can specify boot parameters to set up these services during installation. The same applies if you need IPv6 support during the installation.

6.2.3.1   Providing Data to Access an SMT Server

By default, updates for SUSE Linux Enterprise Server are delivered by the SUSE Customer Center. If your network provides a so called SMT server to provide a local update source, you need to equip the client with the server's URL. Client and server communicate solely via HTTPS protocol, therefore you also need to enter a path to the server's certificate if the certificate was not issued by a certificate authority.

 Note: Non-Interactive Installation Only

Providing parameters for accessing an SMT server is only needed for non-interactive installations. During an interactive installation the data can be provided during the installation (see *Section 6.8, "SUSE Customer Center Registration"* for details).

regurl

> URL of the SMT server. This URL has a fixed format `https://FQN/center/regsvc/`. *FQN* needs to be a fully qualified host name of the SMT server. Example:

> ```
> regurl=https://smt.example.com/center/regsvc/
> ```

regcert

> Location of the SMT server's certificate. Specify one of the following locations:

> **URL**

> > Remote location (HTTP, HTTPS or FTP) from which the certificate can be downloaded. Example:

> > ```
> > regcert=http://smt.example.com/smt-ca.crt
> > ```

> **local path**

> > Absolute path to the certificate on the local machine. Example:

> > ```
> > regcert=/data/inst/smt/smt-ca.cert
> > ```

> **Interactive**

> > Use `ask` to open a pop-up menu during the installation where you can specify the path to the certificate. Do not use this option with AutoYaST. Example

> > ```
> > regcert=ask
> > ```

> **Deactivate certificate installation**

> > Use `done` if the certificate will be installed by an add-on product, or if you are using a certificate issued by an official certificate authority. For example:

> > ```
> > regcert=done
> > ```

 ## Warning: Beware of Typing Errors

> Make sure the values you enter are correct. If `regurl` has not been specified correctly, the registration of the update source will fail. If a wrong value for regcert has been entered, you will be prompted for a local path to the certificate.

> In case regcert is not specified, it will default to `http://FQN/smt.crt` with `FQN` being the name of the SMT server.

6.2.3.2 Configuring an Alternative Data Server for `supportconfig`

The data that supportconfig (see *Book "Administration Guide", Chapter 39 "Gathering System Information for Support"* for more information) gathers is sent to the SUSE Customer Center by default. It is also possible to set up a local server to collect this data. If such a server is available on your network, you need to set the server's URL on the client. This information needs to be entered at the boot prompt.

`supporturl`. URL of the server. The URL has the format `http://FQN/Path/`, where *FQN* is the fully qualified host name of the server and *Path* is the location on the server. For example:

```
supporturl=http://support.example.com/supportconfig/data/
```

6.2.3.3 Using IPv6 During the Installation

By default you can only assign IPv4 network addresses to your machine. To enable IPv6 during installation, enter one of the following parameters at the boot prompt:

Accept IPv4 and IPv6

```
ipv6=1
```

Accept IPv6 only

```
ipv6only=1
```

6.2.3.4 Using a Proxy During the Installation

In networks enforcing the usage of a proxy server for accessing remote Web sites, registration during installation is only possible when configuring a proxy server.

To use a proxy during the installation, press F4 on the boot screen and set the required parameters in the *HTTP Proxy* dialog. Alternatively provide the kernel parameter `proxy` at the boot prompt:

```
1>proxy=http://USER:PASSWORD@proxy.example.com:PORT
```

Specifying *USER* and *PASSWORD* is optional—if the server allows anonymous access, the following data is sufficient: `http://proxy.example.com:PORT`.

6.2.3.5 Enabling SELinux Support

Enabling SELinux upon installation start-up enables you to configure it after the installation has been finished without having to reboot. Use the following parameters:

```
security=selinux selinux=1
```

6.2.3.6 Enabling the Installer Self-Update

During installation and upgrade, YaST can update itself as described in *Section 6.4, "Installer Self-Update"* to solve potential bugs discovered after release. The `self_update` parameter can be used to modify the behavior of this feature.

To enable the installer self-update, set the parameter to `1`:

```
self_update=1
```

To use a user-defined repository, specify a URL:

```
self_update=https://updates.example.com/
```

6.3 Steps of the Installation

The interactive installation of SUSE Linux Enterprise Server split into several steps is listed below. .

After starting the installation, SUSE Linux Enterprise Server loads and configures a minimal Linux system to run the installation procedure. To view the boot messages and copyright notices during this process, press `Esc`. On completion of this process, the YaST installation program starts and displays the graphical installer.

 Tip: Installation Without a Mouse

If the installer does not detect your mouse correctly, use `→|` for navigation, arrow keys to scroll, and `Enter` to confirm a selection. Various buttons or selection fields contain a letter with an underscore. Use `Alt`-`Letter` to select a button or a selection directly instead of navigating there with `→|`.

6.4   Installer Self-Update

During the installation and upgrade process, YaST is able to update itself to solve bugs in the installer that were discovered after the release. This functionality is disabled by default; to enable it, set the boot parameter `self_update` to `1`. For more information, see *Section 6.2.3.6, "Enabling the Installer Self-Update"*.

Although this feature was designed to run without user intervention, it is worth knowing how it works. If you are not interested, you can jump directly to *Section 6.5, "Language, Keyboard and License Agreement"* and skip the rest of this section.

 Tip: Language Selection

The installer self-update is executed before the language selection step. This means that progress and errors which happen during this process are displayed in English by default.

To use another language for this part of the installer, press `F2` in the DVD boot menu and select the language from the list. Alternatively, use the `language` boot parameter (for example, `language=de_DE`).

6.4.1 Self-Update Process

The process can be broken down into two different parts:

1. Determine the update repository location.

2. Download and apply the updates to the installation system.

6.4.1.1 Determining the Update Repository Location

Installer Self-Updates are distributed as regular RPM packages via a dedicated repository, so the first step is to find out the repository URL.

 Important: Installer Self-Update Repository Only

No matter which of the following options you use, only the installer self-update repository URL is expected, for example:

```
self_update=https://updates.suse.com/SUSE/Updates/SLE-SERVER-INSTALLER/12-SP2/
x86_64/update/
```

Do not supply any other repository URL—for example the URL of the software update repository.

YaST will try the following sources of information:

1. The `self_update` boot parameter. (For more details, see *Section 6.2.3.6, "Enabling the Installer Self-Update".*) If you specify a URL, it will take precedence over any other method.

2. The `/general/self_update_url` profile element in case you are using AutoYaST.

3. A registration server. YaST will query the registration server for the URL. The server to be used is determined in the following order:

   a. By evaluating the `regurl` boot parameter (*Section 6.2.3.1, "Providing Data to Access an SMT Server"*).

   b. By evaluating the `/suse_register/reg_server` profile element if you are using AutoYaST.

c. By performing an SLP lookup. If an SLP server is found, YaST will ask you whether it should be used because there is no authentication involved and everybody on the local network could announce a registration server.

d. By querying the SUSE Customer Center.

4. If none of the previous attempts worked, the fallback URL (defined in the installation media) will be used.

6.4.1.2 Downloading and Applying the Updates

When the updates repository is determined, YaST will check whether an update is available. If so, all the updates will be downloaded and applied to the installation system.

Finally, YaST will be restarted to load the new version and the welcome screen will be shown. If no updates were available, the installation will continue without restarting YaST.

 Note: Update Integrity

Update signatures will be checked to ensure integrity and authorship. If a signature is missing or invalid, you will be asked whether you want to apply the update.

6.4.2 Networking during Self-Update

To download installer updates, YaST needs network access. By default, it tries to use DHCP on all network interfaces. If there is a DHCP server in the network, it will work automatically.

If you need a static IP setup, you can use the `ifcfg` boot argument. For more details, see the linuxrc documentation at https://en.opensuse.org/Linuxrc ↗.

6.4.3 Custom Self-Update Repositories

YaST can use a user-defined repository instead of the official one by specifying a URL through the `self_update` boot option. However, the following points should be considered:

* Only HTTP/HTTPS and FTP repositories are supported.

* Only RPM-MD repositories are supported (required by SMT).

- Packages are not installed in the usual way: They are uncompressed only and no scripts are executed.

- No dependency checks are performed. Packages are installed in alphabetical order.

- Files from the packages override the files from the original installation media. This means that the update packages might not need to contain all files, only files that have changed. Unchanged files are omitted to save memory and download bandwidth.

 Note: Only One Repository

Currently, it is not possible to use more than one repository as source for installer self-updates.

6.5 Language, Keyboard and License Agreement

Start the installation of SUSE Linux Enterprise Server by choosing your language. Changing the language will automatically preselect a corresponding keyboard layout. Override this proposal by selecting a different keyboard layout from the drop-down box. The language selected here is also used to assume a time zone for the system clock. This setting can be modified later in the installed system as described in *Chapter 16, Changing Language and Country Settings with YaST*.

Read the license agreement that is displayed beneath the language and keyboard selection thoroughly. Use *License Translations* to access translations. If you agree to the terms, check *I Agree to the License Terms* and click *Next* to proceed with the installation. If you do not agree to the license agreement, you cannot install SUSE Linux Enterprise Server; click *Abort* to terminate the installation.

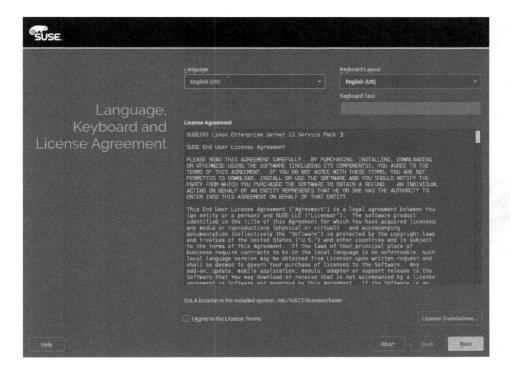

FIGURE 6.3: LANGUAGE, KEYBOARD AND LICENSE AGREEMENT

6.6   IBM z Systems: Disk Activation

When installing on IBM z Systems platforms, the language selection dialog is followed by a dialog to configure the attached hard disks. Select DASD, Fibre Channel Attached SCSI Disks (zFCP), or iSCSI for installation of SUSE Linux Enterprise Server. The DASD and zFCP configuration buttons are only available if the corresponding devices are attached. For instructions on how to configure iSCSI disks, refer to *Book "Storage Administration Guide", Chapter 14 "Mass Storage over IP Networks: iSCSI", Section 14.3 "Configuring iSCSI Initiator"*.

You can also *Change the Network Configuration* in this screen by launching the *Network Settings* dialog. Choose a network interface from the list and click *Edit* to change its settings. Use the tabs to configure DNS and routing. See *Book "Administration Guide", Chapter 16 "Basic Networking", Section 16.4 "Configuring a Network Connection with YaST"* for more details.

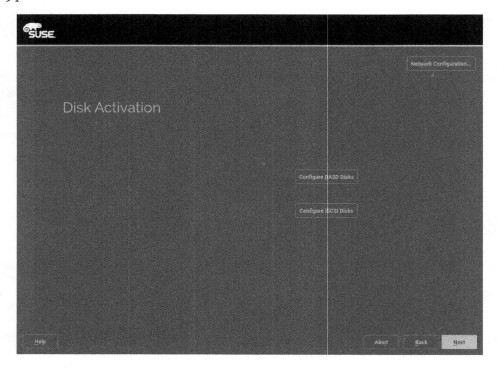

FIGURE 6.4: DISK ACTIVATION

6.6.1 Configuring DASD Disks

After selecting *Configure DASD Disks*, an overview lists all available DASDs. To get a clearer picture of the available devices, use the text box located above the list to specify a range of channels to display. To filter the list according to such a range, select *Filter*.

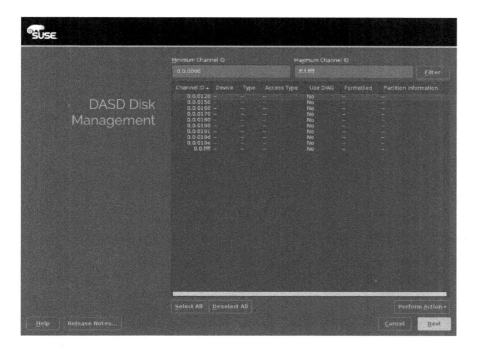

FIGURE 6.5: IBM Z SYSTEMS: SELECTING A DASD

Specify the DASDs to use for the installation by selecting the corresponding entries in the list. Use *Select All* to select all DASDs currently displayed. Activate and make the selected DASDs available for the installation by selecting *Perform Action* › *Activate*. To format the DASDs, select *Perform Action* › *Format*. Alternatively, use the YaST partitioner later as described in *Section 11.1, "Using the YaST Partitioner"*.

6.6.2 Configuring zFCP Disks

To use zFCP disks for the SUSE Linux Enterprise Server installation, select *Configure zFCP Disks* in the selection dialog. This opens a dialog with a list of the zFCP disks available on the system. In this dialog, select *Add* to open another dialog in which to enter zFCP parameters.

To make a zFCP disk available for the SUSE Linux Enterprise Server installation, choose an available *Channel Number* from the drop-down box. *Get WWPNs* (World Wide Port Number) and *Get LUNs* (Logical Unit Number) return lists with available WWPNs and FCP-LUNs, respectively, to choose from. Automatic LUN scanning only works with NPIV enabled.

When completed, exit the zFCP dialog with *Next* and the general hard disk configuration dialog with *Finish* to continue with the rest of the configuration.

6.7 Network Settings

After booting into the installation, the installation routine is set up. During this setup, an attempt to configure at least one network interface with DHCP is made. In case this attempt fails, the *Network Settings* dialog launches. Choose a network interface from the list and click *Edit* to change its settings. Use the tabs to configure DNS and routing. See *Book* "Administration Guide", *Chapter 16* "Basic Networking", Section 16.4 "Configuring a Network Connection with YaST" for more details. On IBM z Systems this dialog does not start automatically. It can be started in the *Disk Activation* step.

In case DHCP was successfully configured during installation setup, you can also access this dialog by clicking *Network Configuration* at the *SUSE Customer Center Registration* step. It lets you change the automatically provided settings.

 Note: Network Interface Configured via linuxrc

If at least one network interface is configured via linuxrc, automatic DHCP configuration is disabled and configuration from linuxrc is imported and used.

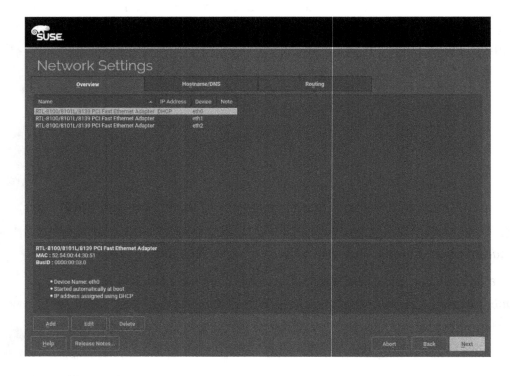

FIGURE 6.6: NETWORK SETTINGS

Tip: Accessing Network Storage or Local RAID

To access a SAN or a local RAID during the installation, you can use the libstorage command line client for this purpose:

1. Switch to a console with `Ctrl`–`Alt`–`F2`.

2. Install the libstoragemgmt extension by running **extend libstoragemgmt**.

3. Now you have access to the **lsmcli** command. For more information, run **lsmcli --help**.

4. To return to the installer, press `Alt`–`F7`

Supported are Netapp Ontap, all SMI-S compatible SAN providers, and LSI MegaRAID.

6.8 SUSE Customer Center Registration

To get technical support and product updates, you need to register and activate your product with the SUSE Customer Center. Registering SUSE Linux Enterprise Server now grants you immediate access to the update repository. This enables you to install the system with the latest updates and patches available. If you are offline or want to skip this step, select *Skip Registration*. You can register your system at any time later from the installed system.

 Note: Network Configuration

After booting into the installation, the installation routine is set up. During this setup, an attempt to configure all network interfaces with DHCP is made. If DHCP is not available or you want to modify the network configuration, click *Network Configuration* in the upper right corner of the *SUSE Customer Center Registration* screen. The YaST module *Network Settings* opens. See *Book "Administration Guide", Chapter 16 "Basic Networking", Section 16.4 "Configuring a Network Connection with YaST"* for details.

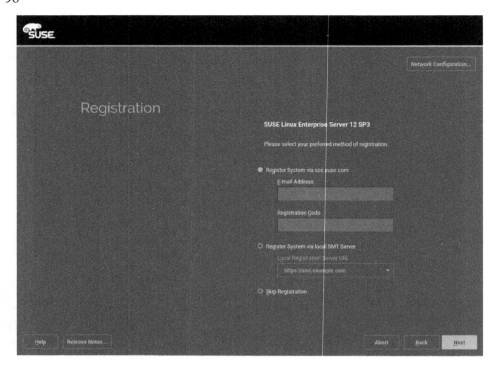

FIGURE 6.7: SUSE CUSTOMER CENTER REGISTRATION

To register your system, provide the *E-mail* address associated with the SUSE account you or your organization uses to manage subscriptions. In case you do not have a SUSE account yet, go to the SUSE Customer Center home page (https://scc.suse.com/ ↗) to create one.

Enter the *Registration Code* you received with your copy of SUSE Linux Enterprise Server. YaST can also read registration codes from a USB storage device such as a flash disk. For details, see *Section 6.8.1, "Loading Registration Codes from USB Storage"*.

Proceed with *Next* to start the registration process. If one or more local registration servers are available on your network, you can choose one of them from a list. By default, SUSE Linux Enterprise Server is registered at the SUSE Customer Center. If your local registration server was not discovered automatically, choose *Cancel*, select *Register System via local SMT Server* and enter the URL of the server. Restart the registration by choosing *Next* again.

During the registration, the online update repositories will be added to your installation setup. When finished, you can choose whether to install the latest available package versions from the update repositories. This ensures that SUSE Linux Enterprise Server is installed with the latest security updates available. If you choose *No*, all packages will be installed from the installation media. Proceed with *Next*.

If the system was successfully registered during installation, YaST will disable repositories from local installation media such as CD/DVD or flash disks when the installation has been completed. This prevents problems if the installation source is no longer available and ensures that you always get the latest updates from the online repositories.

 Tip: Release Notes

From this point on, the Release Notes can be viewed from any screen during the installation process by selecting *Release Notes*.

6.8.1 Loading Registration Codes from USB Storage

To make the registration more convenient, you can also store your registration codes on a USB storage device such as a flash disk. YaST will automatically pre-fill the corresponding text box. This is particularly useful when testing the installation or if you need to register many systems or extensions.

 Note: Limitations

Currently flash disks are only scanned during installation or upgrade, but not when registering a running system.

Create a file named `regcodes.txt` or `regcodes.xml` on the USB disk. If both are present, the XML takes precedence.

In that file, identify the product with the name returned by **zypper search --type product** and assign it a registration code as follows:

EXAMPLE 6.1: regcodes.txt

```
SLES    cc36aae1
SLED    309105d4

sle-we  5eedd26a
sle-live-patching 8c541494
```

EXAMPLE 6.2: regcodes.xml

```
<?xml version="1.0"?>
<profile xmlns="http://www.suse.com/1.0/yast2ns"
 xmlns:config="http://www.suse.com/1.0/configns">
```

```
  <suse_register>
    <addons config:type="list">
      <addon>
<name>SLES</name>
<reg_code>cc36aae1</reg_code>
      </addon>
      <addon>
<name>SLED</name>
<reg_code>309105d4</reg_code>
      </addon>
      <addon>
<name>sle-we</name>
<reg_code>5eedd26a</reg_code>
      </addon>
      <addon>
<name>sle-live-patching</name>
<reg_code>8c541494</reg_code>
      </addon>
    </addons>
  </suse_register>
</profile>
```

Note that SLES and SLED are not extensions, but listing them as add-ons allows for combining several base product registration codes in a single file. See *Book "AutoYaST", Chapter 4 "Configuration and Installation Options", Section 4.3.1 "Extensions"* for details.

6.9   Extension Selection

If you have successfully registered your system in the previous step, a list of available modules and extensions based on SUSE Linux Enterprise Server is shown. Otherwise this configuration step is skipped. It is also possible to add modules and extensions from the installed system, see *Chapter 13, Installing Modules, Extensions, and Third Party Add-On Products* for details.

The list contains free modules for SUSE Linux Enterprise Server, such as the SUSE Linux Enterprise SDK and extensions requiring a registration key that is liable for costs. Click an entry to see its description. Select a module or extension for installation by activating its check mark. This will add its repository from the SUSE Customer Center server to your installation—no additional installation sources are required. Furthermore the installation pattern for the module or extension is added to the default installation to ensure it gets installed automatically.

The amount of available extensions and modules depends on the registration server. A local registration server may only offer update repositories and no additional extensions.

Tip: Modules

Modules are fully supported parts of SUSE Linux Enterprise Server with a different life cycle. They have a clearly defined scope and are delivered via online channel only. Registering at the SUSE Customer Center is a prerequisite for being able to subscribe to these channels.

 Tip: SUSE Linux Enterprise Desktop

As of SUSE Linux Enterprise 12, SUSE Linux Enterprise Desktop is not only available as a separate product, but also as a workstation extension for SUSE Linux Enterprise Server. If you register at the SUSE Customer Center, the SUSE Linux Enterprise Workstation Extension can be selected for installation. Note that installing it requires a valid registration key.

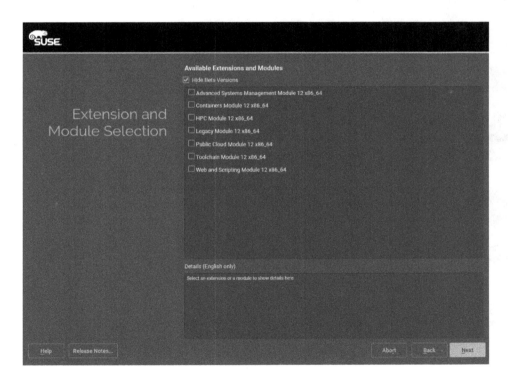

FIGURE 6.8: EXTENSION SELECTION

Proceed with *Next* to the *Add-on Product* dialog, where you can specify sources for additional add-on products not available on the registration server.

If you do not want to install add-ons, proceed with *Next*. Otherwise activate *I would like to install an additional Add-on Product*. Specify the Media Type by choosing from CD, DVD, Hard Disk, USB Mass Storage, a Local Directory or a Local ISO Image. If network access has been configured you can choose from additional remote sources such as HTTP, SLP, FTP, etc. Alternatively you may directly specify a URL. Check *Download Repository Description Files* to download the files describing the repository now. If deactivated, they will be downloaded after the installation starts. Proceed with *Next* and insert a CD or DVD if required.

Depending on the add-on's content, it may be necessary to accept additional license agreements. If you have chosen an add-on product requiring a registration key, you will be asked to enter it at the *Extension and Module Registration Codes* page. Proceed with *Next*.

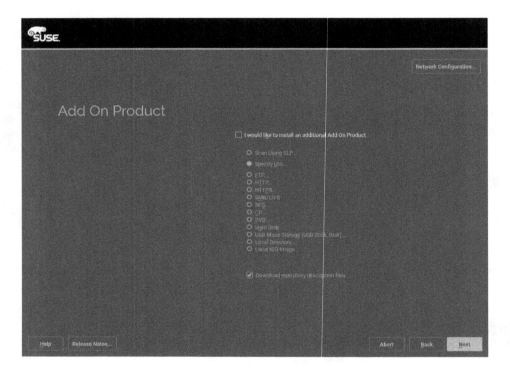

FIGURE 6.9: ADD-ON PRODUCT

 Tip: "No Registration Key" Error

> If you have chosen a product in the *Extension Selection* dialog for which you do not have a valid registration key, choose *Back* until you see the *Extension Selection* dialog. Deselect the module or extension and proceed with *Next*. Modules or extensions can also be installed at any time later from the running system as described in *Chapter 13, Installing Modules, Extensions, and Third Party Add-On Products*.

6.10 System Role

SUSE Linux Enterprise Server supports a broad range of features. To simplify the installation, YaST offers predefined use cases which adjust the system to be installed so it is tailored for the selected scenario. Currently this affects the package set and the suggested partitioning scheme.

Choose the *System Role* that meets your requirements best:

Default System

Select this scenario when installing on a "real" machine or a fully virtualized guest.

KVM Virtualization Host

Select this scenario when installing on a machine that should serve as a KVM host that can run other virtual machines.

Xen Virtualization Host

Select this scenario when installing on a machine that should serve as a Xen host that can run other virtual machines.

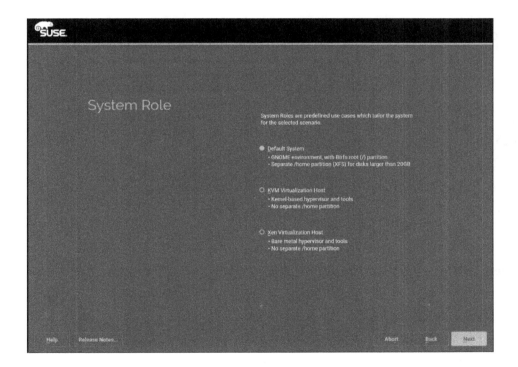

FIGURE 6.10: SYSTEM ROLE SELECTION

6.11 Suggested Partitioning

Define a partition setup for SUSE Linux Enterprise Server in this step. Depending on the system role, the installer creates a proposal for one of the disks available. All proposals contain a root partition formatted with Btrfs (with snapshots enabled) and a swap partition. If you have chosen the system role *Default System* in the previous step, a home partition formatted with XFS will be created, too. On hard disks smaller than 20 GB the proposal does not include a separate home partition. If one or more swap partitions have been detected on the available hard disks, these existing ones will be used (rather than proposing a new swap partition). You have several options to proceed:

Next

> To accept the proposal without any changes, click *Next* to proceed with the installation workflow.

Edit Proposal Settings

> To adjust the proposal choose *Edit Proposal Settings*. The pop-up dialog lets you switch to an *LVM-based Proposal* or an *Encrypted LVM-based Proposal*. You may also adjust file systems for the proposed partitions, create a separate home partition, and enlarge the swap partition (to enable suspend to disk, for example).
> If the root file system format is Btrfs, you can also disable Btrfs snapshots here.

Create Partition Setup

> Use this option to move the proposal described above to a different disk. Select a specific disk from the list. If the chosen hard disk does not contain any partitions yet, the whole hard disk will be used for the proposal. Otherwise, you can choose which existing partition(s) to use. *Edit Proposal Settings* lets you fine-tune the proposal.

Expert Partitioner

> To create a custom partition setup choose *Expert Partitioner*. The Expert Partitioner opens, displaying the current partition setup for all hard disks, including the proposal suggested by the installer. You can *Add*, *Edit*, *Resize*, or *Delete* partitions.
> You can also set up Logical Volumes (LVM), configure software RAID and device mapping (DM), encrypt Partitions, mount NFS shares and manage tmpfs volumes with the Expert Partitioner. To fine-tune settings such as the subvolume and snapshot handling for each Btrfs partition, choose *Btrfs*. For more information about custom partitioning and configuring advanced features, refer to *Section 11.1, "Using the YaST Partitioner"*.

Warning: Custom Partitioning on UEFI Machines

A UEFI machine *requires* an EFI system partition that must be mounted to `/boot/efi`. This partition must be formatted with the `FAT` file system.

If an EFI system partition is already present on your system (for example from a previous Windows installation) use it by mounting it to `/boot/efi` without formatting it.

 ## Warning: Custom Partitioning and Snapper

By default, SUSE Linux Enterprise Server is set up to support snapshots which provide the ability to do rollbacks of system changes. SUSE Linux Enterprise Server uses Snapper with Btrfs for this feature. Refer to *Book "Administration Guide", Chapter 7 "System Recovery and Snapshot Management with Snapper"* for details.

Being able to create system snapshots that enable rollbacks requires most of the system directories to be mounted on a single partition. Refer to *Book "Administration Guide", Chapter 7 "System Recovery and Snapshot Management with Snapper", Section 7.1 "Default Setup"* for more information. This also includes `/usr` and `/var`. Only directories that are excluded from snapshots (see *Book "Administration Guide", Chapter 7 "System Recovery and Snapshot Management with Snapper", Section 7.1.2 "Directories That Are Excluded from Snapshots"* for a list) may reside on separate partitions. Among others, this list includes `/usr/local`, `/var/log`, and `/tmp`.

If you do not plan to use Snapper for system rollbacks, the partitioning restrictions mentioned above do not apply.

 ## Important: Btrfs on an Encrypted Root Partition

The default partitioning setup suggests the root partition as Btrfs with `/boot` being a directory. To encrypt the root partition, make sure to use the GPT partition table type instead of the default MSDOS type. Otherwise the GRUB2 boot loader may not have enough space for the second stage loader.

Note: IBM z Systems: Using Minidisks in z/VM

If SUSE Linux Enterprise Server is installed on minidisks in z/VM, which reside on the same physical disk, the access path of the minidisks (/dev/disk/by-id/) is not unique, because it represents the ID of the physical disk. So if two or more minidisks are on the same physical disk, they all have the same ID.

To avoid problems when mounting minidisks, always mount them either *by path* or *by UUID*.

 ## Warning: IBM z Systems: LVM Root File System

If you configure the system with an LVM root file system, you must place `/boot` on a separate, non-LVM partition, otherwise the system will fail to boot. The recommended size for such a partition is 500 MB and the recommended file system is Ext4.

 ## Note: Supported Software RAID Volumes

Installing to and booting from existing software RAID volumes is supported for Disk Data Format (DDF) volumes and Intel Matrix Storage Manager (IMSM) volumes. IMSM is also known by the following names:

- Intel Rapid Storage Technology

- Intel Matrix Storage Technology

- Intel Application Accelerator / Intel Application Accelerator RAID Edition

 ## Note: Mount Points for FCoE and iSCSI Devices

FCoE and iSCSI devices will appear asynchronously during the boot process. While the initrd guarantees that those devices are set up correctly for the root file system, there are no such guarantees for any other file systems or mount points like `/usr`. Hence any system mount points like `/usr` or `/var` are not supported. To use those devices, ensure correct synchronization of the respective services and devices.

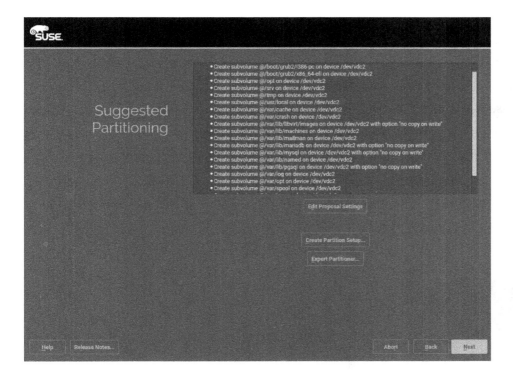

FIGURE 6.11: PARTITIONING

6.12 Clock and Time Zone

In this dialog, select your region and time zone. Both are preselected according to the installation language. To change the preselected values, either use the map or the drop-down boxes for *Region* and *Time Zone*. When using the map, point the cursor at the rough direction of your region and left-click to zoom. Now choose your country or region by left-clicking. Right-click to return to the world map.

To set up the clock, choose whether the *Hardware Clock is Set to UTC*. If you run another operating system on your machine, such as Microsoft Windows, it is likely your system uses local time instead. If you run Linux on your machine, set the hardware clock to UTC and have the switch from standard time to daylight saving time performed automatically.

Important: Set the Hardware Clock to UTC

The switch from standard time to daylight saving time (and vice versa) can only be performed automatically when the hardware clock (CMOS clock) is set to UTC. This also applies if you use automatic time synchronization with NTP, because automatic synchronization will only be performed if the time difference between the hardware and system clock is less than 15 minutes.

Since a wrong system time can cause serious problems (missed backups, dropped mail messages, mount failures on remote file systems, etc.), it is strongly recommended to *always* set the hardware clock to UTC.

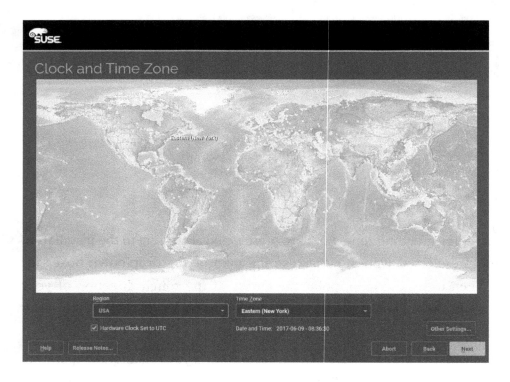

FIGURE 6.12: CLOCK AND TIME ZONE

`POWER, x86_64` If a network is already configured, you can configure time synchronization with an NTP server. Click *Other Settings* to either alter the NTP settings or to *Manually* set the time. See *Book "Administration Guide", Chapter 24 "Time Synchronization with NTP"* for more information on configuring the NTP service. When finished, click *Accept* to continue the installation.

`POWER, x86_64` If running without NTP configured, consider setting `SYSTOHC=no` (`sysconfig` variable) to avoid saving unsynchronized time into the hardware clock.

Note: Time Cannot Be Changed on IBM z Systems

Since the operating system is not allowed to change time and date directly, the *Other Settings* option is not available on IBM z Systems.

6.13 Create New User

Create a local user in this step. After entering the first name and last name, either accept the proposal or specify a new *User name* that will be used to log in. Only use lowercase letters (a-z), digits (0-9) and the characters . (dot), - (hyphen) and _ (underscore). Special characters, umlauts and accented characters are not allowed.

Finally, enter a password for the user. Re-enter it for confirmation (to ensure that you did not type something else by mistake). To provide effective security, a password should be at least six characters long and consist of uppercase and lowercase letters, number and special characters (7-bit ASCII). Umlauts or accented characters are not allowed. Passwords you enter are checked for weakness. When entering a password that is easy to guess (such as a dictionary word or a name) you will see a warning. It is a good security practice to use strong passwords.

 Important: User Name and Password

Remember both your user name and the password because they are needed each time you log in to the system.

If you install SUSE Linux Enterprise Server on a machine with one or more existing Linux installations, YaST allows you to import user data such as user names and passwords. Select *Import User Data from a Previous Installation* and then *Choose Users* for import.

If you do not want to configure any local users (for example when setting up a client on a network with centralized user authentication), skip this step by choosing *Next* and confirming the warning. Network user authentication can be configured at any time later in the installed system; refer to *Chapter 15, Managing Users with YaST* for instructions.

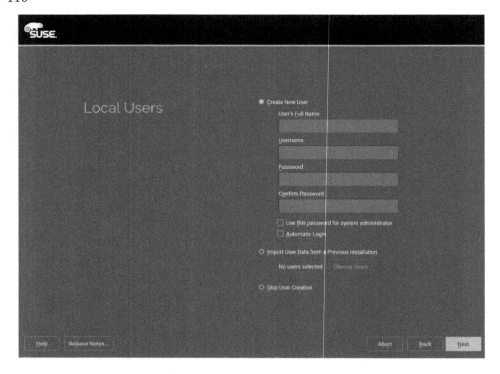

FIGURE 6.13: CREATE NEW USER

Two additional options are available:

Use this Password for System Administrator

If checked, the same password you have entered for the user will be used for the system administrator `root`. This option is suitable for stand-alone workstations or machines in a home network that are administrated by a single user. When not checked, you are prompted for a system administrator password in the next step of the installation workflow (see *Section 6.14, "Password for the System Administrator* `root"`).

Automatic Login

This option automatically logs the current user in to the system when it starts. This is mainly useful if the computer is operated by only one user. For automatic login to work, the option must be explicitly enabled.

6.13.1   Expert Settings

Click *Change* in the Create User dialog to import users from a previous installation (if present). Also change the password encryption type in this dialog.

The default authentication method is *Local (/etc/passwd)*. If a former version of SUSE Linux Enterprise Server or another system using `/etc/passwd` is detected, you may import local users. To do so, check *Read User Data from a Previous Installation* and click *Choose*. In the next dialog, select the users to import and finish with *OK*.

By default the passwords are encrypted with the SHA-512 hash function. Changing this method is not recommended unless needed for compatibility reasons.

6.14 Password for the System Administrator root

If you have not chosen *Use this Password for System Administrator* in the previous step, you will be prompted to enter a password for the System Administrator `root`. Otherwise this configuration step is skipped.

`root` is the name of the superuser, or the administrator of the system. Unlike regular users, `root` has unlimited rights to change the system configuration, install programs, and set up new hardware. If users forget their passwords or have other problems with the system, `root` can help. The `root` account should only be used for system administration, maintenance, and repair. Logging in as `root` for daily work is rather risky: a single mistake could lead to irretrievable loss of system files.

For verification purposes, the password for `root` must be entered twice. Do not forget the `root` password. After having been entered, this password cannot be retrieved.

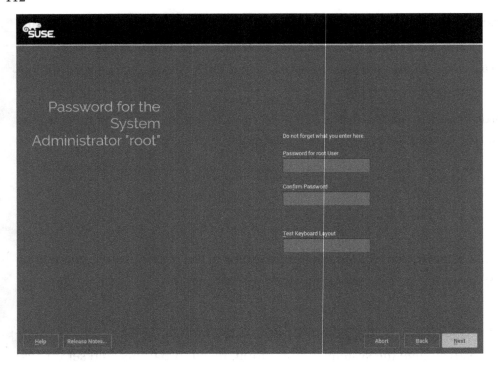

FIGURE 6.14: PASSWORD FOR THE SYSTEM ADMINISTRATOR root

Tip: Passwords and Keyboard Layout

It is recommended to only use characters that are available on an English keyboard. In case of a system error or when you need to start your system in rescue mode a localized keyboard might not be available.

The `root` password can be changed any time later in the installed system. To do so run YaST and start *Security and Users > User and Group Management.*

Important: The root User

The user `root` has all the permissions needed to make changes to the system. To carry out such tasks, the `root` password is required. You cannot carry out any administrative tasks without this password.

6.15 Installation Settings

On the last step before the real installation takes place, you can alter installation settings suggested by the installer. To modify the suggestions, click the respective headline. After having made changes to a particular setting, you are always returned to the Installation Settings window, which is updated accordingly.

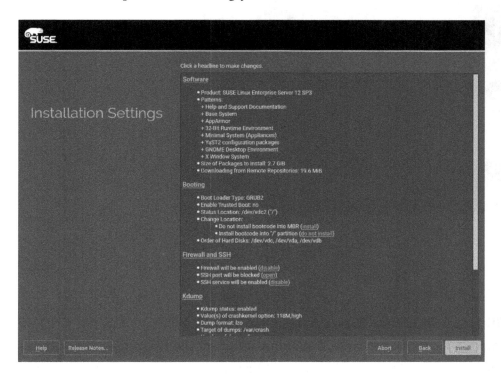

FIGURE 6.15: INSTALLATION SETTINGS

6.15.1 Software

SUSE Linux Enterprise Server contains several software patterns for various application purposes. Click *Software* to open the *Software Selection and System Tasks* screen where you can modify the pattern selection according to your needs. Select a pattern from the list and see a description in the right-hand part of the window. Each pattern contains several software packages needed for specific functions (for example Web and LAMP server or a print server). For a more detailed selection based on software packages to install, select *Details* to switch to the YaST Software Manager.

You can also install additional software packages or remove software packages from your system at any later time with the YaST Software Manager. For more information, refer to *Chapter 12, Installing or Removing Software*.

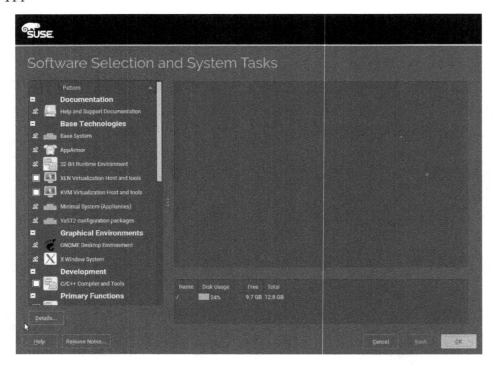

FIGURE 6.16: SOFTWARE SELECTION AND SYSTEM TASKS

 Note: Graphical Desktop

By default SUSE Linux Enterprise Server is installed with X Window and the GNOME desktop environment. If you do not need X Window, deselect the two respective patterns in the *Software Selection and System Tasks* screen. As an alternative to GNOME, the lightweight window manager IceWM can be installed. Select *Details* from the *Software Selection and System Tasks* screen and search for `icewm`.

Tip: IBM z Systems: Hardware Cryptography Support

The hardware cryptography stack is not installed by default. To install it, select *System z HW crypto support* in the *Software Selection and System Tasks* screen.

Tip: Adding Secondary Languages

The language you selected with the first step of the installation will be used as the primary (default) language for the system. You can add secondary languages from within the *Software* dialog by choosing *Details* › *View* › *Languages*.

6.15.2 *Booting*

The installer proposes a boot configuration for your system. Other operating systems found on your computer, such as Microsoft Windows or other Linux installations, will automatically be detected and added to the boot loader. However, SUSE Linux Enterprise Server will be booted by default. Normally, you can leave these settings unchanged. If you need a custom setup, modify the proposal according to your needs. For information, see *Book "Administration Guide", Chapter 12 "The Boot Loader GRUB 2", Section 12.3 "Configuring the Boot Loader with YaST".*

 Important: Software RAID 1

Booting a configuration where `/boot` resides on a software RAID 1 device is supported, but it requires to install the boot loader into the MBR (*Boot Loader Location › Boot from Master Boot Record*). Having `/boot` on software RAID devices with a level other than RAID 1 is not supported. Also see *Book "Storage Administration Guide", Chapter 8 "Configuring Software RAID for the Root Partition".*

6.15.3 *Firewall and SSH*

By default SuSEFirewall2 is enabled on all configured network interfaces. To globally disable the firewall for this computer, click *Disable* (not recommended).

 Note: Firewall Settings

If the firewall is activated, all interfaces are configured to be in the "External Zone", where all ports are closed by default, ensuring maximum security. The only port you can open during the installation is port 22 (SSH), to allow remote access. All other services requiring network access (such as FTP, Samba, Web server, etc.) will only work after having adjusted the firewall settings. Refer to *Book "Security Guide", Chapter 15 "Masquerading and Firewalls"* for more information.

To enable remote access via the secure shell (SSH), make sure the `SSH service` is enabled and the `SSH port` is open.

Tip: Existing SSH Host Keys

If you install SUSE Linux Enterprise Server on a machine with one or more existing Linux installations, the installation routine imports the SSH host key with the most recent access time from an existing installation by default. See also *Section 6.15.7, "Import SSH Host Keys and Configuration"*.

If you are performing a remote administration over VNC, you can also specify whether the machine should be accessible via VNC after the installation. Note that enabling VNC also requires you to set the *Default systemd Target* to *graphical*.

6.15.4 Kdump

Using Kdump, you can save a dump of the kernel (in case of a crash) to analyze what went wrong. Use this dialog to enable and configure Kdump. Find detailed information at *Book "System Analysis and Tuning Guide", Chapter 17 "Kexec and Kdump"*.

6.15.5 IBM z Systems: Blacklist Devices

To save memory, all channels for devices currently not in use are blacklisted by default (each channel that is not blacklisted occupies approximately 50 KB of memory). To configure additional hardware in the installed system using channels that are currently blacklisted, run the respective YaST module to enable the respective channels first.

To disable blacklisting, click *disable*.

6.15.6 Default systemd Target

SUSE Linux Enterprise Server can boot into two different targets (formerly known as "run-levels"). The *graphical* target starts a display manager, whereas the *multi-user* target starts the command line interface.

The default target is *graphical*. In case you have not installed the *X Window System* patterns, you need to change it to *multi-user*. If the system should be accessible via VNC, you need to choose *graphical*.

6.15.7   *Import SSH Host Keys and Configuration*

If an existing Linux installation on your computer was detected, YaST will import the most recent SSH host key found in `/etc/ssh` by default, optionally including other files in the directory as well. This makes it possible to reuse the SSH identity of the existing installation, avoiding the `REMOTE HOST IDENTIFICATION HAS CHANGED` warning on the first connection. Note that this item is not shown in the installation summary if YaST has not discovered any other installations.

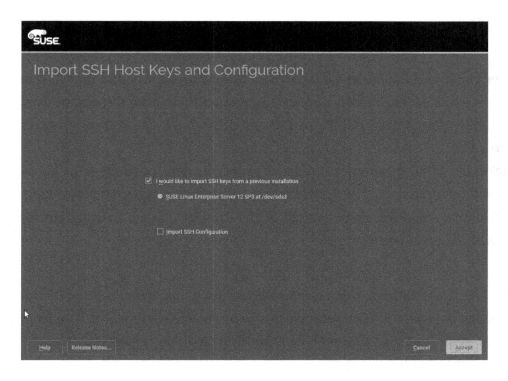

FIGURE 6.17: IMPORT SSH HOST KEYS AND CONFIGURATION

I would like to import SSH keys from a previous install:

    Select this option if you want to import the SSH host key and optionally the configuration of an installed system. You can select the installation to import from in the option list below.

Import SSH Configuration

    Enable this to copy other files in `/etc/ssh` to the installed system in addition to the host keys.

6.15.8 System Information

This screen lists all the hardware information the installer could obtain about your computer. When opened for the first time, the hardware detection is started. Depending on your system, this may take some time. Select any item in the list and click *Details* to see detailed information about the selected item. Use *Save to File* to save a detailed list to either the local file system or a removable device.

Advanced users can also change the *PCI ID Setup* and kernel settings by choosing *Kernel Settings*. A screen with two tabs opens:

PCI ID Setup

Each kernel driver contains a list of device IDs of all devices it supports. If a new device is not in any driver's database, the device is treated as unsupported, even if it can be used with an existing driver. You can add PCI IDs to a device driver here. Only advanced users should attempt to do so.

To add an ID, click *Add* and select whether to *Manually* enter the data, or whether to choose from a list. Enter the required data. The *SysFS Dir* is the directory name from `/sys/bus/pci/drivers` —if empty, the *driver* name is used as the directory name. Existing entries can be managed with *Edit* and *Delete*.

Kernel Settings

Change the *Global I/O Scheduler* here. If *Not Configured* is chosen, the default setting for the respective architecture will be used. This setting can also be changed at any time later from the installed system. Refer to Book *"System Analysis and Tuning Guide", Chapter 12 "Tuning I/O Performance"* for details on I/O tuning.

Also activate the *Enable SysRq Keys* here. These keys will let you issue basic commands (such as rebooting the system or writing kernel dumps) in case the system crashes. Enabling these keys is recommended when doing kernel development. Refer to https://www.kernel.org/doc/html/latest/admin-guide/sysrq.html ↗ for details.

6.16 Performing the Installation

After configuring all installation settings, click *Install* in the Installation Settings window to start the installation. Some software may require a license confirmation. If your software selection includes such software, license confirmation dialogs are displayed. Click *Accept* to install the software package. When not agreeing to the license, click *I Disagree* and the software package will not be installed. In the dialog that follows, confirm with *Install* again.

The installation usually takes between 15 and 30 minutes, depending on the system performance and the selected software scope. After having prepared the hard disk and having saved and restored the user settings, the software installation starts. During this procedure a slide show introduces the features of SUSE Linux Enterprise Server. Choose *Details* to switch to the installation log or *Release Notes* to read important up-to-date information that was not available when the manuals were printed.

After the software installation has completed, the system reboots into the new installation where you can log in. To customize the system configuration or to install additional software packages, start YaST.

 Note: One-Stage Installation

Starting with SUSE Linux Enterprise Server 12 the system installation and basic configuration including the network setup is done in a single stage. After having rebooted into the installed system, you can log in and start using the system. To fine-tune the setup, to configure services or to install additional software, start YaST.

6.16.1 IBM z Systems: IPLing the Installed System

YaST usually reboots into the installed system on the IBM z Systems platform. Exceptions are installations where the boot loader resides on an FCP device in environments with LPAR on a machine older than z196 or with z/VM older than release 5.4. The boot loader gets written to a separate partition mounted as `/boot/zipl/`.

In cases where an automatic reboot is not possible, YaST will show a dialog containing information about from which device to do an IPL. Accept the shutdown option and perform an IPL after the shutdown. The procedure varies according to the type of installation:

LPAR Installation

In the IBM z Systems HMC, select *Load*, select *Clear*, then enter the loading address (the address of the device containing the `/boot/zipl` directory with the boot loader). If using a zFCP disk as the boot device, choose *Load from SCSI* and specify the load address of your FCP adapter plus WWPN and LUN of the boot device. Now start the loading process.

z/VM Installation

Log in to the VM guest (see *Example 4.1, "Configuration of a z/VM Directory"* for the configuration) as `LINUX1` and proceed to IPL the installed system:

```
IPL 151 CLEAR
```

`151` is an example address of the DASD boot device, replace this value with the correct address.

If using a zFCP disk as the boot device, specify both the zFCP WWPN and LUN of the boot device before initiating the IPL. The parameter length is limited to eight characters. Longer numbers must be separated by spaces:

```
SET LOADDEV PORT 50050763 00C590A9 LUN 50010000 00000000
```

Finally, initiate the IPL:

```
IPL FC00
```

`FC00` is an example address of the zFCP adapter, replace this value with the correct address.

KVM Guest Installation

After the installation has finished, the virtual machine is shut down. At this point, log in to the KVM host, edit the virtual machine's description file and restart it to IPL into the installed system:

1. Log in to the KVM host.

2. Edit the domain XML file by running

   ```
   virsh edit s12-1
   ```

   and remove the following lines:

   ```
   <!-- Boot kernel - remove 3 lines after successfull installation -->
   <kernel>/var/lib/libvirt/images/s12-kernel.boot</kernel>
   <initrd>/var/lib/libvirt/images/s12-initrd.boot</initrd>
   <cmdline>linuxrcstderr=/dev/console</cmdline>
   ```

3. Restart the VM Guest to IPL into the installed system:

   ```
   virsh start s12-1 --console
   ```

Note: `cio_ignore` Is Disabled for KVM Installations

The kernel parameter `cio_ignore` prevents the kernel from looking at all the available hardware devices. However, for KVM guests, the hypervisor already takes care to only provide access to the correct devices. Therefore `cio_ignore` is disabled by default when installing a KVM guest (for z/VM and LPAR installations it is activated by default).

6.16.2   IBM z Systems: Connecting to the Installed System

After IPLing the system, establish a connection via VNC, SSH, or X to log in to the installed system. Using either VNC or SSH is recommended. To customize the system configuration or to install additional software packages, start YaST.

6.16.2.1   Using VNC to Connect

A message in the 3270 terminal asks you to connect to the Linux system using a VNC client. However, this message is easily missed, because it is mixed with kernel messages and the terminal process might quit before you notice the message. If nothing happens for five minutes, try to initiate a connection to the Linux system using a VNC viewer.

6.16.2.2   Using SSH to Connect

A message in the 3270 terminal asks you to connect to the Linux system with an SSH client. This message is easily missed, however, because it is mixed with kernel messages and the terminal process might quit before you become aware of the message.

When the message appears, use SSH to log in to the Linux system as `root`. If the connection is denied or times out, wait for the login timeout to expire, then try again (this time depends on server settings).

6.16.2.3 Using X to Connect

When IPLing the installed system, make sure that the X server used for the first phase of the installation is up and still available before booting from the DASD. YaST opens on this X server to finish the installation. Complications may arise if the system is booted up but unable to connect to the X server in a timely fashion.

III Setting Up an Installation Server

7 Setting Up the Server Holding the Installation Sources

SUSE® Linux Enterprise Server can be installed in different ways. Apart from the usual media installation covered in *Chapter 6, Installation with YaST*, you can choose from various network-based approaches or even opt for an unattended installation of SUSE Linux Enterprise Server.

Each method is introduced by means of two short checklists: one listing the prerequisites for this method and the other illustrating the basic procedure. More detail is then provided for all the techniques used in these installation scenarios.

 Note: Terminology

In the following sections, the system to hold your new SUSE Linux Enterprise Server installation is called *target system* or *installation target*. The term *repository* (previously called "installation source") is used for all sources of installation data. This includes physical media, such as CD and DVD, and network servers distributing the installation data in your network.

Depending on the operating system of the machine used as the network installation source for SUSE Linux Enterprise Server, there are several options for the server configuration. The easiest way to set up an installation server is to use YaST on SUSE Linux Enterprise Server or openSUSE.

 Tip: Installation Server Operating System

You can even use a Microsoft Windows machine as the installation server for your Linux deployment. See *Section 7.5, "Managing an SMB Repository"* for details.

7.1 Setting Up an Installation Server Using YaST

YaST offers a graphical tool for creating network repositories. It supports HTTP, FTP, and NFS network installation servers.

1. Log in as `root` to the machine that should act as installation server.

2. Start *YaST* > *Miscellaneous* > *Installation Server*.

3. Select the repository type (HTTP, FTP, or NFS). The selected service is started automatically every time the system starts. If a service of the selected type is already running on your system and you want to configure it manually for the server, deactivate the automatic configuration of the server service with *Do Not Configure Any Network Services*. In both cases, define the directory in which the installation data should be made available on the server.

4. Configure the required repository type. This step relates to the automatic configuration of server services. It is skipped when automatic configuration is deactivated.

   Define an alias for the root directory of the FTP or HTTP server on which the installation data should be found. The repository will later be located under `ftp://Server-IP/Alias/Name` (FTP) or under `http://Server-IP/Alias/Name` (HTTP). *Name* stands for the name of the repository, which is defined in the following step. If you selected NFS in the previous step, define wild cards and export options. The NFS server will be accessible under `nfs://Server-IP/Name`. Details of NFS and exports can be found in Book *"Administration Guide", Chapter 27 "Sharing File Systems with NFS"*.

    Tip: Firewall Settings

   Make sure that the firewall settings of your server system allow traffic on the ports for HTTP, NFS, and FTP. If they currently do not, enable *Open Port in Firewall* or check *Firewall Details* first.

5. Configure the repository. Before the installation media are copied to their destination, define the name of the repository (ideally, an easily remembered abbreviation of the product and version). YaST allows providing ISO images of the media instead of copies of the installation DVDs. If you want this, activate the relevant check box and specify the directory path under which the ISO files can be found locally. Depending on the product to distribute using this installation server, it might be necessary to add additional media, such as service pack DVDs as extra repositories. To announce your installation server in the network via OpenSLP, activate the appropriate option.

Tip: Announcing the Repository

> Consider announcing your repository via OpenSLP if your network setup supports this option. This saves you from entering the network installation path on every target machine. The target systems are booted using the SLP boot option and find the network repository without any further configuration. For details on this option, refer to *Section 9.2, "Booting the Target System for Installation"*.

6. Configuring extra repositories. YaST follows a specific naming convention to configure add-on CDs or service pack CDs repositories. Configuration is accepted only if the repository name of the add-on CDs starts with the repository name of the installation media, In other words, if you chose `SLES12SP1` as repository name for DVD1 than you should chose `SLES12SP1addon` repository name for DVD2. Same applies to SDK CDs.

7. Upload the installation data. The most lengthy step in configuring an installation server is copying the actual installation media. Insert the media in the sequence requested by YaST and wait for the copying procedure to end. When the sources have been fully copied, return to the overview of existing repositories and close the configuration by selecting *Finish*. Your installation server is now fully configured and ready for service. It is automatically started every time the system is started. No further intervention is required. You only need to configure and start this service correctly by hand if you have deactivated the automatic configuration of the selected network service with YaST as an initial step.

To deactivate a repository, select the repository to remove then select *Delete*. The installation data are removed from the system. To deactivate the network service, use the respective YaST module.

If your installation server needs to provide the installation data for more than one product of the product version, start the YaST installation server module and select *Add* in the overview of existing repositories to configure the new repository.

7.2 Setting Up an NFS Repository Manually

Setting up an NFS source for installation is done in two main steps. In the first step, create the directory structure holding the installation data and copy the installation media over to this structure. Second, export the directory holding the installation data to the network.

To create a directory to hold the installation data, proceed as follows:

1. Log in as `root`.

2. Create a directory that will later hold all installation data and change into this directory. For example:

```
root # mkdir /srv/install/PRODUCT/PRODUCTVERSION
root # cd /srv/install/PRODUCT/PRODUCTVERSION
```

Replace *PRODUCT* with an abbreviation of the product name and *PRODUCTVERSION* with a string that contains the product name and version.

3. For each DVD contained in the media kit execute the following commands:

a. Copy the entire content of the installation DVD into the installation server directory:

```
root # cp -a /media/PATH_TO_YOUR_DVD_DRIVE .
```

Replace *PATH_TO_YOUR_DVD_DRIVE* with the actual path under which your DVD drive is addressed. Depending on the type of drive used in your system, this can be `cdrom`, `cdrecorder`, `dvd`, or `dvdrecorder`.

b. Rename the directory to the DVD number:

```
root # mv PATH_TO_YOUR_DVD_DRIVE DVDX
```

Replace *X* with the actual number of your DVD.

On SUSE Linux Enterprise Server, you can export the repository with NFS using YaST. Proceed as follows:

1. Log in as `root`.

2. Start *YaST* › *Network Services* › *NFS Server*.

3. Select *Start* and *Open Port in Firewall* and click *Next*.

4. Select *Add Directory* and browse for the directory containing the installation sources, in this case, *PRODUCTVERSION*.

5. Select *Add Host* and enter the host names of the machines to which to export the installation data. Instead of specifying host names here, you could also use wild cards, ranges of network addresses, or the domain name of your network. Enter the appropriate export options or leave the default, which works fine in most setups. For more information about the syntax used in exporting NFS shares, read the `exports` man page.

6. Click *Finish*. The NFS server holding the SUSE Linux Enterprise Server repository is automatically started and integrated into the boot process.

If you prefer manually exporting the repository via NFS instead of using the YaST NFS Server module, proceed as follows:

1. Log in as `root`.

2. Open the file `/etc/exports` and enter the following line:

```
/PRODUCTVERSION *(ro,root_squash,sync)
```

This exports the directory `/PRODUCTVERSION` to any host that is part of this network or to any host that can connect to this server. To limit the access to this server, use netmasks or domain names instead of the general wild card `*`. Refer to the `export` man page for details. Save and exit this configuration file.

3. To add the NFS service to the list of servers started during system boot, execute the following commands:

```
root # systemctl enable nfsserver
```

4. Start the NFS server with **systemctl start nfsserver**. If you need to change the configuration of your NFS server later, modify the configuration file and restart the NFS daemon with **systemctl restart nfsserver**.

Announcing the NFS server via OpenSLP makes its address known to all clients in your network.

1. Log in as `root`.

2. Create the `/etc/slp.reg.d/install.suse.nfs.reg` configuration file with the following lines:

```
# Register the NFS Installation Server
service:install.suse:nfs://$HOSTNAME/PATH_TO_REPOSITORY/DVD1,en,65535
description=NFS Repository
```

Replace *PATH_TO_REPOSITORY* with the actual path to the installation source on your server.

3. Start the OpenSLP daemon with **systemctl start slpd**.

For more information about OpenSLP, refer to the package documentation located under `/usr/share/doc/packages/openslp/` or refer to *Book "Administration Guide", Chapter 30 "SLP"*. More Information about NFS, refer to *Book "Administration Guide", Chapter 27 "Sharing File Systems with NFS"*.

7.3 Setting Up an FTP Repository Manually

Creating an FTP repository is very similar to creating an NFS repository. An FTP repository can be announced over the network using OpenSLP as well.

1. Create a directory holding the installation sources as described in *Section 7.2, "Setting Up an NFS Repository Manually"*.

2. Configure the FTP server to distribute the contents of your installation directory:

   a. Log in as `root` and install the package `vsftpd` using the YaST software management.

   b. Enter the FTP server root directory:

   ```
   root # cd /srv/ftp
   ```

   c. Create a subdirectory holding the installation sources in the FTP root directory:

   ```
   root # mkdir REPOSITORY
   ```

   Replace *REPOSITORY* with the product name.

   d. Mount the contents of the installation repository into the change root environment of the FTP server:

   ```
   root # mount --bind PATH_TO_REPOSITORY /srv/ftp/REPOSITORY
   ```

   Replace *PATH_TO_REPOSITORY* and *REPOSITORY* with values matching your setup. If you need to make this permanent, add it to `/etc/fstab`.

e. Start vsftpd with **vsftpd**.

3. Announce the repository via OpenSLP, if this is supported by your network setup:

a. Create the `/etc/slp.reg.d/install.suse.ftp.reg` configuration file with the following lines:

```
# Register the FTP Installation Server
service:install.suse:ftp://$HOSTNAME/REPOSITORY/DVD1,en,65535
description=FTP Repository
```

Replace *REPOSITORY* with the actual name to the repository directory on your server. The `service:` line should be entered as one continuous line.

b. Start the OpenSLP daemon with **systemctl start slpd**.

 Tip: Configuring an FTP Server with YaST

If you prefer using YaST instead of manually configuring the FTP installation server, refer to *Book "Administration Guide", Chapter 32 "Setting Up an FTP Server with YaST"* for more information on how to use the YaST FTP server module.

7.4 Setting Up an HTTP Repository Manually

Creating an HTTP repository is very similar to creating an NFS repository. An HTTP repository can be announced over the network using OpenSLP as well.

1. Create a directory holding the installation sources as described in *Section 7.2, "Setting Up an NFS Repository Manually"*.

2. Configure the HTTP server to distribute the contents of your installation directory:

a. Install the Web server Apache as described in *Book "Administration Guide", Chapter 31 "The Apache HTTP Server", Section 31.1.2 "Installation"*.

b. Enter the root directory of the HTTP server (`/srv/www/htdocs`) and create the subdirectory that will hold the installation sources:

```
root # mkdir REPOSITORY
```

Replace *REPOSITORY* with the product name.

c. Create a symbolic link from the location of the installation sources to the root directory of the Web server (`/srv/www/htdocs`):

```
root # ln -s /PATH_TO_REPOSITORY/srv/www/htdocs/REPOSITORY
```

d. Modify the configuration file of the HTTP server (`/etc/apache2/default-server.conf`) to make it follow symbolic links. Replace the following line:

```
Options None
```

with

```
Options Indexes FollowSymLinks
```

e. Reload the HTTP server configuration using **systemctl reload apache2**.

3. Announce the repository via OpenSLP, if this is supported by your network setup:

a. Create the `/etc/slp.reg.d/install.suse.http.reg` configuration file with the following lines:

```
# Register the HTTP Installation Server
service:install.suse:http://$HOSTNAME/REPOSITORY/DVD1/,en,65535
description=HTTP Repository
```

Replace *REPOSITORY* with the actual path to the repository on your server. The `service:` line should be entered as one continuous line.

b. Start the OpenSLP daemon using **systemctl start slpd**.

7.5 Managing an SMB Repository

Using SMB, you can import the installation sources from a Microsoft Windows server and start your Linux deployment even with no Linux machine around.

To set up an exported Windows Share holding your SUSE Linux Enterprise Server repository, proceed as follows:

1. Log in to your Windows machine.

2. Create a new directory that will hold the entire installation tree and name it INSTALL, for example.

3. Export this share according the procedure outlined in your Windows documentation.

4. Enter this share and create a subdirectory, called *PRODUCT*. Replace *PRODUCT* with the actual product name.

5. Enter the `INSTALL/PRODUCT` directory and copy each DVD to a separate directory, such as `DVD1` and `DVD2`.

To use an SMB mounted share as a repository, proceed as follows:

1. Boot the installation target.

2. Select *Installation.*

3. Press `F4` for a selection of the repository.

4. Choose SMB and enter the Windows machine's name or IP address, the share name (`INS‑TALL/PRODUCT/DVD1`, in this example), user name, and password. The syntax looks like this:

```
smb://workdomain;user:password@server/INSTALL/DVD1
```

After you press `Enter`, YaST starts and you can perform the installation.

7.6 Using ISO Images of the Installation Media on the Server

Instead of copying physical media into your server directory manually, you can also mount the ISO images of the installation media into your installation server and use them as a repository. To set up an HTTP, NFS or FTP server that uses ISO images instead of media copies, proceed as follows:

1. Download the ISO images and save them to the machine to use as the installation server.

2. Log in as `root`.

3. Choose and create an appropriate location for the installation data, as described in *Section 7.2, "Setting Up an NFS Repository Manually", Section 7.3, "Setting Up an FTP Repository Manually", or Section 7.4, "Setting Up an HTTP Repository Manually".*

4. Create subdirectories for each DVD.

5. To mount and unpack each ISO image to the final location, issue the following command:

```
root # mount -o loop PATH_TO_ISO PATH_TO_REPOSITORY/PRODUCT/MEDIUMX
```

Replace *PATH_TO_ISO* with the path to your local copy of the ISO image, *PATH_TO_RE-POSITORY* with the source directory of your server, *PRODUCT* with the product name, and *MEDIUMX* with the type (CD or DVD) and number of media you are using.

6. Repeat the previous step to mount all ISO images needed for your product.

7. Start your installation server as usual, as described in *Section 7.2, "Setting Up an NFS Repository Manually"*, *Section 7.3, "Setting Up an FTP Repository Manually"*, or *Section 7.4, "Setting Up an HTTP Repository Manually"*.

To automatically mount the ISO images at boot time, add the respective mount entries to /etc/fstab. An entry according to the previous example would look like the following:

```
PATH_TO_ISO PATH_TO_REPOSITORY/PRODUCTMEDIUM auto loop
```

8 Preparing the Boot of the Target System

SUSE® Linux Enterprise Server can be installed in different ways. Apart from the usual media installation covered in *Chapter 6, Installation with YaST*, you can choose from various network-based approaches or even take a completely hands-off approach to the installation of SUSE Linux Enterprise Server.

The examples use NFS for serving the installation data. If you want to use FTP, SMB or HTTP, see *Chapter 7, Setting Up the Server Holding the Installation Sources*.

 Note: Terminology

In the following sections, the system to hold your new SUSE Linux Enterprise Server installation is called *target system* or *installation target*. The term *repository* (previously called "installation source") is used for all sources of installation data. This includes physical media, such as CD and DVD, and network servers distributing the installation data in your network.

This section covers the configuration tasks needed in complex boot scenarios. It contains ready-to-apply configuration examples for DHCP, PXE boot, TFTP, and Wake on LAN.

The examples assume that the DHCP, TFTP and NFS server reside on the same machine with the IP `192.168.1.1`. All services can reside on different machines without any problems. Make sure to change the IP addresses as required.

8.1 Setting Up a DHCP Server

In addition to providing automatic address allocation to your network clients, the DHCP server announces the IP address of the TFTP server and the file that needs to be pulled in by the installation routines on the target machine. The file that has to be loaded depends on the architecture of the target machine and whether legacy BIOS or UEFI boot is used.

1. Log in as `root` to the machine hosting the DHCP server.

2. Enable the DHCP server by executing **systemctl enable dhcpd**.

3. Append the following lines to a subnet configuration of your DHCP server's configuration file located under `/etc/dhcpd.conf`:

```
# The following lines are optional
option domain-name "my.lab";
option domain-name-servers 192.168.1.1;
option routers 192.168.1.1;
option ntp-servers 192.168.1.1;
ddns-update-style none;
default-lease-time 3600;

# The following lines are required
option arch code 93 = unsigned integer 16; # RFC4578
subnet 192.168.1.0 netmask 255.255.255.0 {
 next-server 192.168.1.1;
 range 192.168.1.100 192.168.1.199;
 default-lease-time 3600;
 max-lease-time 3600;
 if option arch = 00:07 or option arch = 00:09 {
   filename "/EFI/x86/grub.efi";
 }
 else if option arch = 00:0b {
   filename "/EFI/aarch64/bootaa64.efi";
 }
 else  {
   filename "/BIOS/x86/pxelinux.0";
 }
}
```

This configuration example uses the subnet `192.168.1.0/24` with the DHCP, DNS and gateway on the server with the IP `192.168.1.1`. Make sure that all used IP addresses are changed according to your network layout. For more information about the options available in `dhcpd.conf`, refer to the `dhcpd.conf` manual page.

4. Restart the DHCP server by executing **systemctl restart dhcpd**.

If you plan to use SSH for the remote control of a PXE and Wake on LAN installation, specify the IP address DHCP should provide to the installation target. To achieve this, modify the above mentioned DHCP configuration according to the following example:

```
group {
 host test {
   hardware ethernet MAC_ADDRESS;
   fixed-address IP_ADDRESS;
   }
```

```
}
```

The host statement introduces the host name of the installation target. To bind the host name and IP address to a specific host, you must know and specify the system's hardware (MAC) address. Replace all the variables used in this example with the actual values that match your environment.

After restarting the DHCP server, it provides a static IP to the host specified, enabling you to connect to the system via SSH.

8.2   Setting Up a TFTP Server

If using a SUSE based installation, you may use YaST to set up a TFTP Server. Alternatively, set it up manually. The TFTP server delivers the boot image to the target system after it boots and sends a request for it.

8.2.1   Setting Up a TFTP Server Using YaST

1. Log in as `root`.

2. Start *YaST* › *Network Services* › *TFTP Server* and install the requested package.

3. Click *Enable* to make sure that the server is started and included in the boot routines. No further action from your side is required to secure this. xinetd starts tftpd at boot time.

4. Click *Open Port in Firewall* to open the appropriate port in the firewall running on your machine. If there is no firewall running on your server, this option is not available.

5. Click *Browse* to browse for the boot image directory. The default directory `/srv/tftpboot` is created and selected automatically.

6. Click *Finish* to apply your settings and start the server.

8.2.2   Setting Up a TFTP Server Manually

1. Log in as `root` and install the packages `tftp` and `xinetd`.

2. Modify the configuration of xinetd located under `/etc/xinetd.d` to make sure that the TFTP server is started on boot:

   a. If it does not exist, create a file called `tftp` under this directory with **touch tftp**. Then run **chmod 755 tftp**.

   b. Open the file `tftp` and add the following lines:

   ```
   service tftp
   {
           socket_type             = dgram
           protocol                = udp
           wait                    = yes
           user                    = root
           server                  = /usr/sbin/in.tftpd
           server_args             = -s /srv/tftpboot
           disable                 = no
   }
   ```

   c. Save the file and restart xinetd with **systemctl restart xinetd**.

8.3   Installing Files on TFTP Server

The following procedures describe how to prepare the server for target machines with UEFI and BIOS on x86 architectures with 32 and 64 bits. The prepared structure also already provides for AArch64 systems.

8.3.1   Preparing the Structure

In this procedure, replace *OS_VERSION* and *SP_VERSION* with the used operating system and service pack version. For example, use `sles12` and `sp3`.

1. Create a structure in `/srv/tftpboot` to support the various options.

   ```
   root # mkdir -p /srv/tftpboot/BIOS/x86
   root # mkdir -p /srv/tftpboot/EFI/x86/boot
   root # mkdir -p /srv/tftpboot/EFI/aarch64/boot
   root # mkdir -p /srv/install/x86/OS_VERSION/SP_VERSION/cd1
   root # mkdir -p /srv/install/aarch64/OS_VERSION/SP_VERSION/cd1
   ```

2. Download the DVD ISO images of SUSE Linux Enterprise Server 12 SP3 from the SUSE Web site for all architectures you need.

3. Mount the ISO files as described in *Section 7.6, "Using ISO Images of the Installation Media on the Server"*. To have the files available after a reboot, create an entry in `/etc/fstab`. For a standard installation, only DVD 1 is required.

```
root # mount -o loop PATH_TO_ISO /srv/install/ARCH/OS_VERSION/SP_VERSION/cd1/
```

Repeat this step for all required architectures and replace *ARCH* with `x86` or `aarch64` and *PATH_TO_ISO* with the path to the corresponding ISO file.

4. Copy the `kernel`, `initrd` and `message` files required for x86 BIOS and UEFI boot to the appropriate location.

```
root # cd /srv/install/x86/OS_version/SP_version/cd1/boot/x86_64/loader/
root # cp -a linux initrd message /srv/tftpboot/BIOS/x86/
```

5. Ensure that the path `/srv/install` is available via NFS. For details, see *Section 7.2, "Setting Up an NFS Repository Manually"*.

8.3.2 BIOS Files for x86

1. Copy `pxelinux.0` into the TFTP folder and prepare a subfolder for the configuration file.

```
root # cp /usr/share/syslinux/pxelinux.0 /srv/tftpboot/BIOS/x86/
root # mkdir /srv/tftpboot/BIOS/x86/pxelinux.cfg
```

2. Create `/srv/tftpboot/BIOS/x86/pxelinux.cfg/default` and add the following lines:

```
default install

# hard disk
label harddisk
 localboot -2
# install
label install
 kernel linux
 append initrd=initrd install=nfs://192.168.1.1:/srv/install/
x86/OS_version/SP_version/cd1

display message
implicit 0
```

```
prompt 1
timeout 5
```

3. Edit the file `/srv/tftpboot/BIOS/x86/message` to reflect the `default` file you just edited.

```
Welcome to the Installer Environment!

To start the installation enter 'install' and press <return>.

Available boot options:
 harddisk    - Boot from Hard Disk (this is default)
 install     - Installation
```

8.3.3   UEFI Files for x86

In this procedure replace *OS_version* and *SP_version* with the used operating system and service pack version. For example use `sles12` and `sp3`.

1. Copy all required `grub2` files for UEFI booting.

```
root # cd /srv/install/x86/OS_version/SP_version/cd1/EFI/BOOT
root # cp -a bootx64.efi grub.efi MokManager.efi /srv/tftpboot/EFI/x86/
```

2. Copy the kernel and initrd files to the directory structure.

```
root # cd /srv/install/x86/OS_version/SP_version/cd1/boot/x86_64/loader/
root # cp -a linux initrd /srv/tftpboot/EFI/x86/boot
```

3. Create the file `/srv/tftpboot/EFI/x86/grub.cfg` with at least the following content:

```
set timeout=5
menuentry 'Install OS_version SP_version for x86_64' {
  linuxefi /EFI/x86/boot/linux \
    install=nfs://192.168.1.1/srv/install/x86/OS_version/SP_version/cd1
  initrdefi /EFI/x86/boot/initrd
}
```

8.3.4   UEFI Files for AArch64

In this procedure replace *OS_version* and *SP_version* with the used operating system and service pack version. For example use `sles12` and `sp3`.

1. This is done in a way very similar to the x86_64 EFI environment. Start by copying the files required for UEFI booting of a grub2-efi environment.

```
root # cd /srv/install/aarch64/OS_version/SP_version/cd1/EFI/BOOT
root # cp -a bootaa64.efi /srv/tftpboot/EFI/aarch64/
```

2. Copy the kernel and initrd to the directory structure.

```
root # cd /srv/install/aarch64/OS_version/SP_version/cd1/boot/aarch64
root # cp -a linux initrd /srv/tftpboot/EFI/aarch64/boot
```

3. Now create the file /srv/tftpboot/EFI/grub.cfg and add the following content:

```
menuentry 'Install OS_version SP_version' {
  linux /EFI/aarch64/boot/linux network=1 usessh=1 sshpassword="suse" \
   install=nfs://192.168.1.1:/srv/install/aarch64/OS_version/SP_version/cd1 \
   console=ttyAMA0,115200n8
  initrd /EFI/aarch64/boot/initrd
}
```

This addition to the configuration file has a few other options to enable the serial console and allow installation via SSH, which is helpful for systems that do not have a standard KVM console interface. You will notice that this is set up for a specific ARM platform.

8.4 PXELINUX Configuration Options

The options listed here are a subset of all the options available for the PXELINUX configuration file.

APPEND *OPTIONS*

Add one or more options to the kernel command line. These are added for both automatic and manual boots. The options are added at the very beginning of the kernel command line, usually permitting explicitly entered kernel options to override them.

APPEND -

Append nothing. APPEND with a single hyphen as argument in a LABEL section can be used to override a global APPEND.

DEFAULT *KERNEL_OPTIONS...*

Sets the default kernel command line. If PXELINUX boots automatically, it acts as if the entries after DEFAULT had been typed in at the boot prompt, except the auto option is automatically added, indicating an automatic boot.

If no configuration file exists or no DEFAULT entry is defined in the configuration file, the default is the kernel name "linux" with no options.

IFAPPEND *FLAG*

Adds a specific option to the kernel command line depending on the *FLAG* value. The IFAPPEND option is available only on PXELINUX. *FLAG* expects a value, described in *Table 8.1, "Generated and Added Kernel Command Line Options from* IFAPPEND*":*

TABLE 8.1: GENERATED AND ADDED KERNEL COMMAND LINE OPTIONS FROM IFAPPEND

Argument	Generated Kernel Command Line / Description
1	`ip=CLIENT_IP:BOOT_SERVER_IP:GW_IP:NETMASK` The placeholders are replaced based on the input from the DHCP/BOOTP or PXE boot server. Note, this option is not a substitute for running a DHCP client in the booted system. Without regular renewals, the lease acquired by the PXE BIOS will expire, making the IP address available for reuse by the DHCP server.
2	`BOOTIF=MAC_ADDRESS_OF_BOOT_INTERFACE` This option is useful if you want to avoid timeouts when the installation server probes one LAN interface after the other until it gets a reply from a DHCP server. This option allows an initrd program to determine from which interface the system has been booted. linuxrc reads this option and uses this network interface.
4	`SYSUUID=SYSTEM_UUID` Adds UUIDs in lowercase hexadecimals, see `/usr/share/doc/packages/syslinux/pxelinux.txt`

LABEL *LABEL* KERNEL *IMAGE* APPEND *OPTIONS*...

> Indicates that if *LABEL* is entered as the kernel to boot, PXELINUX should instead boot *IMAGE* and the specified APPEND options should be used instead of the ones specified in the global section of the file (before the first LABEL command). The default for *IMAGE* is the same as *LABEL* and, if no APPEND is given, the default is to use the global entry (if any). Up to 128 LABEL entries are permitted.
>
> PXELINUX uses the following syntax:

```
label MYLABEL
  kernel MYKERNEL
  append MYOPTIONS
```

> Labels are mangled as if they were file names and they must be unique after mangling. For example, the two labels "v2.6.30" and "v2.6.31" would not be distinguishable under PXELINUX because both mangle to the same DOS file name.
>
> The kernel does not need to be a Linux kernel. It can also be a boot sector or a COMBOOT file.

LOCALBOOT *TYPE*

> On PXELINUX, specifying LOCALBOOT 0 instead of a KERNEL option means invoking this particular label and causes a local disk boot instead of a kernel boot.

Argument	Description
0	Perform a normal boot
4	Perform a local boot with the Universal Network Driver Interface (UNDI) driver still resident in memory
5	Perform a local boot with the entire PXE stack, including the UNDI driver, still resident in memory

> All other values are undefined. If you do not know what the UNDI or PXE stacks are, specify 0.

TIMEOUT *TIME-OUT*

> Indicates how long to wait at the boot prompt until booting automatically, in units of 1/10 second. The time-out is canceled when the user types anything on the keyboard, assuming the user will complete the command begun. A time-out of zero disables the time-out completely (this is also the default). The maximum possible time-out value is 35996 (just less than one hour).

PROMPT *flag_val*

> If `flag_val` is 0, displays the boot prompt only if Shift or Alt is pressed or Caps Lock or Scroll Lock is set (this is the default). If `flag_val` is 1, always displays the boot prompt.

```
F2  FILENAME
F1  FILENAME
..etc...
F9  FILENAME
F10 FILENAME
```

> Displays the indicated file on the screen when a function key is pressed at the boot prompt. This can be used to implement preboot online help (presumably for the kernel command line options). For backward compatibility with earlier releases, F10 can be also entered as `F0`. Note that there is currently no way to bind file names to F11 and F12.

8.5 Preparing the Target System for PXE Boot

Prepare the system's BIOS for PXE boot by including the PXE option in the BIOS boot order.

 Warning: BIOS Boot Order

> Do not place the PXE option ahead of the hard disk boot option in the BIOS. Otherwise this system would try to re-install itself every time you boot it.

8.6 Preparing the Target System for Wake on LAN

Wake on LAN (WOL) requires the appropriate BIOS option to be enabled prior to the installation. Also, note down the MAC address of the target system. This data is needed to initiate Wake on LAN.

8.7   Wake on LAN

Wake on LAN allows a machine to be turned on by a special network packet containing the machine's MAC address. Because every machine in the world has a unique MAC identifier, you do not need to worry about accidentally turning on the wrong machine.

 Important: Wake on LAN across Different Network Segments

If the controlling machine is not located on the same network segment as the installation target that should be awakened, either configure the WOL requests to be sent as multicasts or remotely control a machine on that network segment to act as the sender of these requests.

Users of SUSE Linux Enterprise Server can use a YaST module called WOL to easily configure Wake on LAN. Users of other versions of SUSE Linux-based operating systems can use a command line tool.

8.8   Wake on LAN with YaST

1. Log in as `root`.

2. Start *YaST* › *Network Services* › *WOL*.

3. Click *Add* and enter the host name and MAC address of the target system.

4. To turn on this machine, select the appropriate entry and click *Wake up*.

8.9   Booting from CD or USB Drive Instead of PXE

You can also use a CD, DVD or USB drive with a small system image instead of booting via PXE. The necessary files will be loaded via NFS when the kernel and initrd are loaded. A bootable image can be created with **mksusecd**. This can be useful if the target machine does not support PXE boot.

Install it with **sudo zypper in mksusecd**. Use the following command to create a bootable ISO image:

```
tux > mksusecd --create image.iso \
```

```
--net=nfs://192.168.1.1:/srv/install/ARCH/OS_VERSION/SP_VERSION/cd1 \
/srv/tftpboot/EFI/ARCH/boot
```

Replace *ARCH* with the folder corresponding to the target system architecture. Also replace *OS_version* and *SP_version* according to your paths in *Section 8.3, "Installing Files on TFTP Server".*

Instead of using an NFS server for the `--net` option, it is also possible to use an HTTP repository, for example the openSUSE repository:

```
tux > mksusecd --create image.iso \
--net=http://download.opensuse.org/tumbleweed/repo/oss/suse \
/srv/tftpboot/EFI/ARCH/boot
```

The `image.iso` can be written to a DVD or CD, or using **dd** to a USB stick:

```
root # dd if=image.iso of=/dev/USB_DEVICE
```

Replace *USB_DEVICE* with the device name of your USB stick. Check the device name thoroughly to ensure that you are not accidentally destroying data on another drive.

146

IV   Remote Installation

9   Remote Installation 147

9 Remote Installation

SUSE® Linux Enterprise Server can be installed in different ways. In addition to the usual media installation covered in *Chapter 6, Installation with YaST*, you can choose from various network-based approaches or even opt for an unattended installation of SUSE Linux Enterprise Server.

Each method is introduced by means of two short checklists: one listing the prerequisites for that method and the other illustrating the basic procedure. More detail is then provided for all the techniques used in these installation scenarios.

 Note: Terminology

In the following sections, the system to hold your new SUSE Linux Enterprise Server installation is called *target system* or *installation target*. The term *repository* (previously called "installation source") is used for all sources of installation data. This includes physical media, such as CD and DVD, and network servers distributing the installation data in your network.

9.1 Installation Scenarios for Remote Installation

This section introduces the most common installation scenarios for remote installations. For each scenario, carefully check the list of prerequisites and follow the procedure outlined for that scenario. If in need of detailed instructions for a particular step, follow the links provided for each one of them.

9.1.1 Simple Remote Installation via VNC—Static Network Configuration

This type of installation still requires some degree of physical access to the target system to boot for installation. The installation is controlled by a remote workstation using VNC to connect to the installation program. User interaction is required as with the manual installation in *Chapter 6, Installation with YaST*.

For this type of installation, make sure that the following requirements are met:

- A repository, either remote or local:

    - Remote repository: NFS, HTTP, FTP, TFTP, or SMB with working network connection.

    - Local repository, for example a DVD.

- Target system with working network connection.

- Controlling system with working network connection and VNC viewer software.

- Physical boot medium (CD, DVD, or flash disk) for booting the target system.

- Valid static IP addresses already assigned to the repository and the controlling system.

- Valid static IP address to assign to the target system.

To perform this kind of installation, proceed as follows:

1. Set up the repository as described in *Chapter 7, Setting Up the Server Holding the Installation Sources*. Choose an NFS, HTTP, FTP, or TFTP network server. For an SMB repository, refer to *Section 7.5, "Managing an SMB Repository"*.

2. Boot the target system using DVD1 of the SUSE Linux Enterprise Server media kit.

3. When the boot screen of the target system appears, use the boot options prompt to set the appropriate VNC options and the address of the repository. This is described in detail in *Section 9.2, "Booting the Target System for Installation"*.

   The target system boots to a text-based environment, giving the network address and display number under which the graphical installation environment can be addressed by any VNC viewer application or browser. VNC installations announce themselves over OpenSLP and if the firewall settings permit. They can be found using `slptool` as described in *Procedure 9.1, "Locating VNC installations via OpenSLP"*.

4. On the controlling workstation, open a VNC viewing application or Web browser and connect to the target system as described in *Section 9.3.1, "VNC Installation"*.

5. Perform the installation as described in *Chapter 6, Installation with YaST*. Reconnect to the target system after it reboots for the final part of the installation.

6. Finish the installation.

9.1.2 Simple Remote Installation via VNC—Dynamic Network Configuration

This type of installation still requires some degree of physical access to the target system to boot for installation. The network configuration is done via DHCP. The installation is controlled from a remote workstation using VNC, but configuration does require user interaction.

For this type of installation, make sure that the following requirements are met:

- Remote repository: NFS, HTTP, FTP, or SMB with working network connection.

- Target system with working network connection.

- Controlling system with working network connection and VNC viewer software.

- Boot the target system using DVD1 of the SUSE Linux Enterprise Server media kit.

- Running DHCP server providing IP addresses.

    To perform this kind of installation, proceed as follows:

1. Set up the repository as described in *Chapter 7, Setting Up the Server Holding the Installation Sources*. Choose an NFS, HTTP, or FTP network server. For an SMB repository, refer to *Section 7.5, "Managing an SMB Repository"*.

2. Boot the target system using DVD1 of the SUSE Linux Enterprise Server media kit.

3. When the boot screen of the target system appears, use the boot options prompt to set the appropriate VNC options and the address of the repository. This is described in detail in *Section 9.2, "Booting the Target System for Installation"*.

    The target system boots to a text-based environment, giving the network address and display number under which the graphical installation environment can be addressed by any VNC viewer application or browser. VNC installations announce themselves over OpenSLP and if the firewall settings permit. They can be found using **slptool** as described in *Procedure 9.1, "Locating VNC installations via OpenSLP"*.

4. On the controlling workstation, open a VNC viewing application or Web browser and connect to the target system as described in *Section 9.3.1, "VNC Installation"*.

5. Perform the installation as described in *Chapter 6, Installation with YaST*. Reconnect to the target system after it reboots for the final part of the installation.

6. Finish the installation.

9.1.3 Remote Installation via VNC—PXE Boot and Wake on LAN

This type of installation is completely hands-off. The target machine is started and booted remotely. User interaction is only needed for the actual installation. This approach is suitable for cross-site deployments.

To perform this type of installation, make sure that the following requirements are met:

- Remote repository: NFS, HTTP, FTP, or SMB with working network connection.

- TFTP server.

- Running DHCP server for your network.

- Target system capable of PXE boot, networking, and Wake on LAN, plugged in and connected to the network.

- Controlling system with working network connection and VNC viewer software.

  To perform this type of installation, proceed as follows:

1. Set up the repository as described in *Chapter 7, Setting Up the Server Holding the Installation Sources*. Choose an NFS, HTTP, or FTP network server or configure an SMB repository as described in *Section 7.5, "Managing an SMB Repository"*.

2. Set up a TFTP server to hold a boot image that can be pulled by the target system. This is described in *Section 8.2, "Setting Up a TFTP Server"*.

3. Set up a DHCP server to provide IP addresses to all machines and reveal the location of the TFTP server to the target system. This is described in *Section 8.1, "Setting Up a DHCP Server"*.

4. Prepare the target system for PXE boot. This is described in further detail in *Section 8.5, "Preparing the Target System for PXE Boot"*.

5. Initiate the boot process of the target system using Wake on LAN. This is described in *Section 8.7, "Wake on LAN"*.

6. On the controlling workstation, open a VNC viewing application or Web browser and connect to the target system as described in *Section 9.3.1, "VNC Installation"*.

7. Perform the installation as described in *Chapter 6, Installation with YaST*. Reconnect to the target system after it reboots for the final part of the installation.

8. Finish the installation.

9.1.4 Simple Remote Installation via SSH—Static Network Configuration

This type of installation still requires some degree of physical access to the target system to boot for installation and to determine the IP address of the installation target. The installation itself is entirely controlled from a remote workstation using SSH to connect to the installer. User interaction is required as with the regular installation described in *Chapter 6, Installation with YaST*.

For this type of installation, make sure that the following requirements are met:

- Remote repository: NFS, HTTP, FTP, or SMB with working network connection.

- Target system with working network connection.

- Controlling system with working network connection and working SSH client software.

- Boot the target system using DVD1 of the SUSE Linux Enterprise Server media kit.

- Valid static IP addresses already assigned to the repository and the controlling system.

- Valid static IP address to assign to the target system.

To perform this kind of installation, proceed as follows:

1. Set up the repository as described in *Chapter 7, Setting Up the Server Holding the Installation Sources*. Choose an NFS, HTTP, or FTP network server. For an SMB repository, refer to *Section 7.5, "Managing an SMB Repository"*.

2. Boot the target system using DVD1 of the SUSE Linux Enterprise Server media kit.

3. When the boot screen of the target system appears, use the boot options prompt to set the appropriate parameters for network connection, address of the repository, and SSH enablement. This is described in detail in *Section 9.2.2, "Using Custom Boot Options"*.
The target system boots to a text-based environment, giving the network address under which the graphical installation environment can be addressed by any SSH client.

4. On the controlling workstation, open a terminal window and connect to the target system as described in *Section 9.3.2.2, "Connecting to the Installation Program"*.

5. Perform the installation as described in *Chapter 6, Installation with YaST*. Reconnect to the target system after it reboots for the final part of the installation.

6. Finish the installation.

9.1.5 Simple Remote Installation via SSH—Dynamic Network Configuration

This type of installation still requires some degree of physical access to the target system to boot for installation and determine the IP address of the installation target. The installation is controlled from a remote workstation using SSH , but configuration does require user interaction.

 Note: Avoid Lost Connections After the Second Step (Installation)

In the network settings dialog, check the *Traditional Method with ifup* and avoid Network-Manager. If not, your SSH connection will be lost during installation. Reset the settings to *User Controlled with NetworkManager* after your installation has finished.

For this type of installation, make sure that the following requirements are met:

- A repository, either remote or local:

    - Remote repository: NFS, HTTP, FTP, TFTP, or SMB with working network connection.

    - Local repository, for example a DVD.

- Target system with working network connection.

- Controlling system with working network connection and working SSH client software.

- Physical boot medium (CD, DVD, or flash disk) for booting the target system.

- Running DHCP server providing IP addresses.

    To perform this kind of installation, proceed as follows:

1. Set up the repository source as described in *Chapter 7, Setting Up the Server Holding the Installation Sources*. Choose an NFS, HTTP, or FTP network server. For an SMB repository, refer to *Section 7.5, "Managing an SMB Repository"*.

2. Boot the target system using DVD1 of the SUSE Linux Enterprise Server media kit.

3. When the boot screen of the target system appears, use the boot options prompt to pass the appropriate parameters for network connection, location of the installation source, and SSH enablement. See *Section 9.2.2, "Using Custom Boot Options"* for detailed instructions on the use of these parameters.

   The target system boots to a text-based environment, giving you the network address under which the graphical installation environment can be addressed by any SSH client.

4. On the controlling workstation, open a terminal window and connect to the target system as described in *Section 9.3.2.2, "Connecting to the Installation Program"*.

5. Perform the installation as described in *Chapter 6, Installation with YaST*. Reconnect to the target system after it reboots for the final part of the installation.

6. Finish the installation.

9.1.6 Remote Installation via SSH—PXE Boot and Wake on LAN

This type of installation is completely hands-off. The target machine is started and booted remotely.

To perform this type of installation, make sure that the following requirements are met:

- Remote repository: NFS, HTTP, FTP, or SMB with working network connection.

- TFTP server.

- Running DHCP server for your network, providing a static IP to the host to install.

- Target system capable of PXE boot, networking, and Wake on LAN, plugged in and connected to the network.

- Controlling system with working network connection and SSH client software.

  To perform this type of installation, proceed as follows:

1. Set up the repository as described in *Chapter 7, Setting Up the Server Holding the Installation Sources*. Choose an NFS, HTTP, or FTP network server. For the configuration of an SMB repository, refer to *Section 7.5, "Managing an SMB Repository"*.

2. Set up a TFTP server to hold a boot image that can be pulled by the target system. This is described in *Section 8.2, "Setting Up a TFTP Server"*.

3. Set up a DHCP server to provide IP addresses to all machines and reveal the location of the TFTP server to the target system. This is described in *Section 8.1, "Setting Up a DHCP Server"*.

4. Prepare the target system for PXE boot. This is described in further detail in *Section 8.5, "Preparing the Target System for PXE Boot"*.

5. Initiate the boot process of the target system using Wake on LAN. This is described in *Section 8.7, "Wake on LAN"*.

6. On the controlling workstation, start an SSH client and connect to the target system as described in *Section 9.3.2, "SSH Installation"*.

7. Perform the installation as described in *Chapter 6, Installation with YaST*. Reconnect to the target system after it reboots for the final part of the installation.

8. Finish the installation.

9.2 Booting the Target System for Installation

There are two different ways to customize the boot process for installation apart from those mentioned under *Section 8.7, "Wake on LAN"* and *Section 8.3.1, "Preparing the Structure"*. You can either use the default boot options and function keys. Alternatively, you can use the boot options prompt in the installation boot screen to specify desired boot options that the installation kernel may require for the specific hardware.

9.2.1 Using the Default Boot Options

The boot options are described in detail in *Chapter 6, Installation with YaST*. Generally, selecting *Installation* starts the installation boot process.

If problems occur, use *Installation—ACPI Disabled* or *Installation—Safe Settings*. For more information about troubleshooting the installation process, refer to *Book "Administration Guide", Chapter 40 "Common Problems and Their Solutions", Section 40.2 "Installation Problems"*.

The menu bar at the bottom of the screen offers some advanced functionality needed in some setups. Using the function keys (F1 ... F12), you can specify additional options to pass to the installation routines without having to know the detailed syntax of these parameters (see *Section 9.2.2, "Using Custom Boot Options"*). A detailed description of the available function keys is available in *Section 6.2.2.1, "The Boot Screen on Machines Equipped with Traditional BIOS"*.

9.2.2 Using Custom Boot Options

Using the appropriate set of boot options helps simplify your installation procedure. Many parameters can also be configured later using the linuxrc routines, but using the boot options is easier. In some automated setups, the boot options can be provided with `initrd` or an `info` file.

The following table lists all installation scenarios mentioned in this chapter with the required parameters for booting and the corresponding boot options. Append all of them in the order they appear in this table to get one boot option string that is handed to the installation routines. For example (all in one line):

```
install=XXX netdevice=XXX hostip=XXX netmask=XXX vnc=XXX VNCPassword=XXX
```

Replace all the values _XXX_ in this command with the values appropriate for your setup.

Chapter 6, Installation with YaST

Parameters Needed for Booting. None

Boot Options. None needed

Section 9.1.1, "Simple Remote Installation via VNC—Static Network Configuration"

PARAMETERS NEEDED FOR BOOTING

- Location of the installation server
- Network device
- IP address
- Netmask
- Gateway
- VNC enablement
- VNC password

BOOT OPTIONS

- `install=(nfs,http,ftp,smb)://PATH_TO_INSTMEDIA`
- `netdevice=NETDEVICE` (only needed if several network devices are available)
- `hostip=IP_ADDRESS`
- `netmask=NETMASK`
- `gateway=IP_GATEWAY`
- `vnc=1`
- `VNCPassword=PASSWORD`

Section 9.1.2, "Simple Remote Installation via VNC—Dynamic Network Configuration"

PARAMETERS NEEDED FOR BOOTING

- Location of the installation server
- VNC enablement
- VNC password

BOOT OPTIONS

- `install=(nfs,http,ftp,smb)://PATH_TO_INSTMEDIA`
- `vnc=1`
- `VNCPassword=PASSWORD`

Section 9.1.3, "Remote Installation via VNC—PXE Boot and Wake on LAN"

PARAMETERS NEEDED FOR BOOTING

- Location of the installation server
- Location of the TFTP server
- VNC enablement
- VNC password

Boot Options. Not applicable; process managed through PXE and DHCP

Section 9.1.4, "Simple Remote Installation via SSH—Static Network Configuration"

PARAMETERS NEEDED FOR BOOTING

- Location of the installation server
- Network device
- IP address
- Netmask
- Gateway
- SSH enablement
- SSH password

BOOT OPTIONS

- `install=(nfs,http,ftp,smb)://PATH_TO_INSTMEDIA`
- `netdevice=NETDEVICE` (only needed if several network devices are available)
- `hostip=IP_ADDRESS`

- `netmask=NETMASK`
- `gateway=IP_GATEWAY`
- `ssh=1`
- `ssh.password=PASSWORD`

Section 9.1.5, "Simple Remote Installation via SSH—Dynamic Network Configuration"

PARAMETERS NEEDED FOR BOOTING

- Location of the installation server
- SSH enablement
- SSH password

BOOT OPTIONS

- `install=(nfs,http,ftp,smb)://PATH_TO_INSTMEDIA`
- `ssh=1`
- `ssh.password=PASSWORD`

Section 9.1.6, "Remote Installation via SSH—PXE Boot and Wake on LAN"

- Location of the installation server
- Location of the TFTP server
- SSH enablement
- SSH password

Boot Options. Not applicable; process managed through PXE and DHCP

 Tip: More Information about linuxrc Boot Options

Find more information about the linuxrc boot options used for booting a Linux system at http://en.opensuse.org/SDB:Linuxrc ↗ .

9.2.2.1 Installing Add-On Products and Driver Updates

SUSE Linux Enterprise Server supports installation of add-on products, such as extensions (for example the SUSE Linux Enterprise High Availability Extension), third-party products as well as drivers or additional software. To automatically install an add-on product when deploying SUSE Linux Enterprise Server remotely, specify the `addon=REPOSITORY` parameter.

REPOSITORY needs to be a hosted repository that can be read by YaST (YaST2 or YUM (rpm-md)). ISO images are currently not supported.

 Tip: Driver Updates

> Driver Updates can be found at http://drivers.suse.com/ ↗. Not all driver updates are provided as repositories—some are only available as ISO images and therefore cannot be installed with the addon parameter. Instructions on how to install driver updates via ISO image are available at http://drivers.suse.com/doc/SolidDriver/Driver_Kits.html ↗.

9.3 Monitoring the Installation Process

There are several options for remotely monitoring the installation process. If the appropriate boot options have been specified while booting for installation, either VNC or SSH can be used to control the installation and system configuration from a remote workstation.

9.3.1 VNC Installation

Using any VNC viewer software, you can remotely control the installation of SUSE Linux Enterprise Server from virtually any operating system. This section introduces the setup using a VNC viewer application or a Web browser.

9.3.1.1 Preparing for VNC Installation

To enable VNC on the installation target, specify the appropriate boot options at the initial boot for installation (see *Section 9.2.2, "Using Custom Boot Options"*). The target system boots into a text-based environment and waits for a VNC client to connect to the installation program.

The installation program announces the IP address and display number needed to connect for installation. If you have physical access to the target system, this information is provided right after the system booted for installation. Enter this data when your VNC client software prompts for it and provide your VNC password.

Because the installation target announces itself via OpenSLP, you can retrieve the address information of the installation target via an SLP browser without the need for any physical contact to the installation itself, provided your network setup and all machines support OpenSLP:

PROCEDURE 9.1: LOCATING VNC INSTALLATIONS VIA OPENSLP

1. Run **slptool findsrvtypes | grep vnc** to get a list of all services offering VNC. The VNC installation targets should be available under a service named YaST.installation.suse.

2. Run **slptool findsrvs** *YaST.installation.suse* to get a list of installations available. Use the IP address and the port (usually 5901) provided with your VNC viewer.

9.3.1.2   Connecting to the Installation Program

To connect to a VNC server (the installation target in this case), start an independent VNC viewer application on any operating system.

Using VNC, you can control the installation of a Linux system from any other operating system, including other Linux flavors, Windows, or macOS.

On a Linux machine, make sure that the package tightvnc is installed. On a Windows machine, install the Windows port of this application, which can be obtained at the TightVNC home page (http://www.tightvnc.com/download.html ↗).

To connect to the installation program running on the target machine, proceed as follows:

1. Start the VNC viewer.

2. Enter the IP address and display number of the installation target as provided by the SLP browser or the installation program itself:

```
IP_ADDRESS:DISPLAY_NUMBER
```

A window opens on your desktop displaying the YaST screens as in a normal local installation.

9.3.2   SSH Installation

Using SSH, you can remotely control the installation of your Linux machine using any SSH client software.

9.3.2.1   Preparing for SSH Installation

In addition to installing the required software package (OpenSSH for Linux and PuTTY for Windows), you need to specify the appropriate boot options to enable SSH for installation. See *Section 9.2.2, "Using Custom Boot Options"* for details. OpenSSH is installed by default on any SUSE Linux–based operating system.

9.3.2.2   Connecting to the Installation Program

1. Retrieve the installation target's IP address. If you have physical access to the target machine, take the IP address the installation routine provides in the console after the initial boot. Otherwise take the IP address that has been assigned to this particular host in the DHCP server configuration.

2. In a command line, enter the following command:

```
ssh -X root@
ip_address_of_target
```

Replace *IP_ADDRESS_OF_TARGET* with the actual IP address of the installation target.

3. When prompted for a user name, enter root .

4. When prompted for the password, enter the password that has been set with the SSH boot option. After you have successfully authenticated, a command line prompt for the installation target appears.

5. Enter **yast** to launch the installation program. A window opens showing the normal YaST screens as described in *Chapter 6, Installation with YaST*.

V Initial System Configuration

10 Setting Up Hardware Components with YaST

YaST allows you to configure hardware items such as audio hardware, your system keyboard layout or printers.

 ## Note: Graphics Card, Monitor, Mouse and Keyboard Settings

Graphics card, monitor, mouse and keyboard can be configured with GNOME tools.

10.1 Setting Up Your System Keyboard Layout

The YaST *System Keyboard Layout* module lets you define the default keyboard layout for the system (also used for the console). Users can modify the keyboard layout in their individual X sessions, using the desktop's tools.

1. Start the YaST *System Keyboard Configuration* dialog by clicking *Hardware > System Keyboard Layout* in YaST. Alternatively, start the module from the command line with **sudo yast2 keyboard**.

2. Select the desired *Keyboard Layout* from the list.

3. Optionally, you can also define the keyboard repeat rate or keyboard delay rate in the *Expert Settings*.

4. Try the selected settings in the *Test* text box.

5. If the result is as expected, confirm your changes and close the dialog. The settings are written to `/etc/sysconfig/keyboard`.

10.2 Setting Up Sound Cards

YaST detects most sound cards automatically and configures them with the appropriate values. To change the default settings, or to set up a sound card that could not be configured automatically, use the YaST sound module. There, you can also set up additional sound cards or switch their order.

To start the sound module, start YaST and click *Hardware > Sound*. Alternatively, start the *Sound Configuration* dialog directly by running **yast2 sound &** as user `root` from a command line.

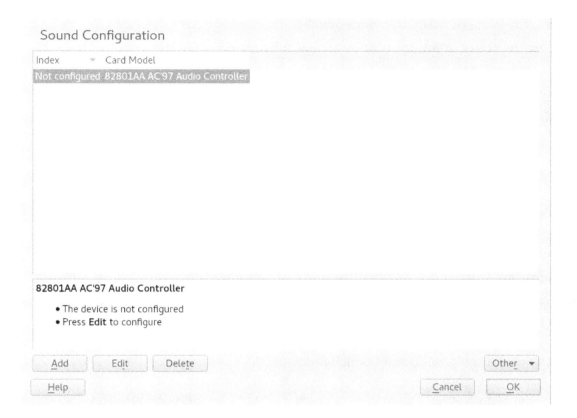

The dialog shows all sound cards that were detected.

If you have added a new sound card or YaST could not automatically configure an existing sound card, follow the steps below. For configuring a new sound card, you need to know your sound card vendor and model. If in doubt, refer to your sound card documentation for the required information. For a reference list of sound cards supported by ALSA with their corresponding sound modules, see http://www.alsa-project.org/main/index.php/Matrix:Main ↗ .

During configuration, you can choose between the following setup options:

Quick Automatic Setup

You are not required to go through any of the further configuration steps—the sound card is configured automatically. You can set the volume or any options you want to change later.

Normal Setup

Allows you to adjust the output volume and play a test sound during the configuration.

Advanced setup with possibility to change options

For experts only. Allows you to customize all parameters of the sound card.

 Important: Advanced Configuration

Only use this option if you know exactly what you are doing. Otherwise leave the parameters untouched and use the normal or the automatic setup options.

1. Start the YaST sound module.

2. To configure a detected, but *Not Configured* sound card, select the respective entry from the list and click *Edit*.
   To configure a new sound card, click *Add*. Select your sound card vendor and model and click *Next*.

3. Choose one of the setup options and click *Next*.

4. If you have chosen *Normal Setup*, you can now *Test* your sound configuration and make adjustments to the volume. You should start at about ten percent volume to avoid damage to your hearing or the speakers.

5. If all options are set according to your wishes, click *Next*.
   The *Sound Configuration* dialog shows the newly configured or modified sound card.

6. To remove a sound card configuration that you no longer need, select the respective entry and click *Delete*.

7. Click *OK* to save the changes and leave the YaST sound module.

PROCEDURE 10.2: MODIFYING SOUND CARD CONFIGURATIONS

1. To change the configuration of an individual sound card (for experts only!), select the sound card entry in the *Sound Configuration* dialog and click *Edit*.
   This takes you to the *Sound Card Advanced Options* where you can fine-tune several parameters. For more information, click *Help*.

2. To adjust the volume of an already configured sound card or to test the sound card, select the sound card entry in the *Sound Configuration* dialog and click *Other*. Select the respective menu item.

Note: YaST Mixer

The YaST mixer settings provide only basic options. They are intended for troubleshooting (for example, if the test sound is not audible). Access the YaST mixer settings from *Other > Volume*. For everyday use and fine-tuning of sound options, use the mixer applet provided by your desktop or the **alsasound** command line tool.

3. For playback of MIDI files, select *Other > Start Sequencer*.

4. When a supported sound card is detected, you can install SoundFonts for playback of MIDI files:

    a. Insert the original driver CD-ROM into your CD or DVD drive.

    b. Select *Other > Install SoundFonts* to copy SF2 SoundFonts™ to your hard disk. The SoundFonts are saved in the directory `/usr/share/sfbank/creative/`.

5. If you have configured more than one sound card in your system you can adjust the order of your sound cards. To set a sound card as primary device, select the sound card in the *Sound Configuration* and click *Other > Set as the Primary Card*. The sound device with index `0` is the default device and thus used by the system and the applications.

6. By default, SUSE Linux Enterprise Server uses the PulseAudio sound system. It is an abstraction layer that helps to mix multiple audio streams, bypassing any restrictions the hardware may have. To enable or disable the PulseAudio sound system, click *Other > PulseAudio Configuration*. If enabled, PulseAudio daemon is used to play sounds. Disable *PulseAudio Support* to use something else system-wide.

The volume and configuration of all sound cards are saved when you click *OK* and leave the YaST sound module. The mixer settings are saved to the file `/etc/asound.state`. The ALSA configuration data is appended to the end of the file `/etc/modprobe.d/sound` and written to `/etc/sysconfig/sound`.

10.3 Setting Up a Printer

YaST can be used to configure a local printer connected to your machine via USB and to set up printing with network printers. It is also possible to share printers over the network. Further information about printing (general information, technical details, and troubleshooting) is available in *Book "Administration Guide", Chapter 17 "Printer Operation"*.

In YaST, click *Hardware > Printer* to start the printer module. By default it opens in the *Printer Configurations* view, displaying a list of all printers that are available and configured. This is especially useful when having access to a lot of printers via the network. From here you can also *Print a Test Page* and configure printers.

 Note: Starting CUPS

To be able to print from your system, CUPS must run. In case it is not running, you are asked to start it. Answer with *Yes*, or you cannot configure printing. In case CUPS is not started at boot time, you will also be asked to enable this feature. It is recommended to say *Yes*, otherwise CUPS would need to be started manually after each reboot.

10.3.1 Configuring Printers

Usually a USB printer is automatically detected. There are two possible reasons it is not automatically detected:

* The USB printer is switched off.

* The communication between printer and computer is not possible. Check the cable and the plugs to make sure that the printer is properly connected. If this is the case, the problem may not be printer-related, but rather a USB-related problem.

Configuring a printer is a three-step process: specify the connection type, choose a driver, and name the print queue for this setup.

For many printer models, several drivers are available. When configuring the printer, YaST defaults to those marked `recommended` as a general rule. Normally it is not necessary to change the driver. However, if you want a color printer to print only in black and white, you can use a driver that does not support color printing. If you experience performance problems with a PostScript printer when printing graphics, try to switch from a PostScript driver to a PCL driver (provided your printer understands PCL).

If no driver for your printer is listed, try to select a generic driver with an appropriate standard language from the list. Refer to your printer's documentation to find out which language (the set of commands controlling the printer) your printer understands. If this does not work, refer to *Section 10.3.1.1, "Adding Drivers with YaST"* for another possible solution.

A printer is never used directly, but always through a print queue. This ensures that simultaneous jobs can be queued and processed one after the other. Each print queue is assigned to a specific driver, and a printer can have multiple queues. This makes it possible to set up a second queue on a color printer that prints black and white only, for example. Refer to *Book "Administration Guide", Chapter 17 "Printer Operation", Section 17.1 "The CUPS Workflow"* for more information about print queues.

PROCEDURE 10.3: ADDING A NEW PRINTER

1. Start the YaST printer module with *Hardware > Printer*.

2. In the *Printer Configurations* screen click *Add*.

3. If your printer is already listed under `Specify the Connection`, proceed with the next step. Otherwise, try to *Detect More* or start the *Connection Wizard*.

4. In the text box under `Find and Assign a Driver` enter the vendor name and the model name and click *Search for*.

5. Choose a driver that matches your printer. It is recommended to choose the driver listed first. If no suitable driver is displayed:

   a. Check your search term

   b. Broaden your search by clicking *Find More*

   c. Add a driver as described in *Section 10.3.1.1, "Adding Drivers with YaST"*

6. Specify the `Default paper size`.

7. In the *Set Arbitrary Name* field, enter a unique name for the print queue.

8. The printer is now configured with the default settings and ready to use. Click *OK* to return to the *Printer Configurations* view. The newly configured printer is now visible in the list of printers.

10.3.1.1 Adding Drivers with YaST

Not all printer drivers available for SUSE Linux Enterprise Server are installed by default. If no suitable driver is available in the *Find and Assign a Driver* dialog when adding a new printer install a driver package containing drivers for your printers:

PROCEDURE 10.4: INSTALLING ADDITIONAL DRIVER PACKAGES

1. Start the YaST printer module with *Hardware > Printer*.

2. In the *Printer Configurations* screen, click *Add*.

3. In the `Find and Assign a Driver` section, click *Driver Packages*.

4. Choose one or more suitable driver packages from the list. Do *not* specify the path to a printer description file.

5. Choose *OK* and confirm the package installation.

6. To directly use these drivers, proceed as described in *Procedure 10.3, "Adding a New Printer"*.

PostScript printers do not need printer driver software. PostScript printers need only a PostScript Printer Description (PPD) file which matches the particular model. PPD files are provided by the printer manufacturer.

If no suitable PPD file is available in the *Find and Assign a Driver* dialog when adding a PostScript printer install a PPD file for your printer:

Several sources for PPD files are available. It is recommended to first try additional driver packages that are shipped with SUSE Linux Enterprise Server but not installed by default (see below for installation instructions). If these packages do not contain suitable drivers for your printer, get PPD files directly from your printer vendor or from the driver CD of a PostScript printer. For details, see *Book "Administration Guide", Chapter 17 "Printer Operation", Section 17.8.2 "No Suitable PPD File Available for a PostScript Printer"*. Alternatively, find PPD files at http://www.linuxfoundation.org/collaborate/workgroups/openprinting/database/databaseintro ↗, the "OpenPrinting.org printer database". When downloading PPD files from OpenPrinting, keep in mind that it always shows the latest Linux support status, which is not necessarily met by SUSE Linux Enterprise Server.

1. Start the YaST printer module with *Hardware* › *Printer*.

2. In the *Printer Configurations* screen, click *Add*.

3. In the `Find and Assign a Driver` section, click *Driver Packages*.

4. Enter the full path to the PPD file into the text box under `Make a Printer Description File Available`.

5. Click *OK* to return to the `Add New Printer Configuration` screen.

6. To directly use this PPD file, proceed as described in *Procedure 10.3, "Adding a New Printer"*.

10.3.1.2   Editing a Local Printer Configuration

By editing an existing configuration for a printer you can change basic settings such as connection type and driver. It is also possible to adjust the default settings for paper size, resolution, media source, etc. You can change identifiers of the printer by altering the printer description or location.

1. Start the YaST printer module with *Hardware* › *Printer*.

2. In the *Printer Configurations* screen, choose a local printer configuration from the list and click *Edit*.

3. Change the connection type or the driver as described in *Procedure 10.3, "Adding a New Printer"*. This should only be necessary in case you have problems with the current configuration.

4. Optionally, make this printer the default by checking *Default Printer*.

5. Adjust the default settings by clicking *All Options for the Current Driver*. To change a setting, expand the list of options by clicking the relative + sign. Change the default by clicking an option. Apply your changes with *OK*.

10.3.2 Configuring Printing via the Network with YaST

Network printers are not detected automatically. They must be configured manually using the YaST printer module. Depending on your network setup, you can print to a print server (CUPS, LPD, SMB, or IPX) or directly to a network printer (preferably via TCP). Access the configuration view for network printing by choosing *Printing via Network* from the left pane in the YaST printer module.

10.3.2.1 Using CUPS

In a Linux environment CUPS is usually used to print via the network. The simplest setup is to only print via a single CUPS server which can directly be accessed by all clients. Printing via more than one CUPS server requires a running local CUPS daemon that communicates with the remote CUPS servers.

 Important: Browsing Network Print Queues

CUPS servers announce their print queues over the network either via the traditional CUPS browsing protocol or via Bonjour/DND-SD. Clients need to be able to browse these lists, so users can select specific printers to send their print jobs to. To be able to browse network print queues, the service `cups-browsed` provided by the package `cups-filters-cups-browsed` must run on all clients that print via CUPS servers. `cups-browsed` is started automatically when configuring network printing with YaST.

In case browsing does not work after having started `cups-browsed`, the CUPS server(s) probably announce the network print queues via Bonjour/DND-SD. In this case you need to additionally install the package `avahi` and start the associated service with **sudo systemctl start avahi-daemon** on all clients.

PROCEDURE 10.6: PRINTING VIA A SINGLE CUPS SERVER

1. Start the YaST printer module with *Hardware › Printer*.

2. From the left pane, launch the *Print via Network* screen.

3. Check *Do All Your Printing Directly via One Single CUPS Server* and specify the name or IP address of the server.

4. Click *Test Server* to make sure you have chosen the correct name or IP address.

5. Click OK to return to the *Printer Configurations* screen. All printers available via the CUPS server are now listed.

1. Start the YaST printer module with *Hardware > Printer*.

2. From the left pane, launch the *Print via Network* screen.

3. Check *Accept Printer Announcements from CUPS Servers*.

4. Under `General Settings` specify which servers to use. You may accept connections from all networks available or from specific hosts. If you choose the latter option, you need to specify the host names or IP addresses.

5. Confirm by clicking *OK* and then *Yes* when asked to start a local CUPS server. After the server has started YaST will return to the *Printer Configurations* screen. Click *Refresh list* to see the printers detected by now. Click this button again, in case more printer are to be available.

10.3.2.2   Using Print Servers other than CUPS

If your network offers print services via print servers other than CUPS, start the YaST printer module with *Hardware > Printer* and launch the *Print via Network* screen from the left pane. Start the *Connection Wizard* and choose the appropriate *Connection Type*. Ask your network administrator for details on configuring a network printer in your environment.

10.3.3   Sharing Printers Over the Network

Printers managed by a local CUPS daemon can be shared over the network and so turn your machine into a CUPS server. Usually you share a printer by enabling CUPS' so-called "browsing mode". If browsing is enabled, the local print queues are made available on the network for listening to remote CUPS daemons. It is also possible to set up a dedicated CUPS server that manages all print queues and can directly be accessed by remote clients. In this case it is not necessary to enable browsing.

1. Start the YaST printer module with *Hardware > Printer*.

2. Launch the *Share Printers* screen from the left pane.

3. Select *Allow Remote Access*. Also check *For computers within the local network* and enable browsing mode by also checking *Publish printers by default within the local network*.

4. Click *OK* to restart the CUPS server and to return to the *Printer Configurations* screen.

5. Regarding CUPS and firewall settings, see http://en.opensuse.org/SD-B:CUPS_and_SANE_Firewall_settings↗.

11 Advanced Disk Setup

Sophisticated system configurations require specific disk setups. All common partitioning tasks can be done with YaST. To get persistent device naming with block devices, use the block devices below `/dev/disk/by-id` or `/dev/disk/by-uuid`. Logical Volume Management (LVM) is a disk partitioning scheme that is designed to be much more flexible than the physical partitioning used in standard setups. Its snapshot functionality enables easy creation of data backups. Redundant Array of Independent Disks (RAID) offers increased data integrity, performance, and fault tolerance. SUSE Linux Enterprise Server also supports multipath I/O (see *Book "Storage Administration Guide", Chapter 16 "Managing Multipath I/O for Devices"* for details). There is also the option to use iSCSI as a networked disk (read more about iSCSI in *Book "Storage Administration Guide", Chapter 14 "Mass Storage over IP Networks: iSCSI"*).

11.1 Using the YaST Partitioner

With the expert partitioner, shown in *Figure 11.1, "The YaST Partitioner"*, manually modify the partitioning of one or several hard disks. You can add, delete, resize, and edit partitions, or access the soft RAID, and LVM configuration.

 Warning: Repartitioning the Running System

> Although it is possible to repartition your system while it is running, the risk of making a mistake that causes data loss is very high. Try to avoid repartitioning your installed system and always do a complete backup of your data before attempting to do so.

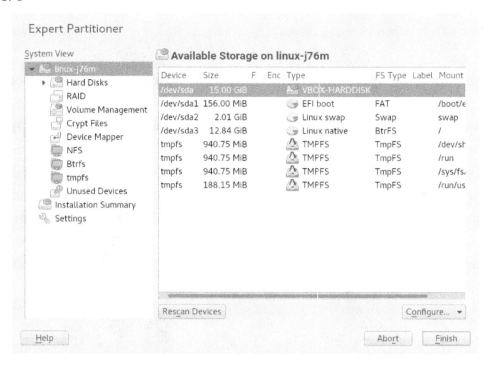

FIGURE 11.1: THE YAST PARTITIONER

 Tip: IBM z Systems: Device Names

> IBM z Systems recognizes only DASD and SCSI hard disks. IDE hard disks are not supported. This is why these devices appear in the partition table as `dasda` or `sda` for the first recognized device.

All existing or suggested partitions on all connected hard disks are displayed in the list of *Available Storage* in the YaST *Expert Partitioner* dialog. Entire hard disks are listed as devices without numbers, such as `/dev/sda` (or `/dev/dasda`). Partitions are listed as parts of these devices, such as `/dev/sda1` (or `/dev/dasda1`, respectively). The size, type, encryption status, file system, and mount point of the hard disks and their partitions are also displayed. The mount point describes where the partition appears in the Linux file system tree.

Several functional views are available on the left hand *System View*. These views can be used to collect information about existing storage configurations, configure functions (like `RAID`, `Volume Management`, `Crypt Files`), and view file systems with additional features, such as Btrfs, NFS, or `TMPFS`.

If you run the expert dialog during installation, any free hard disk space is also listed and automatically selected. To provide more disk space to SUSE® Linux Enterprise Server, free the needed space starting from the bottom toward the top of the list (starting from the last partition of a hard disk toward the first).

11.1.1   Partition Types

 Tip: IBM z Systems: Hard Disks

On IBM z Systems platforms, SUSE Linux Enterprise Server supports SCSI hard disks and DASDs (direct access storage devices). While SCSI disks can be partitioned as described below, DASDs can have no more than three partition entries in their partition tables.

Every hard disk has a partition table with space for four entries. Every entry in the partition table corresponds to a primary partition or an extended partition. Only one extended partition entry is allowed, however.

A primary partition simply consists of a continuous range of cylinders (physical disk areas) assigned to a particular operating system. With primary partitions you would be limited to four partitions per hard disk, because more do not fit in the partition table. This is why extended partitions are used. Extended partitions are also continuous ranges of disk cylinders, but an extended partition may be divided into *logical partitions* itself. Logical partitions do not require entries in the partition table. In other words, an extended partition is a container for logical partitions.

If you need more than four partitions, create an extended partition as the fourth partition (or earlier). This extended partition should occupy the entire remaining free cylinder range. Then create multiple logical partitions within the extended partition. The maximum number of logical partitions is 63, independent of the disk type. It does not matter which types of partitions are used for Linux. Primary and logical partitions both function normally.

 Tip: GPT Partition Table

If you need to create more than 4 primary partitions on one hard disk, you need to use the GPT partition type. This type removes the primary partitions number restriction, and supports partitions bigger than 2 TB as well.

To use GPT, run the YaST Partitioner, click the relevant disk name in the *System View* and choose *Expert* › *Create New Partition Table* › *GPT*.

11.1.2 Creating a Partition

To create a partition from scratch select *Hard Disks* and then a hard disk with free space. The actual modification can be done in the *Partitions* tab:

1. Select *Add* and specify the partition type (primary or extended). Create up to four primary partitions or up to three primary partitions and one extended partition. Within the extended partition, create several logical partitions (see *Section 11.1.1, "Partition Types"*).

2. Specify the size of the new partition. You can either choose to occupy all the free unpartitioned space, or enter a custom size.

3. Select the file system to use and a mount point. YaST suggests a mount point for each partition created. To use a different mount method, like mount by label, select *Fstab Options*. For more information on supported file systems, see `root`.

4. Specify additional file system options if your setup requires them. This is necessary, for example, if you need persistent device names. For details on the available options, refer to *Section 11.1.3, "Editing a Partition"*.

5. Click *Finish* to apply your partitioning setup and leave the partitioning module.
   If you created the partition during installation, you are returned to the installation overview screen.

11.1.2.1 Btrfs Partitioning

The default file system for the root partition is Btrfs (see *Book "Administration Guide", Chapter 7 "System Recovery and Snapshot Management with Snapper"* and *Book "Storage Administration Guide", Chapter 1 "Overview of File Systems in Linux"* for more information on Btrfs). The root file system is the default subvolume and it is not listed in the list of created subvolumes. As a default Btrfs subvolume, it can be mounted as a normal file system.

Important: Btrfs on an Encrypted Root Partition

The default partitioning setup suggests the root partition as Btrfs with `/boot` being a directory. To encrypt the root partition encrypted, make sure to use the GPT partition table type instead of the default MSDOS type. Otherwise the GRUB2 boot loader may not have enough space for the second stage loader.

It is possible to create snapshots of Btrfs subvolumes—either manually, or automatically based on system events. For example when making changes to the file system, **zypper** invokes the **snapper** command to create snapshots before and after the change. This is useful if you are not satisfied with the change **zypper** made and want to restore the previous state. As **snapper** invoked by **zypper** creates snapshots of the *root* file system by default, it makes sense to exclude specific directories from being included into snapshots. This is the reason why YaST suggests creating the following separate subvolumes.

`/boot/grub2/i386-pc`, `/boot/grub2/x86_64-efi`, `/boot/grub2/powerpc-ieee1275`, `/boot/grub2/s390x-emu`

A rollback of the boot loader configuration is not supported. The directories listed above are architecture-specific. The first two directories are present on AMD64/Intel 64 machines, the latter two on IBM POWER and on IBM z Systems, respectively.

`/home`

If `/home` does not reside on a separate partition, it is excluded to avoid data loss on rollbacks.

`/opt`, `/var/opt`

Third-party products usually get installed to `/opt`. It is excluded to avoid uninstalling these applications on rollbacks.

`/srv`

Contains data for Web and FTP servers. It is excluded to avoid data loss on rollbacks.

`/tmp`, `/var/tmp`, `/var/cache`, `/var/crash`

All directories containing temporary files and caches are excluded from snapshots.

`/usr/local`

This directory is used when manually installing software. It is excluded to avoid uninstalling these installations on rollbacks.

`/var/lib/libvirt/images`

The default location for virtual machine images managed with libvirt. Excluded to ensure virtual machine images are not replaced with older versions during a rollback. By default, this subvolume is created with the option `no copy on write`.

`/var/lib/mailman`, `/var/spool`

Directories containing mails or mail queues are excluded to avoid a loss of mails after a rollback.

`/var/lib/named`

Contains zone data for the DNS server. Excluded from snapshots to ensure a name server can operate after a rollback.

`/var/lib/mariadb`, `/var/lib/mysql`, `/var/lib/pgqsl`

These directories contain database data. By default, these subvolumes are created with the option `no copy on write`.

`/var/log`

Log file location. Excluded from snapshots to allow log file analysis after the rollback of a broken system.

 Tip: Size of Btrfs Partition

Since saved snapshots require more disk space, it is recommended to reserve enough space for Btrfs. Suggested size for a root Btrfs partition with default subvolumes is 20GB.

11.1.2.1.1 Managing Btrfs Subvolumes using YaST

Subvolumes of a Btrfs partition can be now managed with the YaST *Expert partitioner* module. You can add new or remove existing subvolumes.

PROCEDURE 11.1: BTRFS SUBVOLUMES WITH YAST

1. Start the YaST *Expert Partitioner* with *System › Partitioner*.

2. Choose *Btrfs* in the left *System View* pane.

3. Select the Btrfs partition whose subvolumes you need to manage and click *Edit*.

4. Click *Subvolume Handling*. You can see a list off all existing subvolumes of the selected Btrfs partition. You can notice several `@/.snapshots/xyz/snapshot` entries—each of these subvolumes belongs to one existing snapshot.

5. Depending on whether you want to add or remove subvolumes, do the following:

    a. To remove a subvolume, select it from the list of *Exisitng Subvolumes* and click *Remove.*

    b. To add a new subvolume, enter its name to the *New Subvolume* text box and click *Add new.*

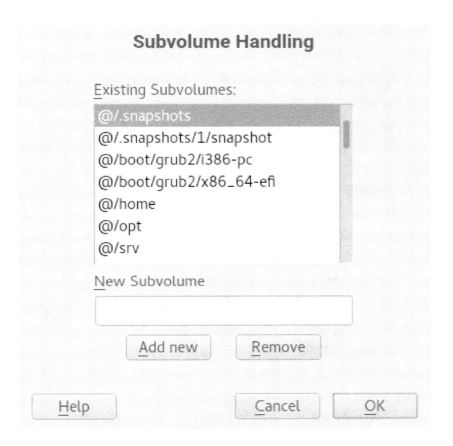

FIGURE 11.2: BTRFS SUBVOLUMES IN YAST PARTITIONER

6. Confirm with *OK* and *Finish.*

7. Leave the partitioner with *Finish.*

11.1.3 Editing a Partition

When you create a new partition or modify an existing partition, you can set various parameters. For new partitions, the default parameters set by YaST are usually sufficient and do not require any modification. To edit your partition setup manually, proceed as follows:

1. Select the partition.

2. Click *Edit* to edit the partition and set the parameters:

   File System ID

   Even if you do not want to format the partition at this stage, assign it a file system ID to ensure that the partition is registered correctly. Typical values are *Linux*, *Linux swap*, *Linux LVM*, and *Linux RAID*.

   File System

   To change the partition file system, click *Format Partition* and select file system type in the *File System* list.

   SUSE Linux Enterprise Server supports several types of file systems. Btrfs is the Linux file system of choice for the root partition because of its advanced features. It supports copy-on-write functionality, creating snapshots, multi-device spanning, sub-volumes, and other useful techniques. XFS, Ext3 and JFS are journaling file systems. These file systems can restore the system very quickly after a system crash, using write processes logged during the operation. Ext2 is not a journaling file system, but it is adequate for smaller partitions because it does not require much disk space for management.

   The default file system for the root partition is Btrfs. The default file system for additional partitions is XFS.

   Swap is a special format that allows the partition to be used as a virtual memory. Create a swap partition of at least 256 MB. However, if you use up your swap space, consider adding more memory to your system instead of adding more swap space.

    Warning: Changing the File System

   Changing the file system and reformatting partitions irreversibly deletes all data from the partition.

   For details on the various file systems, refer to *Storage Administration Guide*.

Encrypt Device

If you activate the encryption, all data is written to the hard disk in encrypted form. This increases the security of sensitive data, but reduces the system speed, as the encryption takes some time to process. More information about the encryption of file systems is provided in *Book "Security Guide", Chapter 11 "Encrypting Partitions and Files"*.

Mount Point

Specify the directory where the partition should be mounted in the file system tree. Select from YaST suggestions or enter any other name.

Fstab Options

Specify various parameters contained in the global file system administration file (`/etc/fstab`). The default settings should suffice for most setups. You can, for example, change the file system identification from the device name to a volume label. In the volume label, use all characters except `/` and space.

To get persistent devices names, use the mount option *Device ID, UUID* or *LABEL*. In SUSE Linux Enterprise Server, persistent device names are enabled by default.

 Note: IBM z Systems: Mounting by Path

Since mounting by ID causes problems on IBM z Systems when using disk-to-disk copying for cloning purposes, devices are mounted by path in `/etc/fstab` on IBM z Systems by default.

If you prefer to mount the partition by its label, you need to define one in the *Volume label* text entry. For example, you could use the partition label `HOME` for a partition intended to mount to `/home`.

If you intend to use quotas on the file system, use the mount option *Enable Quota Support*. This must be done before you can define quotas for users in the YaST *User Management* module. For further information on how to configure user quota, refer to *Section 15.3.4, "Managing Quotas"*.

3. Select *Finish* to save the changes.

Note: Resize File Systems

To resize an existing file system, select the partition and use *Resize*. Note, that it is not possible to resize partitions while mounted. To resize partitions, unmount the relevant partition before running the partitioner.

11.1.4   Expert Options

After you select a hard disk device (like *sda*) in the *System View* pane, you can access the *Expert* menu in the lower right part of the *Expert Partitioner* window. The menu contains the following commands:

Create New Partition Table

This option helps you create a new partition table on the selected device.

 Warning: Creating a New Partition Table

Creating a new partition table on a device irreversibly removes all the partitions and their data from that device.

Clone This Disk

This option helps you clone the device partition layout (but not the data) to other available disk devices.

11.1.5   Advanced Options

After you select the host name of the computer (the top-level of the tree in the *System View* pane), you can access the *Configure* menu in the lower right part of the *Expert Partitioner* window. The menu contains the following commands:

Configure iSCSI

To access SCSI over IP block devices, you first need to configure iSCSI. This results in additionally available devices in the main partition list.

Configure Multipath

Selecting this option helps you configure the multipath enhancement to the supported mass storage devices.

11.1.6 More Partitioning Tips

The following section includes a few hints and tips on partitioning that should help you make the right decisions when setting up your system.

 Tip: Cylinder Numbers

Note, that different partitioning tools may start counting the cylinders of a partition with `0` or with `1`. When calculating the number of cylinders, you should always use the difference between the last and the first cylinder number and add one.

11.1.6.1 Using swap

Swap is used to extend the available physical memory. It is then possible to use more memory than physical RAM available. The memory management system of kernels before 2.4.10 needed swap as a safety measure. Then, if you did not have twice the size of your RAM in swap, the performance of the system suffered. These limitations no longer exist.

Linux uses a page called "Least Recently Used" (LRU) to select pages that might be moved from memory to disk. Therefore, running applications have more memory available and caching works more smoothly.

If an application tries to allocate the maximum allowed memory, problems with swap can arise. There are three major scenarios to look at:

System with no swap

The application gets the maximum allowed memory. All caches are freed, and thus all other running applications are slowed. After a few minutes, the kernel's out-of-memory kill mechanism activates and kills the process.

System with medium sized swap (128 MB–512 MB)

At first, the system slows like a system without swap. After all physical RAM has been allocated, swap space is used as well. At this point, the system becomes very slow and it becomes impossible to run commands from remote. Depending on the speed of the hard disks that run the swap space, the system stays in this condition for about 10 to 15 minutes until the out-of-memory kill mechanism resolves the issue. Note that you will need a certain amount of swap if the computer needs to perform a "suspend to disk". In that case, the swap size should be large enough to contain the necessary data from memory (512 MB–1 GB).

System with lots of swap (several GB)

It is better to not have an application that is out of control and swapping excessively in this case. If you use such application, the system will need many hours to recover. In the process, it is likely that other processes get timeouts and faults, leaving the system in an undefined state, even after terminating the faulty process. In this case, do a hard machine reboot and try to get it running again. Lots of swap is only useful if you have an application that relies on this feature. Such applications (like databases or graphics manipulation programs) often have an option to directly use hard disk space for their needs. It is advisable to use this option instead of using lots of swap space.

If your system is not out of control, but needs more swap after some time, it is possible to extend the swap space online. If you prepared a partition for swap space, add this partition with YaST. If you do not have a partition available, you can also use a swap file to extend the swap. Swap files are generally slower than partitions, but compared to physical RAM, both are extremely slow so the actual difference is negligible.

PROCEDURE 11.2: ADDING A SWAP FILE MANUALLY

To add a swap file in the running system, proceed as follows:

1. Create an empty file in your system. For example, if you want to add a swap file with 128 MB swap at `/var/lib/swap/swapfile`, use the commands:

```
mkdir -p /var/lib/swap
dd if=/dev/zero of=/var/lib/swap/swapfile bs=1M count=128
```

2. Initialize this swap file with the command

```
mkswap /var/lib/swap/swapfile
```

 Note: Changed UUID for Swap Partitions when Formatting via `mkswap`

Do not reformat existing swap partitions with **mkswap** if possible. Reformatting with **mkswap** will change the UUID value of the swap partition. Either reformat via YaST (will update `/etc/fstab`) or adjust `/etc/fstab` manually.

3. Activate the swap with the command

```
swapon /var/lib/swap/swapfile
```

To disable this swap file, use the command

```
swapoff /var/lib/swap/swapfile
```

4. Check the current available swap spaces with the command

```
cat /proc/swaps
```

Note that at this point, it is only temporary swap space. After the next reboot, it is no longer used.

5. To enable this swap file permanently, add the following line to `/etc/fstab`:

```
/var/lib/swap/swapfile swap swap defaults 0 0
```

11.1.7   Partitioning and LVM

From the *Expert partitioner*, access the LVM configuration by clicking the *Volume Management* item in the *System View* pane. However, if a working LVM configuration already exists on your system, it is automatically activated upon entering the initial LVM configuration of a session. In this case, all disks containing a partition (belonging to an activated volume group) cannot be repartitioned. The Linux kernel cannot reread the modified partition table of a hard disk when any partition on this disk is in use. If you already have a working LVM configuration on your system, physical repartitioning should not be necessary. Instead, change the configuration of the logical volumes.

At the beginning of the physical volumes (PVs), information about the volume is written to the partition. To reuse such a partition for other non-LVM purposes, it is advisable to delete the beginning of this volume. For example, in the VG `system` and PV `/dev/sda2`, do this with the command **dd** `if=/dev/zero of=/dev/sda2 bs=512 count=1`.

 Warning: File System for Booting

The file system used for booting (the root file system or `/boot`) must not be stored on an LVM logical volume. Instead, store it on a normal physical partition.

To change your `/usr` or `swap`, refer to , *Updating Init RAM Disk When Switching to Logical Volumes*. For more details about LVM, see *Book "Storage Administration Guide"*.

11.2   LVM Configuration

This section explains specific steps to take when configuring LVM. If you need information about the Logical Volume Manager in general, refer to the *Book "Storage Administration Guide", Chapter 5 "LVM Configuration", Section 5.1 "Understanding the Logical Volume Manager"*.

 ## Warning: Back up Your Data

Using LVM is sometimes associated with increased risk such as data loss. Risks also include application crashes, power failures, and faulty commands. Save your data before implementing LVM or reconfiguring volumes. Never work without a backup.

11.2.1   LVM Configuration with YaST

The YaST LVM configuration can be reached from the YaST Expert Partitioner (see *Section 11.1, "Using the YaST Partitioner"*) within the *Volume Management* item in the *System View* pane. The Expert Partitioner allows you to edit and delete existing partitions and create new ones that need to be used with LVM. The first task is to create PVs that provide space to a volume group:

1. Select a hard disk from *Hard Disks*.

2. Change to the *Partitions* tab.

3. Click *Add* and enter the desired size of the PV on this disk.

4. Use *Do not format partition* and change the *File System ID* to *0x8E Linux LVM*. Do not mount this partition.

5. Repeat this procedure until you have defined all the desired physical volumes on the available disks.

11.2.1.1   Creating Volume Groups

If no volume group exists on your system, you must add one (see *Figure 11.3, "Creating a Volume Group"*). It is possible to create additional groups by clicking *Volume Management* in the *System View* pane, and then on *Add Volume Group*. One single volume group is usually sufficient.

1. Enter a name for the VG, for example, `system`.

2. Select the desired *Physical Extend Size*. This value defines the size of a physical block in the volume group. All the disk space in a volume group is handled in blocks of this size.

3. Add the prepared PVs to the VG by selecting the device and clicking *Add*. Selecting several devices is possible by holding `Ctrl` while selecting the devices.

4. Select *Finish* to make the VG available to further configuration steps.

FIGURE 11.3: CREATING A VOLUME GROUP

If you have multiple volume groups defined and want to add or remove PVs, select the volume group in the *Volume Management* list and click *Resize*. In the following window, you can add or remove PVs to the selected volume group.

11.2.1.2   Configuring Logical Volumes

After the volume group has been filled with PVs, define the LVs which the operating system should use in the next dialog. Choose the current volume group and change to the *Logical Volumes* tab. *Add*, *Edit*, *Resize*, and *Delete* LVs as needed until all space in the volume group has been occupied. Assign at least one LV to each volume group.

FIGURE 11.4: LOGICAL VOLUME MANAGEMENT

Click *Add* and go through the wizard-like pop-up that opens:

1. Enter the name of the LV. For a partition that should be mounted to /home, a name like HOME could be used.

2. Select the type of the LV. It can be either *Normal Volume, Thin Pool,* or *Thin Volume.* Note that you need to create a thin pool first, which can store individual thin volumes. The big advantage of thin provisioning is that the total sum of all thin volumes stored in a thin pool can exceed the size of the pool itself.

3. Select the size and the number of stripes of the LV. If you have only one PV, selecting more than one stripe is not useful.

4. Choose the file system to use on the LV and the mount point.

By using stripes it is possible to distribute the data stream in the LV among several PVs (striping). However, striping a volume can only be done over different PVs, each providing at least the amount of space of the volume. The maximum number of stripes equals to the number of PVs, where Stripe "1" means "no striping". Striping only makes sense with PVs on different hard disks, otherwise performance will decrease.

 Warning: Striping

YaST cannot, at this point, verify the correctness of your entries concerning striping. Any mistake made here is apparent only later when the LVM is implemented on disk.

If you have already configured LVM on your system, the existing logical volumes can also be used. Before continuing, assign appropriate mount points to these LVs. With *Finish*, return to the YaST Expert Partitioner and finish your work there.

11.3 Soft RAID Configuration with YaST

This section describes actions required to create and configure various types of RAID. In case you need background information about RAID, refer to *Book "Storage Administration Guide", Chapter 7 "Software RAID Configuration", Section 7.1 "Understanding RAID Levels"*.

11.3.1 Soft RAID Configuration with YaST

The YaST *RAID* configuration can be reached from the YaST Expert Partitioner, described in *Section 11.1, "Using the YaST Partitioner"*. This partitioning tool enables you to edit and delete existing partitions and create new ones to be used with soft RAID:

1. Select a hard disk from *Hard Disks*.

2. Change to the *Partitions* tab.

3. Click *Add* and enter the desired size of the raid partition on this disk.

4. Use *Do not Format the Partition* and change the *File System ID* to *0xFD Linux RAID*. Do not mount this partition.

5. Repeat this procedure until you have defined all the desired physical volumes on the available disks.

For RAID 0 and RAID 1, at least two partitions are needed—for RAID 1, usually exactly two and no more. If RAID 5 is used, at least three partitions are required, RAID 6 and RAID 10 require at least four partitions. It is recommended to use partitions of the same size only. The RAID partitions should be located on different hard disks to decrease the risk of losing data if one is defective (RAID 1 and 5) and to optimize the performance of RAID 0. After creating all the partitions to use with RAID, click *RAID › Add RAID* to start the RAID configuration.

In the next dialog, choose between RAID levels 0, 1, 5, 6 and 10. Then, select all partitions with either the "Linux RAID" or "Linux native" type that should be used by the RAID system. No swap or DOS partitions are shown.

 Tip: Classify Disks

For RAID types where the order of added disks matters, you can mark individual disks with one of the letters A to E. Click the *Classify* button, select the disk and click of the *Class X* buttons, where X is the letter you want to assign to the disk. Assign all available RAID disks this way, and confirm with *OK*. You can easily sort the classified disks with the *Sorted* or *Interleaved* buttons, or add a sort pattern from a text file with *Pattern File*.

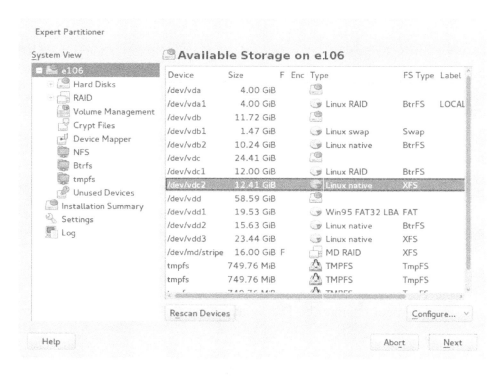

FIGURE 11.5: RAID PARTITIONS

To add a previously unassigned partition to the selected RAID volume, first click the partition then *Add*. Assign all partitions reserved for RAID. Otherwise, the space on the partition remains unused. After assigning all partitions, click *Next* to select the available *RAID Options*.

In this last step, set the file system to use, encryption and the mount point for the RAID volume. After completing the configuration with *Finish*, see the `/dev/md0` device and others indicated with *RAID* in the expert partitioner.

11.3.2 Troubleshooting

Check the file `/proc/mdstat` to find out whether a RAID partition has been damaged. If Th system fails, shut down your Linux system and replace the defective hard disk with a new one partitioned the same way. Then restart your system and enter the command **mdadm /dev/mdX --add /dev/sdX**. Replace 'X' with your particular device identifiers. This integrates the hard disk automatically into the RAID system and fully reconstructs it.

Note that although you can access all data during the rebuild, you may encounter some performance issues until the RAID has been fully rebuilt.

11.3.3 For More Information

Configuration instructions and more details for soft RAID can be found in the HOWTOs at:

* `/usr/share/doc/packages/mdadm/Software-RAID.HOWTO.html`

* http://raid.wiki.kernel.org ↗

Linux RAID mailing lists are available, such as http://marc.info/?l=linux-raid ↗ .

12 Installing or Removing Software

Use YaST's software management module to search for software components you want to add or remove. YaST resolves all dependencies for you. To install packages not shipped with the installation media, add additional software repositories to your setup and let YaST manage them. Keep your system up-to-date by managing software updates with the update applet.

Change the software collection of your system with the YaST Software Manager. This YaST module is available in two flavors: a graphical variant for X Window and a text-based variant to be used on the command line. The graphical flavor is described here—for details on the text-based YaST, see *Book "Administration Guide", Chapter 5 "YaST in Text Mode"*.

 Note: Confirmation and Review of Changes

> When installing, updating or removing packages, any changes in the Software Manager are first applied after clicking *Accept* or *Apply*. YaST maintains a list with all actions, allowing you to review and modify your changes before applying them to the system.

12.1 Definition of Terms

Repository

> A local or remote directory containing packages, plus additional information about these packages (package metadata).

(Repository) Alias/Repository Name

> A short name for a repository (called `Alias` within Zypper and *Repository Name* within YaST). It can be chosen by the user when adding a repository and must be unique.

Repository Description Files

> Each repository provides files describing content of the repository (package names, versions, etc.). These repository description files are downloaded to a local cache that is used by YaST.

Product

> Represents a whole product, for example SUSE® Linux Enterprise Server.

Pattern

A pattern is an installable group of packages dedicated to a certain purpose. For example, the `Laptop` pattern contains all packages that are needed in a mobile computing environment. Patterns define package dependencies (such as required or recommended packages) and come with a preselection of packages marked for installation. This ensures that the most important packages needed for a certain purpose are available on your system after installation of the pattern. If necessary, you can manually select or deselect packages within a pattern.

Package

A package is a compressed file in `rpm` format that contains the files for a particular program.

Patch

A patch consists of one or more packages and may be applied by means of delta RPMs. It may also introduce dependencies to packages that are not installed yet.

Resolvable

A generic term for product, pattern, package or patch. The most commonly used type of resolvable is a package or a patch.

Delta RPM

A delta RPM consists only of the binary diff between two defined versions of a package, and therefore has the smallest download size. Before being installed, the full RPM package is rebuilt on the local machine.

Package Dependencies

Certain packages are dependent on other packages, such as shared libraries. In other terms, a package may `require` other packages—if the required packages are not available, the package cannot be installed. In addition to dependencies (package requirements) that must be fulfilled, some packages `recommend` other packages. These recommended packages are only installed if they are actually available, otherwise they are ignored and the package recommending them is installed nevertheless.

12.2   Using the YaST Software Manager

Start the software manager from the *YaST Control Center* by choosing *Software > Software Management*.

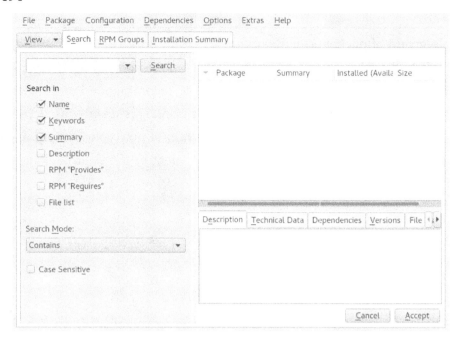

12.2.1   Views for Searching Packages or Patterns

The YaST software manager can install packages or patterns from all currently enabled repositories. It offers different views and filters to make it easier to find the software you are searching for. The *Search* view is the default view of the window. To change view, click *View* and select one of the following entries from the drop-down box. The selected view opens in a new tab.

Patterns

Lists all patterns available for installation on your system.

Package Groups

Lists all packages sorted by groups such as *Graphics*, *Programming*, or *Security*.

RPM Groups

Lists all packages sorted by functionality with groups and subgroups. For example *Networking › Email › Clients*.

Languages

A filter to list all packages needed to add a new system language.

Repositories

> A filter to list packages by repository. To select more than one repository, hold the `Ctrl` key while clicking repository names. The "pseudo repository" *@System* lists all packages currently installed.

Search

> Lets you search for a package according to certain criteria. Enter a search term and press `Enter`. Refine your search by specifying where to *Search In* and by changing the *Search Mode*. For example, if you do not know the package name but only the name of the application that you are searching for, try including the package *Description* in the search process.

Installation Summary

> If you have already selected packages for installation, update or removal, this view shows the changes that will be applied to your system when you click *Accept*. To filter for packages with a certain status in this view, activate or deactivate the respective check boxes. Press `Shift`-`F1` for details on the status flags.

 Tip: Finding Packages Not Belonging to an Active Repository

> To list all packages that do not belong to an active repository, choose *View* › *Repositories* › *@System* and then choose *Secondary Filter* › *Unmaintained Packages*. This is useful, for example, if you have deleted a repository and want to make sure no packages from that repository remain installed.

12.2.2   Installing and Removing Packages or Patterns

Certain packages are dependent on other packages, such as shared libraries. On the other hand, some packages cannot coexist with others on the system. If possible, YaST automatically resolves these dependencies or conflicts. If your choice results in a dependency conflict that cannot be automatically solved, you need to solve it manually as described in *Section 12.2.4, "Checking Software Dependencies"*.

 Note: Removal of Packages

> When removing any packages, by default YaST only removes the selected packages. If you want YaST to also remove any other packages that become unneeded after removal of the specified package, select *Options* › *Cleanup when deleting packages* from the main menu.

1. Search for packages as described in *Section 12.2.1, "Views for Searching Packages or Patterns"*.

2. The packages found are listed in the right pane. To install a package or remove it, right-click it and choose *Install* or *Delete*. If the relevant option is not available, check the package status indicated by the symbol in front of the package name—press `Shift`-`F1` for help.

 Tip: Applying an Action to All Packages Listed

> To apply an action to all packages listed in the right pane, go to the main menu and choose an action from *Package > All in This List*.

3. To install a pattern, right-click the pattern name and choose *Install*.

4. It is not possible to remove a pattern per se. Instead, select the packages of a pattern you want to remove and mark them for removal.

5. To select more packages, repeat the steps mentioned above.

6. Before applying your changes, you can review or modify them by clicking *View > Installation Summary*. By default, all packages that will change status, are listed.

7. To revert the status for a package, right-click the package and select one of the following entries: *Keep* if the package was scheduled to be deleted or updated, or *Do Not Install* if it was scheduled for installation. To abandon all changes and quit the Software Manager, click *Cancel* and *Abandon*.

8. When you are finished, click *Accept* to apply your changes.

9. In case YaST found dependencies on other packages, a list of packages that have additionally been chosen for installation, update or removal is presented. Click *Continue* to accept them.
    After all selected packages are installed, updated or removed, the YaST Software Manager automatically terminates.

 Note: Installing Source Packages

Installing source packages with YaST Software Manager is not possible at the moment. Use the command line tool **zypper** for this purpose. For more information, see *Book "Administration Guide", Chapter 6 "Managing Software with Command Line Tools", Section 6.1.2.5 "Installing or Downloading Source Packages"*.

12.2.3   Updating Packages

Instead of updating individual packages, you can also update all installed packages or all packages from a certain repository. When mass updating packages, the following aspects are generally considered:

- priorities of the repositories that provide the package,

- architecture of the package (for example, AMD64/Intel 64),

- version number of the package,

- package vendor.

Which of the aspects has the highest importance for choosing the update candidates depends on the respective update option you choose.

1. To update all installed packages to the latest version, choose *Package › All Packages › Update if Newer Version Available* from the main menu.

   All repositories are checked for possible update candidates, using the following policy: YaST first tries to restrict the search to packages with the same architecture and vendor like the installed one. If the search is positive, the "best" update candidate from those is selected according to the process below. However, if no comparable package of the same vendor can be found, the search is expanded to all packages with the same architecture. If still no comparable package can be found, all packages are considered and the "best" update candidate is selected according to the following criteria:

   1. Repository priority: Prefer the package from the repository with the highest priority.

   2. If more than one package results from this selection, choose the one with the "best" architecture (best choice: matching the architecture of the installed one).

   If the resulting package has a higher version number than the installed one, the installed package will be updated and replaced with the selected update candidate.

   This option tries to avoid changes in architecture and vendor for the installed packages, but under certain circumstances, they are tolerated.

Note: Update Unconditionally

If you choose *Package > All Packages > Update Unconditionally* instead, the same criteria apply but any candidate package found is installed unconditionally. Thus, choosing this option might actually lead to downgrading some packages.

2. To make sure that the packages for a mass update derive from a certain repository:

   a. Choose the repository from which to update as described in *Section 12.2.1, "Views for Searching Packages or Patterns"* .

   b. On the right hand side of the window, click *Switch system packages to the versions in this repository*. This explicitly allows YaST to change the package vendor when replacing the packages.
   When you proceed with *Accept*, all installed packages will be replaced by packages deriving from this repository, if available. This may lead to changes in vendor and architecture and even to downgrading some packages.

   c. To refrain from this, click *Cancel switching system packages to the versions in this repository*. Note that you can only cancel this until you click the *Accept* button.

3. Before applying your changes, you can review or modify them by clicking *View > Installation Summary*. By default, all packages that will change status, are listed.

4. If all options are set according to your wishes, confirm your changes with *Accept* to start the mass update.

12.2.4 Checking Software Dependencies

Most packages are dependent on other packages. If a package, for example, uses a shared library, it is dependent on the package providing this library. On the other hand, some packages cannot coexist, causing a conflict (for example, you can only install one mail transfer agent: sendmail or postfix). When installing or removing software, the Software Manager makes sure no dependencies or conflicts remain unsolved to ensure system integrity.

In case there exists only one solution to resolve a dependency or a conflict, it is resolved automatically. Multiple solutions always cause a conflict which needs to be resolved manually. If solving a conflict involves a vendor or architecture change, it also needs to be solved manually. When clicking *Accept* to apply any changes in the Software Manager, you get an overview of all actions triggered by the automatic resolver which you need to confirm.

By default, dependencies are automatically checked. A check is performed every time you change a package status (for example, by marking a package for installation or removal). This is generally useful, but can become exhausting when manually resolving a dependency conflict. To disable this function, go to the main menu and deactivate *Dependencies › Autocheck*. Manually perform a dependency check with *Dependencies › Check Now*. A consistency check is always performed when you confirm your selection with *Accept*.

To review a package's dependencies, right-click it and choose *Show Solver Information*. A map showing the dependencies opens. Packages that are already installed are displayed in a green frame.

 ## Note: Manually Solving Package Conflicts

Unless you are very experienced, follow the suggestions YaST makes when handling package conflicts, otherwise you may not be able to resolve them. Keep in mind that every change you make, potentially triggers other conflicts, so you can easily end up with a steadily increasing number of conflicts. In case this happens, *Cancel* the Software Manager, *Abandon* all your changes and start again.

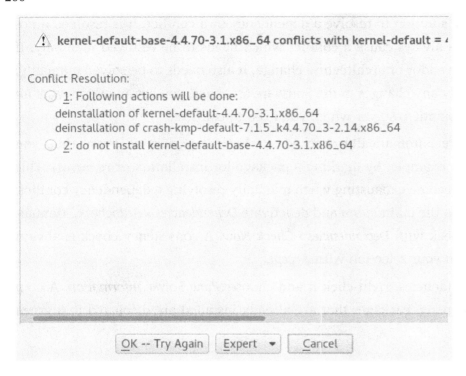

FIGURE 12.1: CONFLICT MANAGEMENT OF THE SOFTWARE MANAGER

12.2.4.1 Handling of Package Recommendations

In addition to the hard dependencies required to run a program (for example a certain library), a package can also have weak dependencies, that add for example extra functionality or translations. These weak dependencies are called package recommendations.

The way package recommendations are handled has slightly changed starting with SUSE Linux Enterprise Server 12 SP1. Nothing has changed when installing a new package—recommended packages are still installed by default.

Prior to SUSE Linux Enterprise Server 12 SP1, missing recommendations for already installed packages were installed automatically. Now these packages will no longer be installed automatically. To switch to the old default, set `PKGMGR_REEVALUATE_RECOMMENDED="yes"` in `/etc/sysconfig/yast2`. To install all missing recommendations for already installed packages, start *YaST* › *Software Manager* and choose *Extras* › *Install All Matching Recommended Packages*.

To disable the installation of recommended packages when installing new packages, deactivate *Dependencies* › *Install Recommended Packages* in the YaST Software Manager. If using the command line tool Zypper to install packages, use the option `--no-recommends`.

12.3 Managing Software Repositories and Services

To install third-party software, add additional software repositories to your system. By default, the product repositories such as SUSE Linux Enterprise Server-DVD 12 SP3 and a matching update repository are automatically configured after you have registered your system. For more information about registration, see *Section 6.8, "SUSE Customer Center Registration"* **or** *Section 19.9, "Registering Your System"*. Depending on the initially selected product, an additional repository containing translations, dictionaries, etc. might also be configured.

To manage repositories, start YaST and select *Software > Software Repositories*. The *Configured Software Repositories* dialog opens. Here, you can also manage subscriptions to so-called *Services* by changing the *View* at the right corner of the dialog to *All Services*. A Service in this context is a *Repository Index Service* (RIS) that can offer one or more software repositories. Such a Service can be changed dynamically by its administrator or vendor.

Each repository provides files describing content of the repository (package names, versions, etc.). These repository description files are downloaded to a local cache that is used by YaST. To ensure their integrity, software repositories can be signed with the GPG Key of the repository maintainer. Whenever you add a new repository, YaST offers the ability to import its key.

 ## Warning: Trusting External Software Sources

Before adding external software repositories to your list of repositories, make sure this repository can be trusted. SUSE is not responsible for any problems arising from software installed from third-party software repositories.

12.3.1 Adding Software Repositories

You can either add repositories from DVD/CD, removable mass storage devices (such as flash disks), a local directory, an ISO image or a network source.

To add repositories from the *Configured Software Repositories* dialog in YaST proceed as follows:

1. Click *Add*.

2. Select one of the options listed in the dialog:

FIGURE 12.2: ADDING A SOFTWARE REPOSITORY

- To scan your network for installation servers announcing their services via SLP, select *Scan Using SLP* and click *Next*.

- To add a repository from a removable medium, choose the relevant option and insert the medium or connect the USB device to the machine, respectively. Click *Next* to start the installation.

- For the majority of repositories, you will be asked to specify the path (or URL) to the media after selecting the respective option and clicking *Next*. Specifying a *Repository Name* is optional. If none is specified, YaST will use the product name or the URL as repository name.

The option *Download Repository Description Files* is activated by default. If you deactivate the option, YaST will automatically download the files later, if needed.

3. Depending on the repository you have added, you may be prompted to import the repository's GPG key or asked to agree to a license.
   After confirming these messages, YaST will download and parse the metadata. It will add the repository to the list of *Configured Repositories*.

4. If needed, adjust the repository *Properties* as described in *Section 12.3.2, "Managing Repository Properties".*

5. Confirm your changes with *OK* to close the configuration dialog.

6. After having successfully added the repository, the software manager starts and you can install packages from this repository. For details, refer to *Chapter 12, Installing or Removing Software*.

12.3.2 Managing Repository Properties

The *Configured Software Repositories* overview of the *Software Repositories* lets you change the following repository properties:

Status

The repository status can either be *Enabled* or *Disabled*. You can only install packages from repositories that are enabled. To turn a repository off temporarily, select it and deactivate *Enable*. You can also double-click a repository name to toggle its status. To remove a repository completely, click *Delete*.

Refresh

When refreshing a repository, its content description (package names, versions, etc.) is downloaded to a local cache that is used by YaST. It is sufficient to do this once for static repositories such as CDs or DVDs, whereas repositories whose content changes often should be refreshed frequently. The easiest way to keep a repository's cache up-to-date is to choose *Automatically Refresh*. To do a manual refresh click *Refresh* and select one of the options.

Keep Downloaded Packages

Packages from remote repositories are downloaded before being installed. By default, they are deleted upon a successful installation. Activating *Keep Downloaded Packages* prevents the deletion of downloaded packages. The download location is configured in `/etc/zypp/zypp.conf`, by default it is `/var/cache/zypp/packages`.

Priority

The *Priority* of a repository is a value between `1` and `200`, with `1` being the highest priority and `200` the lowest priority. Any new repositories that are added with YaST get a priority of `99` by default. If you do not care about a priority value for a certain repository, you can also set the value to `0` to apply the default priority to that repository (`99`). If a package is available in more than one repository, then the repository with the highest priority takes precedence. This is useful if you want to avoid downloading packages unnecessarily from the Internet by giving a local repository (for example, a DVD) a higher priority.

Important: Priority Compared to Version

The repository with the highest priority takes precedence in any case. Therefore, make sure that the update repository always has the highest priority, otherwise you might install an outdated version that will not be updated until the next online update.

Name and URL

To change a repository name or its URL, select it from the list with a single-click and then click *Edit*.

12.3.3   Managing Repository Keys

To ensure their integrity, software repositories can be signed with the GPG Key of the repository maintainer. Whenever you add a new repository, YaST offers to import its key. Verify it as you would do with any other GPG key and make sure it does not change. If you detect a key change, something might be wrong with the repository. Disable the repository as an installation source until you know the cause of the key change.

To manage all imported keys, click *GPG Keys* in the *Configured Software Repositories* dialog. Select an entry with the mouse to show the key properties at the bottom of the window. *Add*, *Edit* or *Delete* keys with a click on the respective buttons.

12.4   Keeping the System Up-to-date

SUSE offers a continuous stream of software security patches for your product. They can be installed using the *Book "Administration Guide", Chapter 3 "YaST Online Update"* module. It also offers advanced features to customize the patch installation.

The GNOME desktop also provides a tool for installing patches and for installing package updates of packages that are already installed. In contrast to a *Patch*, a package update is only related to *one* package and provides a newer version of a package. The GNOME tool lets you install both patches and package updates with a few clicks as described in *Section 12.4.2, "Installing Patches and Package Updates"*.

12.4.1   The GNOME Software Updater

Whenever new patches or package updates are available, GNOME shows a notification about this at the bottom of the desktop (or on the locked screen).

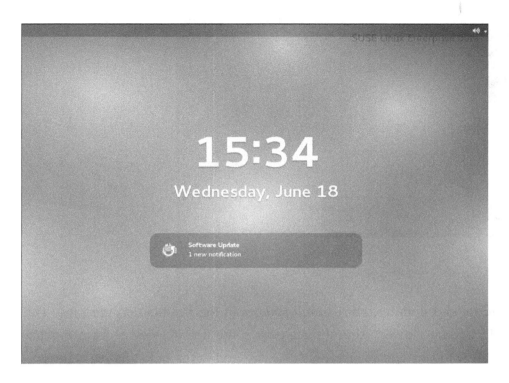

FIGURE 12.3: UPDATE NOTIFICATION ON GNOME LOCK SCREEN

12.4.2   Installing Patches and Package Updates

Whenever new patches or package updates are available, GNOME shows a notification about this at the bottom of the desktop (or on the locked screen).

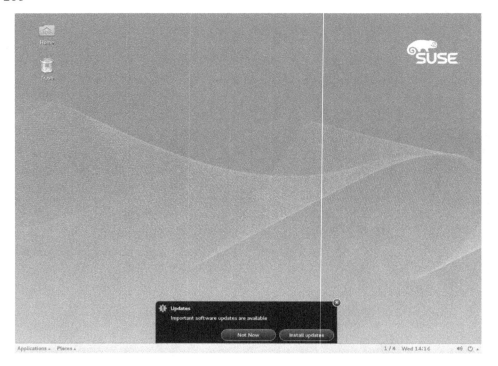

FIGURE 12.4: UPDATE NOTIFICATION ON GNOME DESKTOP

1. To install the patches and updates, click *Install updates* in the notification message. This opens the GNOME update viewer. Alternatively, open the update viewer from *Applications* › *System Tools* › *Software Update* or press `Alt`–`F2` and enter **gpk-update-viewer**.

2. All *Security Updates* and *Important Updates* are preselected. It is strongly recommended to install these patches. *Other Updates* can be manually selected by activating the respective check boxes. Get detailed information on a patch or package update by clicking its title.

3. Click *Install Updates* to start the installation. You will be prompted for the `root` password.

4. Enter the `root` password in the authentication dialog and proceed.

FIGURE 12.5: GNOME UPDATE VIEWER

12.4.3   Configuring the GNOME Software Updater

To configure notifications, select *Applications › System Settings › Notification › Software Update* and adjust the desired settings.

To configure how often to check for updates or to activate or deactivate repositories, select *Applications › System Tools › Settings › Software Settings*. The tabs of the configuration dialog let you modify the following settings:

UPDATE SETTINGS

Check for Updates

Choose how often a check for updates is performed: *Hourly, Daily, Weekly,* or *Never.*

Check for Major Upgrades

Choose how often a check for major upgrades is performed: *Daily, Weekly,* or *Never.*

Check for updates when using mobile broadband

This configuration option is only available on mobile computers. Turned off by default.

Check for updates on battery power

This configuration option is only available on mobile computers. Turned off by default.

SOFTWARE SOURCES

Repositories

Lists the repositories that will be checked for available patches and package updates. You can enable or disable certain repositories.

 Important: Keep Update Repository Enabled

To make sure that you are notified about any patches that are security-relevant, keep the `Updates` repository for your product enabled.

More options are configurable using **gconf-editor**: *apps* › *gnome-packagekit.*

13 Installing Modules, Extensions, and Third Party Add-On Products

Modules and extensions add parts or functionality to the system. Modules are fully supported parts of SUSE Linux Enterprise Server with a different life cycle and update timeline. They are a set of packages, have a clearly defined scope and are delivered via online channel only.

Extensions, such as the Workstation Extension or the High Availability Extension, add extra functionality to the system and require an own registration key that is liable for costs. Extensions are delivered via online channel or physical media. Registering at the SUSE Customer Center or a local registration server is a prerequisite for subscribing to the online channels. The Package Hub (*Section 13.4, "SUSE Package Hub"*) and SUSE Software Development Kit (*Section 13.3, "SUSE Software Development Kit (SDK) 12 SP3"*) extensions are exceptions which do not require a registration key and are not covered by SUSE support agreements.

A list of modules and extensions for your product is available after having registered your system at SUSE Customer Center or a local registration server. If you skipped the registration step during the installation, you can register your system at any time using the *SUSE Customer Center Configuration* module in YaST. For details, refer to *Section 19.9, "Registering Your System"*.

Some add-on products are also provided by third parties, for example, binary-only drivers that are needed by certain hardware to function properly. If you have such hardware, refer to the release notes for more information about availability of binary drivers for your system. The release notes are available from http://www.suse.com/releasenotes/ ↗, from YaST or from `/usr/share/doc/re-` `lease-notes/` in your installed system.

13.1 Installing Modules and Extensions from Online Channels

The following procedure requires that you have registered your system with SUSE Customer Center, or a local registration server. When registering your system, you will see a list of extensions and modules immediately after having completed *Step 4* of *Section 19.9, "Registering Your System"*. In that case, skip the next steps and proceed with *Step 2*.

 Note: Viewing Already Installed Add-Ons

To view already installed add-ons, start YaST and select *Software › Add-Ons*

PROCEDURE 13.1: INSTALLING ADD-ONS AND EXTENSIONS FROM ONLINE CHANNELS WITH YAST

1. Start YaST and select *Software › Add System Extensions or Modules*.
    YaST connects to the registration server and displays a list of *Available Extensions and Modules*.

     Note: Available Extensions and Modules

    The amount of available extensions and modules depends on the registration server. A local registration server may only offer update repositories and no additional extensions.

     Note: Module Life Cycles

    Life cycle end dates of modules are available at https://scc.suse.com/docs/lifecycle/sle/12/modules ↗.

2. Click an entry to see its description.

3. Select one or multiple entries for installation by activating their check marks.

FIGURE 13.1: INSTALLATION OF SYSTEM EXTENSIONS

4. Click *Next* to proceed.

5. Depending on the repositories to be added for the extension or module, you may be prompted to import the repository's GPG key or asked to agree to a license.
   After confirming these messages, YaST will download and parse the metadata. The repositories for the selected extensions will be added to your system—no additional installation sources are required.

6. If needed, adjust the repository *Properties* as described in *Section 12.3.2, "Managing Repository Properties".*

 ## Note: For More Information

White paper SUSE Linux Enterprise Server 12 Modules (https://www.suse.com/docrep/documents/huz0a6bf9a/suse_linux_enterprise_server_12_modules_white_paper.pdf) ↗ .

13.2 Installing Extensions and Third Party Add-On Products from Media

When installing an extension or add-on product from media, you can select various types of product media, like DVD/CD, removable mass storage devices (such as flash disks), or a local directory or ISO image. The media can also be provided by a network server, for example, via HTTP, FTP, NFS, or Samba.

1. Start YaST and select *Software › Add-On Products*. Alternatively, start the YaST *Add-On Products* module from the command line with **sudo yast2 add-on**.

   The dialog will show an overview of already installed add-on products, modules and extensions.

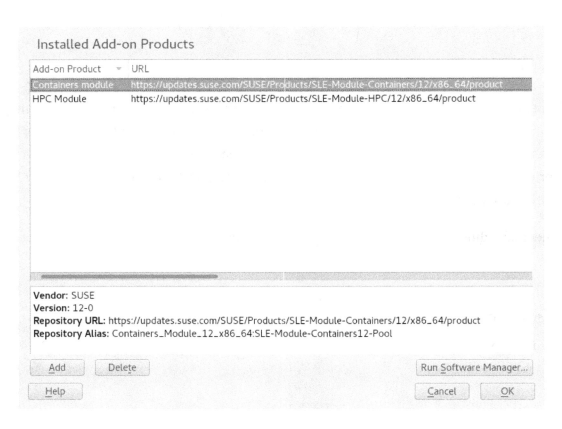

FIGURE 13.2: LIST OF INSTALLED ADD-ON PRODUCTS, MODULES AND EXTENSIONS

2. Choose *Add* to install a new add-on product.

3. In the *Add-On Product* dialog, select the option that matches the type of medium from which you want to install:

FIGURE 13.3: INSTALLATION OF AN ADD-ON PRODUCT OR AN EXTENSION

- To scan your network for installation servers announcing their services via SLP, select *Scan Using SLP* and click *Next*.

- To add a repository from a removable medium, choose the relevant option and insert the medium or connect the USB device to the machine, respectively. Click *Next* to start the installation.

- For most media types, you will prompted to specify the path (or URL) to the media after selecting the respective option and clicking *Next*. Specifying a *Repository Name* is optional. If none is specified, YaST will use the product name or the URL as the repository name.

The option *Download Repository Description Files* is activated by default. If you deactivate the option, YaST will automatically download the files later, if needed.

4. Depending on the repository you have added, you may be prompted to import the repository's GPG key or asked to agree to a license.
After confirming these messages, YaST will download and parse the metadata. It will add the repository to the list of *Configured Repositories*.

5. If needed, adjust the repository *Properties* as described in *Section 12.3.2, "Managing Repository Properties"*.

6. Confirm your changes with *OK* to close the configuration dialog.

7. After having successfully added the repository for the add-on media, the software manager starts and you can install packages. For details, refer to *Chapter 12, Installing or Removing Software*.

13.3 SUSE Software Development Kit (SDK) 12 SP3

SUSE Software Development Kit 12 SP3 is a module for SUSE Linux Enterprise 12 SP3. It is a complete tool kit for application development. In fact, to provide a comprehensive build system, SUSE Software Development Kit 12 SP3 includes all the open source tools that were used to build the SUSE Linux Enterprise Server product. It provides you as a developer, independent software vendor (ISV), or independent hardware vendor (IHV) with all the tools needed to port applications to all the platforms supported by SUSE Linux Enterprise Desktop and SUSE Linux Enterprise Server.

The SUSE Software Development Kit does not require a registration key and is not covered by SUSE support agreements.

SUSE Software Development Kit also contains integrated development environments (IDEs), debuggers, code editors, and other related tools. It supports most major programming languages, including C, C++, Java, and most scripting languages. For your convenience, SUSE Software Development Kit includes multiple Perl packages that are not included in SUSE Linux Enterprise.

The SDK is a module for SUSE Linux Enterprise and is available via an online channel from the SUSE Customer Center. Alternatively, go to http://download.suse.com/ ⌐, search for SUSE Linux Enterprise Software Development Kit and download it from there. Refer to *Chapter 13, Installing Modules, Extensions, and Third Party Add-On Products* for details.

13.4 SUSE Package Hub

In the list of *Available Extensions and Modules* you find the SUSE Package Hub. It is available without any additional fee. It provides a large set of additional community packages for SUSE Linux Enterprise that can easily be installed but are *not* supported by SUSE.

More information about SUSE Package Hub and how to contribute is available at https://pack-agehub.suse.com/ ↗

 Important: SUSE Package Hub is Not Supported

Be aware that packages provided in the SUSE Package Hub are not officially supported by SUSE. SUSE only provides support for enabling the Package Hub repository and help with installation or deployment of the RPM packages.

14 Installing Multiple Kernel Versions

SUSE Linux Enterprise Server supports the parallel installation of multiple kernel versions. When installing a second kernel, a boot entry and an initrd are automatically created, so no further manual configuration is needed. When rebooting the machine, the newly added kernel is available as an additional boot option.

Using this functionality, you can safely test kernel updates while being able to always fall back to the proven former kernel. To do this, do not use the update tools (such as the YaST Online Update or the updater applet), but instead follow the process described in this chapter.

 Warning: Support Entitlement

Be aware that you lose your entire support entitlement for the machine when installing a self-compiled or a third-party kernel. Only kernels shipped with SUSE Linux Enterprise Server and kernels delivered via the official update channels for SUSE Linux Enterprise Server are supported.

 Tip: Check Your Boot Loader Configuration Kernel

It is recommended to check your boot loader configuration after having installed another kernel to set the default boot entry of your choice. See *Book "Administration Guide", Chapter 12 "The Boot Loader GRUB 2", Section 12.3 "Configuring the Boot Loader with YaST"* for more information.

14.1 Enabling and Configuring Multiversion Support

Installing multiple versions of a software package (multiversion support) is enabled by default since SUSE Linux Enterprise Server 12. To verify this setting, proceed as follows:

1. Open `/etc/zypp/zypp.conf` with the editor of your choice as `root`.

2. Search for the string `multiversion`. If multiversion is enabled for all kernel packages capable of this feature, the following line appears uncommented:

```
multiversion = provides:multiversion(kernel)
```

3. To restrict multiversion support to certain kernel flavors, add the package names as a comma-separated list to the `multiversion` option in `/etc/zypp/zypp.conf`—for example

```
multiversion = kernel-default,kernel-default-base,kernel-source
```

4. Save your changes.

 Warning: Kernel Module Packages (KMP)

Make sure that required vendor provided kernel modules (Kernel Module Packages) are also installed for the new updated kernel. The kernel update process will not warn about eventually missing kernel modules because package requirements are still fulfilled by the old kernel that is kept on the system.

14.1.1 Automatically Deleting Unused Kernels

When frequently testing new kernels with multiversion support enabled, the boot menu quickly becomes confusing. Since a `/boot` partition usually has limited space you also might run into trouble with `/boot` overflowing. While you can delete unused kernel versions manually with YaST or Zypper (as described below), you can also configure `libzypp` to automatically delete kernels no longer used. By default no kernels are deleted.

1. Open `/etc/zypp/zypp.conf` with the editor of your choice as `root`.

2. Search for the string `multiversion.kernels` and activate this option by uncommenting the line. This option takes a comma-separated list of the following values:

   `3.12.24-7.1`: keep the kernel with the specified version number

   `latest`: keep the kernel with the highest version number

   `latest-N`: keep the kernel with the Nth highest version number

   `running`: keep the running kernel

`oldest`: keep the kernel with the lowest version number (the one that was originally shipped with SUSE Linux Enterprise Server)

`oldest+N`. keep the kernel with the Nth lowest version number

Here are some examples

`multiversion.kernels = latest,running`

> Keep the latest kernel and the one currently running. This is similar to not enabling the multiversion feature, except that the old kernel is removed *after the next reboot* and not immediately after the installation.

`multiversion.kernels = latest,latest-1,running`

> Keep the last two kernels and the one currently running.

`multiversion.kernels = latest,running,3.12.25.rc7-test`

> Keep the latest kernel, the one currently running, and *3.12.25.rc7-test*.

 Tip: Keep the Running Kernel

> Unless you are using a special setup, always keep the kernel marked `running`.
>
> If you do not keep the running kernel, it will be deleted when updating the kernel. In turn, this means that all of the running kernel's modules are also deleted and cannot be loaded anymore.
>
> If you decide not to keep the running kernel, always reboot immediately after a kernel upgrade to avoid issues with modules.

14.1.2   Use Case: Deleting an Old Kernel after Reboot Only

You want to make sure that an old kernel will only be deleted after the system has rebooted successfully with the new kernel.

Change the following line in `/etc/zypp/zypp.conf`:

```
multiversion.kernels = latest,running
```

The previous parameters tell the system to keep the latest kernel and the running one only if they differ.

14.1.3   Use Case: Keeping Older Kernels as Fallback

You want to keep one or more kernel versions to have one or more "spare" kernels.

This can be useful if you need kernels for testing. If something goes wrong (for example, your machine does not boot), you still can use one or more kernel versions which are known to be good.

Change the following line in /etc/zypp/zypp.conf:

```
multiversion.kernels = latest,latest-1,latest-2,running
```

When you reboot your system after the installation of a new kernel, the system will keep three kernels: the current kernel (configured as latest,running) and its two immediate predecessors (configured as latest-1 and latest-2).

14.1.4   Use Case: Keeping a Specific Kernel Version

You make regular system updates and install new kernel versions. However, you are also compiling your own kernel version and want to make sure that the system will keep them.

Change the following line in /etc/zypp/zypp.conf:

```
multiversion.kernels = latest,3.12.28-4.20,running
```

When you reboot your system after the installation of a new kernel, the system will keep two kernels: the new and running kernel (configured as latest,running) and your self-compiled kernel (configured as 3.12.28-4.20).

14.2   Installing/Removing Multiple Kernel Versions with YaST

1. Start YaST and open the software manager via *Software › Software Management*.

2. List all packages capable of providing multiple versions by choosing *View › Package Groups › Multiversion Packages*.

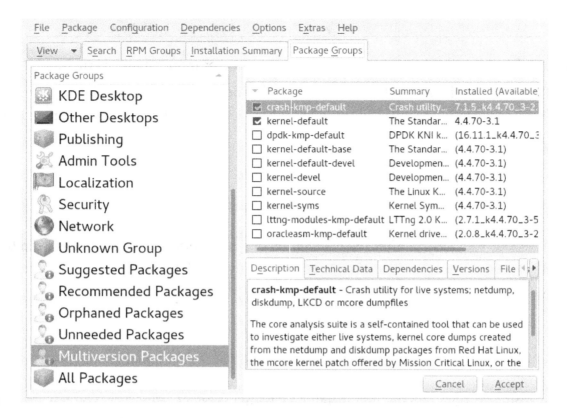

FIGURE 14.1: THE YAST SOFTWARE MANAGER: MULTIVERSION VIEW

3. Select a package and open its *Version* tab in the bottom pane on the left.

4. To install a package, click the check box next to it. A green check mark indicates it is selected for installation.

   To remove an already installed package (marked with a white check mark), click the check box next to it until a red X indicates it is selected for removal.

5. Click *Accept* to start the installation.

14.3 Installing/Removing Multiple Kernel Versions with Zypper

1. Use the command **zypper se -s 'kernel*'** to display a list of all kernel packages available:

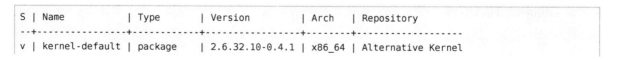

```
S | Name           | Type      | Version          | Arch   | Repository
--+----------------+-----------+------------------+--------+-------------------
v | kernel-default | package   | 2.6.32.10-0.4.1  | x86_64 | Alternative Kernel
```

```
i | kernel-default | package    | 2.6.32.9-0.5.1  | x86_64 | (System Packages)
  | kernel-default | srcpackage | 2.6.32.10-0.4.1 | noarch | Alternative Kernel
i | kernel-default | package    | 2.6.32.9-0.5.1  | x86_64 | (System Packages)
...
```

2. Specify the exact version when installing:

```
zypper in kernel-default-2.6.32.10-0.4.1
```

3. When uninstalling a kernel, use the commands **zypper se -si 'kernel*'** to list all kernels installed and **zypper rm** *PACKAGENAME-VERSION* to remove the package.

15 Managing Users with YaST

During installation, you could have created a local user for your system. With the YaST module *User and Group Management* you can add more users or edit existing ones. It also lets you configure your system to authenticate users with a network server.

15.1 User and Group Administration Dialog

To administer users or groups, start YaST and click *Security and Users > User and Group Management*. Alternatively, start the *User and Group Administration* dialog directly by running **sudo yast2 users &** from a command line.

FIGURE 15.1: YAST USER AND GROUP ADMINISTRATION

Every user is assigned a system-wide user ID (UID). Apart from the users which can log in to your machine, there are also several *system users* for internal use only. Each user is assigned to one or more groups. Similar to *system users*, there are also *system groups* for internal use.

Depending on the set of users you choose to view and modify with, the dialog (local users, network users, system users), the main window shows several tabs. These allow you to execute the following tasks:

Managing User Accounts

From the *Users* tab create, modify, delete or temporarily disable user accounts as described in *Section 15.2, "Managing User Accounts"*. Learn about advanced options like enforcing password policies, using encrypted home directories, or managing disk quotas in *Section 15.3, "Additional Options for User Accounts"*.

Changing Default Settings

Local users accounts are created according to the settings defined on the *Defaults for New Users* tab. Learn how to change the default group assignment, or the default path and access permissions for home directories in *Section 15.4, "Changing Default Settings for Local Users"*.

Assigning Users to Groups

Learn how to change the group assignment for individual users in *Section 15.5, "Assigning Users to Groups"*.

Managing Groups

From the *Groups* tab, you can add, modify or delete existing groups. Refer to *Section 15.6, "Managing Groups"* for information on how to do this.

Changing the User Authentication Method

When your machine is connected to a network that provides user authentication methods like NIS or LDAP, you can choose between several authentication methods on the *Authentication Settings* tab. For more information, refer to *Section 15.7, "Changing the User Authentication Method"*.

For user and group management, the dialog provides similar functionality. You can easily switch between the user and group administration view by choosing the appropriate tab at the top of the dialog.

Filter options allow you to define the set of users or groups you want to modify: On the *Users* or *Group* tab, click *Set Filter* to view and edit users or groups according to certain categories, such as *Local Users* or *LDAP Users*, for example (if you are part of a network which uses LDAP). With *Set Filter › Customize Filter* you can also set up and use a custom filter.

Depending on the filter you choose, not all of the following options and functions will be available from the dialog.

15.2 Managing User Accounts

YaST offers to create, modify, delete or temporarily disable user accounts. Do not modify user accounts unless you are an experienced user or administrator.

 Note: Changing User IDs of Existing Users

File ownership is bound to the user ID, not to the user name. After a user ID change, the files in the user's home directory are automatically adjusted to reflect this change. However, after an ID change, the user no longer owns the files he created elsewhere in the file system unless the file ownership for those files are manually modified.

In the following, learn how to set up default user accounts. For further options, refer to *Section 15.3, "Additional Options for User Accounts"*.

PROCEDURE 15.1: ADDING OR MODIFYING USER ACCOUNTS

1. Open the YaST *User and Group Administration* dialog and click the *Users* tab.

2. With *Set Filter* define the set of users you want to manage. The dialog lists users in the system and the groups the users belong to.

3. To modify options for an existing user, select an entry and click *Edit*.
   To create a new user account, click *Add*.

4. Enter the appropriate user data on the first tab, such as *Username* (which is used for login) and *Password*. This data is sufficient to create a new user. If you click *OK* now, the system will automatically assign a user ID and set all other values according to the default.

5. Activate *Receive System Mail* if you want any kind of system notifications to be delivered to this user's mailbox. This creates a mail alias for `root` and the user can read the system mail without having to first log in as `root`.
   The mails sent by system services are stored in the local mailbox `/var/spool/mail/`*USERNAME*, where *USERNAME* is the login name of the selected user. To read e-mails, you can use the `mail` command.

6. To adjust further details such as the user ID or the path to the user's home directory, do so on the *Details* tab.
   If you need to relocate the home directory of an existing user, enter the path to the new home directory there and move the contents of the current home directory with *Move to New Location*. Otherwise, a new home directory is created without any of the existing data.

7. To force users to regularly change their password or set other password options, switch to *Password Settings* and adjust the options. For more details, refer to *Section 15.3.2, "Enforcing Password Policies"*.

8. If all options are set according to your wishes, click *OK*.

9. Click *OK* to close the administration dialog and to save the changes. A newly added user can now log in to the system using the login name and password you created. Alternatively, to save all changes without exiting the *User and Group Administration* dialog, click *Expert Options* > *Write Changes Now*.

 Tip: Matching User IDs

For a new (local) user on a laptop which also needs to integrate into a network environment where this user already has a user ID, it is useful to match the (local) user ID to the ID in the network. This ensures that the file ownership of the files the user creates "offline" is the same as if he had created them directly on the network.

PROCEDURE 15.2: DISABLING OR DELETING USER ACCOUNTS

1. Open the YaST *User and Group Administration* dialog and click the *Users* tab.

2. To temporarily disable a user account without deleting it, select the user from the list and click *Edit*. Activate *Disable User Login*. The user cannot log in to your machine until you enable the account again.

3. To delete a user account, select the user from the list and click *Delete*. Choose if you also want to delete the user's home directory or if you want to retain the data.

15.3 Additional Options for User Accounts

In addition to the settings for a default user account, SUSE® Linux Enterprise Server offers further options, such as options to enforce password policies, use encrypted home directories or define disk quotas for users and groups.

15.3.1 Automatic Login and Passwordless Login

If you use the GNOME desktop environment you can configure *Auto Login* for a certain user and *Passwordless Login* for all users. Auto login causes a user to become automatically logged in to the desktop environment on boot. This functionality can only be activated for one user at a time. Login without password allows all users to log in to the system after they have entered their user name in the login manager.

 Warning: Security Risk

Enabling *Auto Login* or *Passwordless Login* on a machine that can be accessed by more than one person is a security risk. Without the need to authenticate, any user can gain access to your system and your data. If your system contains confidential data, do not use this functionality.

to activate auto login or login without password, access these functions in the YaST *User and Group Administration* with *Expert Options* › *Login Settings*.

15.3.2 Enforcing Password Policies

On any system with multiple users, it is a good idea to enforce at least basic password security policies. Users should change their passwords regularly and use strong passwords that cannot easily be exploited. For local users, proceed as follows:

PROCEDURE 15.3: CONFIGURING PASSWORD SETTINGS

1. Open the YaST *User and Group Administration* dialog and select the *Users* tab.

2. Select the user for which to change the password options and click *Edit*.

3. Switch to the *Password Settings* tab. The user's last password change is displayed on the tab.

4. To make the user change his password at next login, activate *Force Password Change*.

5. To enforce password rotation, set a *Maximum Number of Days for the Same Password* and a *Minimum Number of Days for the Same Password*.

6. To remind the user to change his password before it expires, set the number of *Days before Password Expiration to Issue Warning*.

7. To restrict the period of time the user can log in after his password has expired, change the value in *Days after Password Expires with Usable Login*.

8. You can also specify a certain expiration date for the complete account. Enter the *Expiration Date* in YYYY-MM-DD format. Note that this setting is not password-related but rather applies to the account itself.

9. For more information about the options and about the default values, click *Help*.

10. Apply your changes with *OK*.

15.3.3   Managing Encrypted Home Directories

To protect data in home directories against theft and hard disk removal, you can create encrypted home directories for users. These are encrypted with LUKS (Linux Unified Key Setup), which results in an image and an image key being generated for the user. The image key is protected with the user's login password. When the user logs in to the system, the encrypted home directory is mounted and the contents are made available to the user.

With YaST, you can create encrypted home directories for new or existing users. To encrypt or modify encrypted home directories of already existing users, you need to know the user's current login password. By default, all existing user data is copied to the new encrypted home directory, but it is not deleted from the unencrypted directory.

 Warning: Security Restrictions

Encrypting a user's home directory does not provide strong security from other users. If strong security is required, the system should not be physically shared.

Find background information about encrypted home directories and which actions to take for stronger security in *Book "Security Guide", Chapter 11 "Encrypting Partitions and Files", Section 11.2 "Using Encrypted Home Directories"*.

PROCEDURE 15.4: CREATING ENCRYPTED HOME DIRECTORIES

1. Open the YaST *User and Group Management* dialog and click the *Users* tab.

2. To encrypt the home directory of an existing user, select the user and click *Edit*. Otherwise, click *Add* to create a new user account and enter the appropriate user data on the first tab.

3. In the *Details* tab, activate *Use Encrypted Home Directory*. With *Directory Size in MB*, specify the size of the encrypted image file to be created for this user.

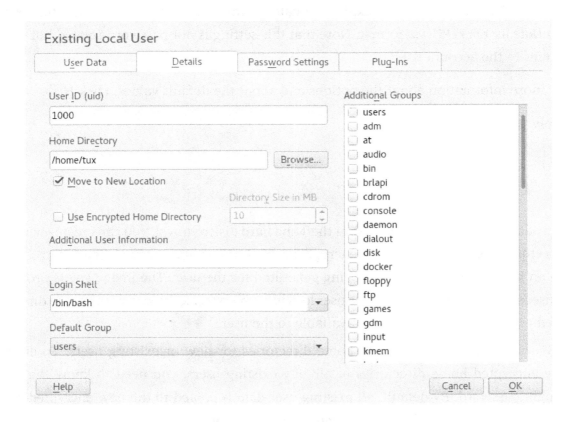

4. Apply your settings with *OK*.

5. Enter the user's current login password to proceed if YaST prompts for it.

6. Click *OK* to close the administration dialog and save the changes.
   Alternatively, to save all changes without exiting the *User and Group Administration* dialog, click *Expert Options › Write Changes Now*.

PROCEDURE 15.5: MODIFYING OR DISABLING ENCRYPTED HOME DIRECTORIES

Of course, you can also disable the encryption of a home directory or change the size of the image file at any time.

1. Open the YaST *User and Group Administration* dialog in the *Users* view.

2. Select a user from the list and click *Edit*.

3. to disable the encryption, switch to the *Details* tab and disable *Use Encrypted Home Directory*.

If you need to enlarge or reduce the size of the encrypted image file for this user, change the *Directory Size in MB*.

4. Apply your settings with *OK*.

5. Enter the user's current login password to proceed if YaST prompts for it.

6. Click *OK* to close the administration dialog and save the changes.

   Alternatively, to save all changes without exiting the *User and Group Administration* dialog, click *Expert Options › Write Changes Now*.

15.3.4 Managing Quotas

To prevent system capacities from being exhausted without notification, system administrators can set up quotas for users or groups. Quotas can be defined for one or more file systems and restrict the amount of disk space that can be used and the number of inodes (index nodes) that can be created there. Inodes are data structures on a file system that store basic information about a regular file, directory, or other file system object. They store all attributes of a file system object (like user and group ownership, read, write, or execute permissions), except file name and contents.

SUSE Linux Enterprise Server allows usage of `soft` and `hard` quotas. Additionally, grace intervals can be defined that allow users or groups to temporarily violate their quotas by certain amounts.

Soft Quota

Defines a warning level at which users are informed that they are nearing their limit. Administrators will urge the users to clean up and reduce their data on the partition. The soft quota limit is usually lower than the hard quota limit.

Hard Quota

Defines the limit at which write requests are denied. When the hard quota is reached, no more data can be stored and applications may crash.

Grace Period

Defines the time between the overflow of the soft quota and a warning being issued. Usually set to a rather low value of one or several hours.

To configure quotas for certain users and groups, you need to enable quota support for the respective partition in the YaST Expert Partitioner first.

 Note: Quotas Btrfs Partitions

Quotas for Btrfs partitions are handled differently. For more information, see *Book "Storage Administration Guide", Chapter 1 "Overview of File Systems in Linux", Section 1.2.5 "Btrfs Quota Support for Subvolumes"*.

1. In YaST, select *System* › *Partitioner* and click *Yes* to proceed.

2. In the *Expert Partitioner*, select the partition for which to enable quotas and click *Edit*.

3. Click *Fstab Options* and activate *Enable Quota Support*. If the `quota` package is not already installed, it will be installed once you confirm the respective message with *Yes*.

4. Confirm your changes and leave the *Expert Partitioner*.

5. Make sure the service `quotaon` is running by entering the following command:

```
systemctl status quotaon
```

It should be marked as being `active`. If this is not the case, start it with the command **systemctl start quotaon**.

PROCEDURE 15.7: SETTING UP QUOTAS FOR USERS OR GROUPS

Now you can define soft or hard quotas for specific users or groups and set time periods as grace intervals.

1. In the YaST *User and Group Administration*, select the user or the group you want to set the quotas for and click *Edit*.

2. On the *Plug-Ins* tab, select the *Manage User Quota* entry and click *Launch* to open the *Quota Configuration* dialog.

3. From *File System*, select the partition to which the quota should apply.

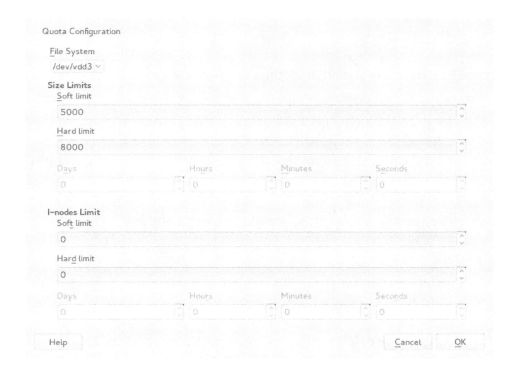

4. Below *Size Limits*, restrict the amount of disk space. Enter the number of 1 KB blocks the user or group may have on this partition. Specify a *Soft Limit* and a *Hard Limit* value.

5. Additionally, you can restrict the number of inodes the user or group may have on the partition. Below *Inodes Limits*, enter a *Soft Limit* and *Hard Limit*.

6. You can only define grace intervals if the user or group has already exceeded the soft limit specified for size or inodes. Otherwise, the time-related text boxes are not activated. Specify the time period for which the user or group is allowed to exceed the limits set above.

7. Confirm your settings with *OK*.

8. Click *OK* to close the administration dialog and save the changes.
   Alternatively, to save all changes without exiting the *User and Group Administration* dialog, click *Expert Options* › *Write Changes Now*.

SUSE Linux Enterprise Server also ships command-line tools like `repquota` or `warnquota`. System administrators can use this tools to control the disk usage or send e-mail notifications to users exceeding their quota. Using **quota_nld**, administrators can also forward kernel messages about exceeded quotas to D-BUS. For more information, refer to the `repquota`, the `warnquota` and the **quota_nld** man page.

15.4 Changing Default Settings for Local Users

When creating new local users, several default settings are used by YaST. These include, for example, the primary group and the secondary groups the user belongs to, or the access permissions of the user's home directory. You can change these default settings to meet your requirements:

1. Open the YaST *User and Group Administration* dialog and select the *Defaults for New Users* tab.

2. To change the primary group the new users should automatically belong to, select another group from *Default Group*.

3. To modify the secondary groups for new users, add or change groups in *Secondary Groups*. The group names must be separated by commas.

4. If you do not want to use /home/*USERNAME* as default path for new users' home directories, modify the *Path Prefix for Home Directory*.

5. To change the default permission modes for newly created home directories, adjust the umask value in *Umask for Home Directory*. For more information about umask, refer to *Book "Security Guide", Chapter 10 "Access Control Lists in Linux"* and to the **umask** man page.

6. For information about the individual options, click *Help*.

7. Apply your changes with *OK*.

15.5 Assigning Users to Groups

Local users are assigned to several groups according to the default settings which you can access from the *User and Group Administration* dialog on the *Defaults for New Users* tab. In the following, learn how to modify an individual user's group assignment. If you need to change the default group assignments for new users, refer to *Section 15.4, "Changing Default Settings for Local Users"*.

PROCEDURE 15.8: CHANGING A USER'S GROUP ASSIGNMENT

1. Open the YaST *User and Group Administration* dialog and click the *Users* tab. It lists users and the groups the users belong to.

2. Click *Edit* and switch to the *Details* tab.

3. To change the primary group the user belongs to, click *Default Group* and select the group from the list.

4. To assign the user additional secondary groups, activate the corresponding check boxes in the *Additional Groups* list.

5. Click *OK* to apply your changes.

6. Click *OK* to close the administration dialog and save the changes.
Alternatively, to save all changes without exiting the *User and Group Administration* dialog, click *Expert Options* › *Write Changes Now*.

15.6   Managing Groups

With YaST you can also easily add, modify or delete groups.

PROCEDURE 15.9: CREATING AND MODIFYING GROUPS

1. Open the YaST *User and Group Management* dialog and click the *Groups* tab.

2. With *Set Filter* define the set of groups you want to manage. The dialog lists groups in the system.

3. To create a new group, click *Add*.

4. To modify an existing group, select the group and click *Edit*.

5. In the following dialog, enter or change the data. The list on the right shows an overview of all available users and system users which can be members of the group.

234

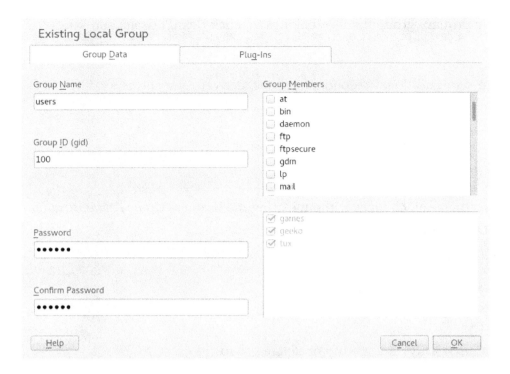

6. To add existing users to a new group select them from the list of possible *Group Members* by checking the corresponding box. To remove them from the group deactivate the box.

7. Click *OK* to apply your changes.

8. Click *OK* to close the administration dialog and save the changes.
   Alternatively, to save all changes without exiting the *User and Group Administration* dialog, click *Expert Options* › *Write Changes Now*.

To delete a group, it must not contain any group members. To delete a group, select it from the list and click *Delete*. Click *OK* to close the administration dialog and save the changes. Alternatively, to save all changes without exiting the *User and Group Administration* dialog, click *Expert Options* › *Write Changes Now*.

234

Managing Groups   SLES 12 SP3

15.7 Changing the User Authentication Method

When your machine is connected to a network, you can change the authentication method. The following options are available:

NIS

Users are administered centrally on a NIS server for all systems in the network. For details, see Book *"Security Guide", Chapter 3 "Using NIS"*.

LDAP

Users are administered centrally on an LDAP server for all systems in the network. For details about LDAP, see Book *"Security Guide", Chapter 5 "LDAP—A Directory Service"*.

You can manage LDAP users with the YaST user module. All other LDAP settings, including the default settings for LDAP users, need to be defined with the YaST LDAP client module as described in Book *"Security Guide", Chapter 4 "Setting Up Authentication Servers and Clients Using YaST", Section 4.2 "Configuring an Authentication Client with YaST"*.

Kerberos

With Kerberos, a user registers once and then is trusted in the entire network for the rest of the session.

Samba

SMB authentication is often used in mixed Linux and Windows networks. For details, see Book *"Administration Guide", Chapter 28 "Samba"*.

To change the authentication method, proceed as follows:

1. Open the *User and Group Administration* dialog in YaST.

2. Click the *Authentication Settings* tab to show an overview of the available authentication methods and the current settings.

3. To change the authentication method, click *Configure* and select the authentication method you want to modify. This takes you directly to the client configuration modules in YaST. For information about the configuration of the appropriate client, refer to the following sections:

   NIS: Book *"Security Guide", Chapter 3 "Using NIS", Section 3.2 "Configuring NIS Clients"*

   LDAP: Book *"Security Guide", Chapter 4 "Setting Up Authentication Servers and Clients Using YaST", Section 4.2 "Configuring an Authentication Client with YaST"*

Samba: *Book "Administration Guide", Chapter 28 "Samba", Section 28.5.1 "Configuring a Samba Client with YaST"*

4. After accepting the configuration, return to the *User and Group Administration* overview.

5. Click *OK* to close the administration dialog.

16 Changing Language and Country Settings with YaST

Working in different countries or having to work in a multilingual environment requires your computer to be set up to support this. SUSE® Linux Enterprise Server can handle different locales in parallel. A locale is a set of parameters that defines the language and country settings reflected in the user interface.

The main system language was selected during installation and keyboard and time zone settings were adjusted. However, you can install additional languages on your system and determine which of the installed languages should be the default.

For those tasks, use the YaST language module as described in *Section 16.1, "Changing the System Language"*. Install secondary languages to get optional localization if you need to start applications or desktops in languages other than the primary one.

Apart from that, the YaST timezone module allows you to adjust your country and timezone settings accordingly. It also lets you synchronize your system clock against a time server. For details, refer to *Section 16.2, "Changing the Country and Time Settings"*.

16.1 Changing the System Language

Depending on how you use your desktop and whether you want to switch the entire system to another language or only the desktop environment itself, there are several ways to do this:

Changing the System Language Globally

Proceed as described in *Section 16.1.1, "Modifying System Languages with YaST"* and *Section 16.1.2, "Switching the Default System Language"* to install additional localized packages with YaST and to set the default language. Changes are effective after the next login. To ensure that the entire system reflects the change, reboot the system or close and restart all running services, applications, and programs.

Changing the Language for the Desktop Only

Provided you have previously installed the desired language packages for your desktop environment with YaST as described below, you can switch the language of your desktop using the desktop's control center. After the X server has been restarted, your entire desktop reflects your new choice of language. Applications not belonging to your desktop framework are not affected by this change and may still appear in the language that was set in YaST.

Temporarily Switching Languages for One Application Only

You can also run a single application in another language (that has already been installed with YaST). To do so, start it from the command line by specifying the language code as described in *Section 16.1.3, "Switching Languages for Standard X and GNOME Applications"*.

16.1.1 Modifying System Languages with YaST

YaST knows two different language categories:

Primary Language

The primary language set in YaST applies to the entire system, including YaST and the desktop environment. This language is used whenever available unless you manually specify another language.

Secondary Languages

Install secondary languages to make your system multilingual. Languages installed as secondary languages can be selected manually for a specific situation. For example, use a secondary language to start an application in a certain language to do word processing in this language.

Before installing additional languages, determine which of them should be the default system language (primary language).

To access the YaST language module, start YaST and click *System > Language*. Alternatively, start the *Languages* dialog directly by running `sudo yast2 language &` from a command line.

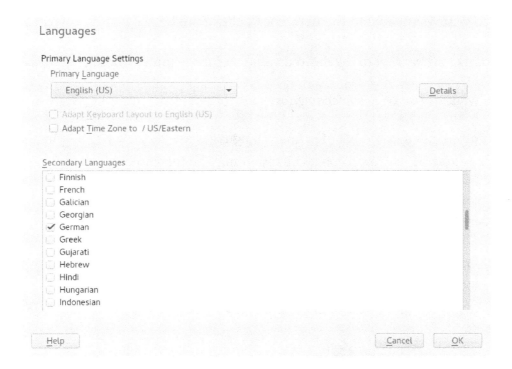

PROCEDURE 16.1: INSTALLING ADDITIONAL LANGUAGES

When installing additional languages, YaST also allows you to set different locale settings for the user `root`, see *Step 4*. The option *Locale Settings for User root* determines how the locale variables (`LC_*`) in the file `/etc/sysconfig/language` are set for `root`. You can either set them to the same locale as for normal users, keep it unaffected by any language changes or only set the variable `RC_LC_CTYPE` to the same values as for the normal users. This variable sets the localization for language-specific function calls.

1. To add additional languages in the YaST language module, select the *Secondary Languages* you want to install.

2. To make a language the default language, set it as *Primary Language*.

3. Additionally, adapt the keyboard to the new primary language and adjust the time zone, if appropriate.

 Tip: Advanced Settings

For advanced keyboard or time zone settings, select *Hardware › System Keyboard Layout* or *System › Date and Time* in YaST to start the respective dialogs. For more information, refer to *Section 10.1, "Setting Up Your System Keyboard Layout"* and *Section 16.2, "Changing the Country and Time Settings"*.

4. To change language settings specific to the user `root`, click *Details*.

    a. Set *Locale Settings for User root* to the desired value. For more information, click *Help*.

    b. Decide if you want to *Use UTF-8 Encoding* for `root` or not.

5. If your locale was not included in the list of primary languages available, try specifying it with *Detailed Locale Setting*. However, some localization may be incomplete.

6. Confirm your changes in the dialogs with *OK*. If you have selected secondary languages, YaST installs the localized software packages for the additional languages.

The system is now multilingual. However, to start an application in a language other than the primary one, you need to set the desired language explicitly as explained in *Section 16.1.3, "Switching Languages for Standard X and GNOME Applications"*.

16.1.2 Switching the Default System Language

1. To globally switch the default system language, start the YaST language module.

2. Select the desired new system language as *Primary Language*.

 Important: Deleting Former System Languages

    If you switch to a different primary language, the localized software packages for the former primary language will be removed from the system. To switch the default system language but keep the former primary language as additional language, add it as *Secondary Language* by enabling the respective check box.

3. Adjust the keyboard and time zone options as desired.

4. Confirm your changes with *OK*.

5. After YaST has applied the changes, restart current X sessions (for example, by logging out and logging in again) to make YaST and the desktop applications reflect your new language settings.

16.1.3   Switching Languages for Standard X and GNOME Applications

After you have installed the respective language with YaST, you can run a single application in another language.

Start the application from the command line by using the following command:

```
LANG=LANGUAGE application
```

For example, to start f-spot in German, run **LANG=de_DE f-spot**. For other languages, use the appropriate language code. Get a list of all language codes available with the **locale** -av command.

16.2   Changing the Country and Time Settings

Using the YaST date and time module, adjust your system date, clock and time zone information to the area you are working in. To access the YaST module, start YaST and click *System › Date and Time*. Alternatively, start the *Clock and Time Zone* dialog directly by running **sudo yast2 timezone &** from a command line.

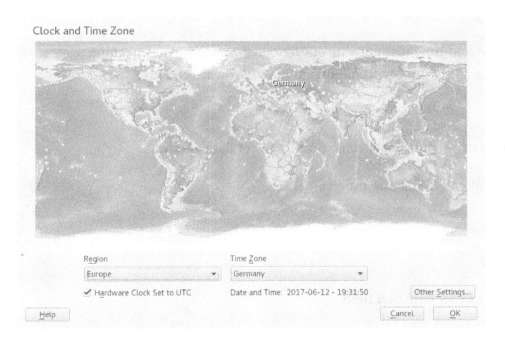

First, select a general region, such as *Europe*. Choose an appropriate country that matches the one you are working in, for example, *Germany*.

Depending on which operating systems run on your workstation, adjust the hardware clock settings accordingly:

- If you run another operating system on your machine, such as Microsoft Windows*, it is likely your system does not use UTC, but local time. In this case, deactivate *Hardware Clock Set To UTC*.

- If you only run Linux on your machine, set the hardware clock to UTC and have the switch from standard time to daylight saving time performed automatically.

 Important: Set the Hardware Clock to UTC

The switch from standard time to daylight saving time (and vice versa) can only be performed automatically when the hardware clock (CMOS clock) is set to UTC. This also applies if you use automatic time synchronization with NTP, because automatic synchronization will only be performed if the time difference between the hardware and system clock is less than 15 minutes.

Since a wrong system time can cause serious problems (missed backups, dropped mail messages, mount failures on remote file systems, etc.) it is strongly recommended to *always* set the hardware clock to UTC.

You can change the date and time manually or opt for synchronizing your machine against an NTP server, either permanently or only for adjusting your hardware clock.

PROCEDURE 16.2: MANUALLY ADJUSTING TIME AND DATE

1. In the YaST timezone module, click *Other Settings* to set date and time.

2. Select *Manually* and enter date and time values.

3. Confirm your changes.

PROCEDURE 16.3: SETTING DATE AND TIME WITH NTP SERVER

1. Click *Other Settings* to set date and time.

2. Select *Synchronize with NTP Server*.

3. Enter the address of an NTP server, if not already populated.

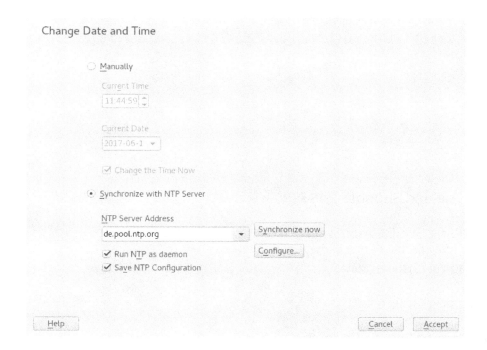

4. Click *Synchronize Now* to get your system time set correctly.

5. To use NTP permanently, enable *Save NTP Configuration*.

6. With the *Configure* button, you can open the advanced NTP configuration. For details, see *Book "Administration Guide", Chapter 24 "Time Synchronization with NTP", Section 24.1 "Configuring an NTP Client with YaST"*.

7. Confirm your changes.

VI Updating and Upgrading SUSE Linux Enterprise

17 Life Cycle and Support

This chapter provides background information on terminology, SUSE product lifecycles and Service Pack releases, and recommended upgrade policies.

17.1 Terminology

This section uses several terms. To understand the information, read the definitions below:

Backporting

Backporting is the act of adapting specific changes from a newer version of software and applying it to an older version. The most commonly used case is fixing security holes in older software components. Usually it is also part of a maintenance model to supply enhancements or (less commonly) new features.

Delta RPM

A delta RPM consists only of the binary diff between two defined versions of a package, and therefore has the smallest download size. Before being installed, the full RPM package is rebuilt on the local machine.

Downstream

A metaphor of how software is developed in the open source world (compare it with *upstream*). The term *downstream* refers to people or organizations like SUSE who integrate the source code from upstream with other software to build a distribution which is then used by end users. Thus, the software flows downstream from its developers via the integrators to the end users.

Extensions,
Add-On Products

Extensions and third party add-on products provide additional functionality of product value to SUSE Linux Enterprise Server. They are provided by SUSE and by SUSE partners, and they are registered and installed on top of the base product SUSE Linux Enterprise Server.

LTSS

LTSS is the abbreviation for Long Term Service Pack Support, which is available as an extension for SUSE Linux Enterprise Server.

Major Release,
General Availability (GA) Version

The major release of SUSE Linux Enterprise (or any software product) is a new version which brings new features and tools, decommissions previously deprecated components and comes with backward-incompatible changes. Major releases for example are SUSE Linux Enterprise 11 or 12.

Migration

Updating to a Service Pack (SP) by using the online update tools or an installation medium to install the respective patches. It updates all packages of the installed system to the latest state.

Migration Targets

Set of compatible products to which a system can be migrated, containing the version of the products/extensions and the URL of the repository. Migration targets can change over time and depend on installed extensions. Multiple migration targets can be selected, for example SLE 12 SP2 and SES2 or SLE 12 SP2 and SES3.

Modules

Modules are fully supported parts of SUSE Linux Enterprise Server with a different life cycle. They have a clearly defined scope and are delivered via online channel only. Registering at the SUSE Customer Center, SMT (Subscription Management Tool), or SUSE Manager is a prerequisite for being able to subscribe to these channels.

Package

A package is a compressed file in `rpm` format that contains all files for a particular program, including optional components like configuration, examples, and documentation.

Patch

A patch consists of one or more packages and may be applied by means of delta RPMs. It may also introduce dependencies to packages that are not installed yet.

Service Packs (SP)

Combines several patches into a form that is easy to install or deploy. Service packs are numbered and usually contain security fixes, updates, upgrades, or enhancements of programs.

Upstream

A metaphor of how software is developed in the open source world (compare it with *down-stream*). The term *upstream* refers to the original project, author or maintainer of a software that is distributed as source code. Feedback, patches, feature enhancements, or other improvements flow from end users or contributors to upstream developers. They decide if the request will be integrated or rejected.

If the project members decide to integrate the request, it will show up in newer versions of the software. An accepted request will benefit all parties involved.

If a request is not accepted, it may be for different reasons. Either it is in a state that is not compliant with the project's guidelines, it is invalid, it is already integrated, or it is not in the interest or roadmap of the project. An unaccepted request makes it harder for upstream developers as they need to synchronize their patches with the upstream code. This practice is generally avoided, but sometimes it is still needed.

Update

Installation of a newer *minor* version of a package, which usually contains security or bug fixes.

Upgrade

Installation of a newer *major* version of a package or distribution, which brings *new features*.

17.2   Product Life Cycle

SUSE has the following life cycle for products:

- SUSE Linux Enterprise Server has a 13-year life cycle: 10 years of general support and 3 years of extended support.

- SUSE Linux Enterprise Desktop has a 10-year life cycle: 7 years of general support and 3 years of extended support.

- Major releases are made every 4 years. Service packs are made every 12-14 months.

SUSE supports previous service packs for 6 months after the release of the new service pack. *Figure 17.1, "Major Releases and Service Packs"* depicts some mentioned aspects.

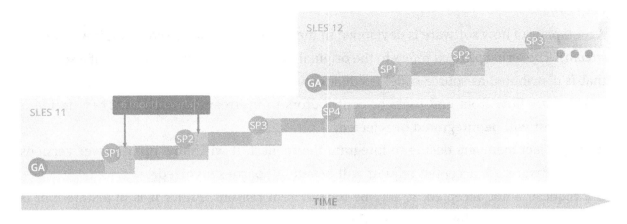

FIGURE 17.1: MAJOR RELEASES AND SERVICE PACKS

If you need additional time to design, validate and test your upgrade plans, Long Term Service Pack Support can extend the support you get by an additional 12 to 36 months in 12-month increments, giving you a total of between 2 and 5 years of support on any service pack (see *Figure 17.2, "Long Term Service Pack Support"*).

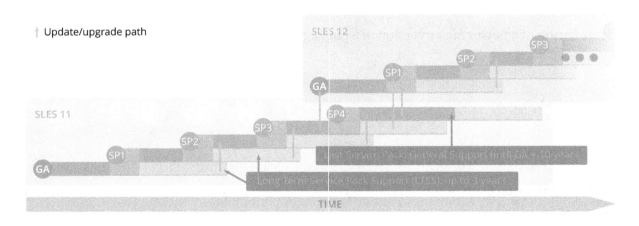

FIGURE 17.2: LONG TERM SERVICE PACK SUPPORT

For more information refer to https://www.suse.com/products/long-term-service-pack-support/ ↗.

For the life cycles of all products refer to https://www.suse.com/lifecycle/ ↗.

17.3 Module Life Cycles

With SUSE Linux Enterprise 12, SUSE introduces modular packaging. The modules are distinct sets of packages grouped into their own maintenance channel and updated independently of service pack life cycles. This allows you to get timely and easy access to the latest technology in areas where innovation is occurring at a rapid pace. For information about the life cycles of modules refer to https://scc.suse.com/docs/lifecycle/sle/12/modules ↗ .

17.4 Generating Periodic Life Cycle Report

SUSE Linux Enterprise Server can regularly check for changes in the support status of all installed products and send the report via e-mail in case of changes. To generate the report, install the `zypper-lifecycle-plugin` with **zypper in zypper-lifecycle-plugin**.

Enable the report generation on your system with **systemctl**:

```
root # systemctl enable lifecycle-report
```

The recipient and subject of the report e-mail, as well as the report generation period can be configured in the file `/etc/sysconfig/lifecycle-report` with any text editor. The settings `MAIL_TO` and `MAIL_SUBJ` define the mail recipient and subject, while `DAYS` sets the interval at which the report is generated.

The report displays changes in the support status after the change occurred and not in advance. If the change occurs right after the generation of the last report, it can take up to 14 days until you are notified of the change. Take this into account when setting the `DAYS` option. Change the following configuration entries to fit your requirements:

```
MAIL_TO='root@localhost'
MAIL_SUBJ='Lifecycle report'
DAYS=14
```

The latest report is available in the file `/var/lib/lifecycle/report`. The file contains two sections. The first section informs about the end of support for used products. The second section lists packages with their support end dates and update availability.

17.5 Support Levels

The range for extended support levels starts from year 10 and ends in year 13. These contain continued L3 engineering level diagnosis and reactive critical bug fixes. With these support levels, you will receive updates for trivially exploitable root exploits in the kernel and other root exploits directly executable without user interaction. Furthermore, they support existing workloads, software stacks, and hardware with limited package exclusion list. Find an overview in *Table 17.1, "Security Updates and Bug Fixes"*.

TABLE 17.1: SECURITY UPDATES AND BUG FIXES

	General Support for Most Recent Service Pack (SP)			General Support for Previous SP, with LTSS	Extended Support with LTSS
Feature	Year 1-5	Year 6-7	Year 8-10	Year 4-10	Year 10-13
Technical Services	Yes	Yes	Yes	Yes	Yes
Access to Patches and Fixes	Yes	Yes	Yes	Yes	Yes
Access to Documentation and Knowledge Base	Yes	Yes	Yes	Yes	Yes
Support for Existing Stacks and Workloads	Yes	Yes	Yes	Yes	Yes

Feature	General Support for Most Recent Service Pack (SP)			General Support for Previous SP, with LTSS	Extended Support with LTSS
	Year 1-5	Year 6-7	Year 8-10	Year 4-10	Year 10-13
Support for New Deployments	Yes	Yes	Limited (Based on partner and customer requests)	Limited (Based on partner and customer requests)	No
Enhancement Requests	Yes	Limited (Based on partner and customer requests)	Limited (Based on partner and customer requests)	No	No
Hardware Enablement and Optimization	Yes	Limited (Based on partner and customer requests)	Limited (Based on partner and customer requests)	No	No
Driver updates via SUSE Solid-Driver Program (formerly PLDP)	Yes	Yes	Limited (Based on partner and customer requests)	Limited (Based on partner and customer requests)	No
Backport of Fixes from Recent SP	Yes	Yes	Limited (Based on partner and customer requests)	N/A	N/A

	General Support for Most Recent Service Pack (SP)			General Support for Previous SP, with LTSS	Extended Support with LTSS
Feature	**Year 1-5**	**Year 6-7**	**Year 8-10**	**Year 4-10**	**Year 10-13**
Critical Security Updates	Yes	Yes	Yes	Yes	Yes
Defect Resolution	Yes	Yes	Limited (Severity Level 1 and 2 defects only)	Limited (Severity Level 1 and 2 defects only)	Limited (Severity Level 1 and 2 defects only)

17.6 Repository Model

The repository layout corresponds to the product lifecycles. The following sections contain a list of all relevant repositories.

DESCRIPTION OF REQUIRED REPOSITORIES

Updates

Maintenance updates to packages in the corresponding `Core` or `Pool` repository.

Pool

Containing all binary RPMs from the installation media, plus pattern information and support status metadata.

DESCRIPTION OF OPTIONAL REPOSITORIES

Debuginfo-Pool,

Debuginfo-Updates

These repositories contain static content. Of these two, only the `Debuginfo-Updates` repository receives updates. Enable these repositories if you need to install libraries with debug information in case of an issue.

17.6.1 Required Repositories for SUSE Linux Enterprise Server

SLES 11 SP3

> SLES11-SP3-Pool
> SLES11-SP3-Updates

SLES 11 SP4

> SLES11-SP4-Pool
> SLES11-SP4-Updates

SLES 12

> SLES12-GA-Pool
> SLES12-GA-Updates

SLES 12 SP1

> SLES12-SP1-Pool
> SLES12-SP1-Updates

SLES 12 SP2

> SLES12-SP2-Pool
> SLES12-SP2-Updates

SLES 12 SP3

> SLES12-SP3-Pool
> SLES12-SP3-Updates

17.6.2 Optional Repositories for SUSE Linux Enterprise Server

SLES 11 SP3

> SLES11-SP3-Debuginfo-Core
> SLES11-SP3-Debuginfo-Updates
> SLES11-SP3-Extension-Store
> SLES11-SP3-Extra

SLES 12

```
SLES12-GA-Debuginfo-Core
SLES12-GA-Debuginfo-Updates
```

SLES 12 SP1

```
SLES12-SP1-Debuginfo-Core
SLES12-SP1-Debuginfo-Updates
```

SLES 12 SP2

```
SLES12-SP2-Debuginfo-Core
SLES12-SP2-Debuginfo-Updates
```

SLES 12 SP3

```
SLES12-SP3-Debuginfo-Core
SLES12-SP3-Debuginfo-Updates
```

17.6.3   Module-Specific Repositories for SUSE Linux Enterprise Server

The following listing contains only the core repositories for each module, but not `Debuginfo` or `Source` repositories.

Modules Available for SLES 12 GA/SP1/SP2/SP3

- Advanced Systems Management Module: CFEngine, Puppet and the Machinery tool

```
SLE-Module-Adv-Systems-Management12-Pool
SLE-Module-Adv-Systems-Management12-Updates
```

- Containers Module: Docker, tools, prepackaged images

```
SLE-Module-Containers12-Pool
SLE-Module-Containers12-Updates
```

- Legacy Module: Sendmail, old IMAP stack, old Java, … (not available on AArch64)

```
SLE-Module-Legacy12-Pool
SLE-Module-Legacy12-Updates
```

- Public Cloud Module: public cloud initialization code and tools

```
SLE-Module-Public-Cloud12-Pool
SLE-Module-Public-Cloud12-Updates
```

- Toolchain Module: GNU Compiler Collection (GCC)

```
SLE-Module-Toolchain12-Pool
SLE-Module-Toolchain12-Updates
```

- Web and Scripting Module: PHP, Python, Ruby on Rails

```
SLE-Module-Web-Scripting12-Pool
SLE-Module-Web-Scripting12-Updates
```

Modules Available for SLES 12 GA/SP1

- Certifications Module: FIPS 140-2 certification-specific packages (not available on AArch64 and POWER)

```
SLE-Module-Certifications12-Pool
SLE-Module-Certifications12-Updates
```

Modules Available for SLES 12 SP2/SP3

- HPC Module: tools and libraries related to High Performance Computing

```
SLE-Module-HPC12-Pool
SLE-Module-HPC12-Updates
```

17.6.4   Required Repositories for SUSE Linux Enterprise Desktop

SLED 11 SP3

```
SLED11-SP3-Pool
SLED11-SP3-Updates
```

SLED 11 SP4

```
SLED11-SP4-Pool
SLED11-SP4-Updates
```

SLED 12

> SLED12-GA-Pool
> SLED12-GA-Updates

SLED 12 SP1

> SLED12-SP1-Pool
> SLED12-SP1-Updates

SLED 12 SP2

> SLED12-SP2-Pool
> SLED12-SP2-Updates

SLED 12 SP3

> SLED12-SP3-Pool
> SLED12-SP3-Updates

17.6.5   Optional Repositories for SUSE Linux Enterprise Desktop

SLED 11 SP3

> SLED11-SP3-Debuginfo-Core
> SLED11-SP3-Debuginfo-Updates
> SLED11-SP3-Extension-Store
> SLED11-SP3-Extra

SLED 12

> SLED12-GA-Debuginfo-Core
> SLED12-GA-Debuginfo-Updates

SLED 12 SP1

> SLED12-SP1-Debuginfo-Core
> SLED12-SP1-Debuginfo-Updates

SLED 12 SP2

> SLED12-SP2-Debuginfo-Core
> SLED12-SP2-Debuginfo-Updates

SLED 12 SP3

```
SLED12-SP3-Debuginfo-Core
SLED12-SP3-Debuginfo-Updates
```

17.6.6   Origin of Packages

SUSE Linux Enterprise 11 SP3/SP4.   With the update to SP3 there are only two repositories available: `SLES11-SP3-Pool` and `SLES11-SP3-Updates`. Since SP4, any previous repositories are not visible anymore.

SUSE Linux Enterprise 12 and SP1/SP2.   With the update to SUSE Linux Enterprise 12 there are only two repositories available: `SLES12-GA-Pool` and `SLES12-GA-Updates`. Any previous repositories from SUSE Linux Enterprise 11 are not visible anymore.

17.6.7   Register and Unregister Repositories with SUSEConnect

On registration, the system receives repositories from the SUSE Customer Center (see https:// scc.suse.com/ ↗) or a local registration proxy like SMT. The repository names map to specific URIs in the customer center. To list all available repositories on your system, use **zypper** as follows:

```
root # zypper repos -u
```

This gives you a list of all available repositories on your system. Each repository is listed by its alias, name and whether it is enabled and will be refreshed. The option `-u` gives you also the URI from where it originated.

To register your machine, run SUSEConnect, for example:

```
root # SUSEConnect -r REGCODE
```

If you want to unregister your machine, from SP1 and above you can use SUSEConnect too:

```
root # SUSEConnect --de-register
```

To check your locally installed products and their status, use the following command:

```
root # SUSEConnect -s
```

18 Upgrading SUSE Linux Enterprise

SUSE® Linux Enterprise (SLE) allows to upgrade an existing system to the new version, for example, going from SLE 11 SP4 to the latest SLE 12 service pack. No new installation is needed. Existing data, such as home and data directories and system configuration, is kept intact. You can update from a local CD or DVD drive or from a central network installation source.

This chapter explains how to manually upgrade your SUSE Linux Enterprise system, be it by DVD, network, an automated process, or SUSE Manager.

18.1 Supported Upgrade Paths to SLE 12 SP3

 Important: Cross-architecture Upgrades Are Not Supported

Cross-architecture upgrades, such as upgrading from a 32-bit version of SUSE Linux Enterprise Server to the 64-bit version, or upgrading from big endian to little endian are *not* supported!

Specifically, SLE 11 on POWER (big endian) to SLE 12 SP2 on POWER (new: little endian!), is *not* supported.

Also, since SUSE Linux Enterprise 12 is 64-bit only, upgrades from any 32-bit SUSE Linux Enterprise 11 systems to SUSE Linux Enterprise 12 and later are *not* supported.

To make a cross-architecture upgrade, you need to perform a new installation.

Before you perform any migration, read *Section 18.3, "Preparing the System"*.

 Note: Skipping Service Packs

Consecutively installing all Service Packs is the safest upgrade path. In some cases it is supported to skip 1 or 2 Service Packs when upgrading. However, we recommend to *not* skip any Service Pack.

Note: Upgrading Major Releases

We recommend to do a fresh install when upgrading to a new Major Release, for example from SUSE Linux Enterprise 11 to SUSE Linux Enterprise 12.

Upgrading from SUSE Linux Enterprise 10 (any Service Pack)

There is no supported direct migration path to SUSE Linux Enterprise 12. We recommend a fresh installation in this case.

Upgrading from SUSE Linux Enterprise 11 GA / SP1 / SP2 / SP3

There is no supported direct migration path to SUSE Linux Enterprise 12. You need at least SLE 11 SP4 before you can proceed to SLE 12 SP3.

If you cannot do a fresh install, first upgrade your installed SLE 11 Service Pack to SLE 11 SP4. These steps are described in the SUSE Linux Enterprise 11 Deployment Guide (https://www.suse.com/documentation/sles11/) ↗.

Then proceed with *Section 18.2, "Online and Offline Upgrade"*.

Upgrading from SUSE Linux Enterprise 11 SP4

Upgrading from SLE 11 SP4 to SLE 12 SP3 is only supported via an offline upgrade. Refer to *Section 18.2, "Online and Offline Upgrade"* for details.

Upgrading from SUSE Linux Enterprise 12 GA to SP3

A direct upgrade from SLE 12 GA to SP3 is not supported. Upgrade to SLE 12 SP2 first.

Upgrading from SUSE Linux Enterprise 12 SP1 / SP2 to SP3

Upgrading from SUSE Linux Enterprise 12 SP1 or SP2 to SP3 is supported.

Upgrading from SUSE Linux Enterprise 12 LTSS GA / SP1 LTSS / SP2 to SP3

Updating any previous SLE 12 LTSS version to SP3 is supported.

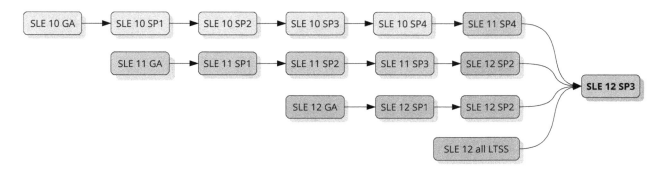

FIGURE 18.1: OVERVIEW OF SHORTEST UPGRADE PATHS

18.2 Online and Offline Upgrade

SUSE supports two different upgrade and migration methods. For more information about the terminology, see *Section 17.1, "Terminology"*. The methods are:

Online

> All upgrades that are executed from the running system are considered to be online. Examples: Connected through SUSE Customer Center, Subscription Management Tool (SMT), SUSE Manager using Zypper or YaST.
>
> When migrating between Service Packs of the same major release, we suggest following *Section 20.4, "Upgrading with the Online Migration Tool (YaST)"* or *Section 20.5, "Upgrading with Zypper"*.

Offline

> Offline methods usually boot another operating system from which the installed SLE version is upgraded. Examples are: DVD, flash disk, ISO image, AutoYaST, "plain RPM" or PXE boot.

Upgrading from SUSE Linux Enterprise 11 SP4 to SUSE Linux Enterprise 12 SP3 is only supported via an offline upgrade. See *Chapter 19, Upgrading Offline*

Upgrading from any SUSE Linux Enterprise 12 LTSS version or SUSE Linux Enterprise 12 SP1 or SP2 to SP3 is supported using all offline and online methods. See *Chapter 19, Upgrading Offline* and *Chapter 20, Upgrading Online*.

18.3 Preparing the System

Before starting the upgrade procedure, make sure your system is properly prepared. Among others, preparation involves backing up data and checking the release notes.

18.3.1 Make Sure the Current System is Up-To-Date

Upgrading the system is only supported from the most recent patch-level. Make sure the latest system updates are installed by either running **`zypper patch`** or by starting the YaST module *Online-Update*.

18.3.2   Read the Release Notes

In the release notes you can find additional information on changes since the previous release of SUSE Linux Enterprise Server. Check the release notes to see whether:

- your hardware needs special considerations;

- any used software packages have changed significantly;

- special precautions are necessary for your installation.

The release notes also provide information that could not make it into the manual on time. They also contain notes about known issues.

If you are skipping one or more Service Packs, check the release notes of the skipped Service Packs as well. The release notes usually only contain the changes between two subsequent releases. You can miss important changes if you are only reading the current release notes.

Find the release notes locally in the directory `/usr/share/doc/release-notes` or online at https://www.suse.com/releasenotes/ ↗.

18.3.3   Make a Backup

Before updating, copy existing configuration files to a separate medium (such as tape device, removable hard disk, etc.) to back up the data. This primarily applies to files stored in `/etc` and some directories and files in `/var` and `/opt`. You may also want to write the user data in `/home` (the `HOME` directories) to a backup medium. Back up this data as `root`. Only `root` has read permissions for all local files.

If you have selected *Update an Existing System* as the installation mode in YaST, you can choose to do a (system) backup at a later point in time. You can choose to include all modified files and files from the `/etc/sysconfig` directory. However, this is not a complete backup, as all the other important directories mentioned above are missing. Find the backup in the `/var/adm/backup` directory.

18.3.3.1   Listing Installed Packages and Repositories

It is often useful to have a list of installed packages, for example when doing a fresh install of a new major SLE release or reverting to the old version.

Be aware that not all installed packages or used repositories are available in newer releases of SUSE Linux Enterprise. Some may have been renamed and others replaced. It is also possible that some packages are still available for legacy purposes while another package is used by default. Therefore some manual editing of the files might be necessary. This can be done with any text editor.

Create a file named `repositories.bak` containing a list of all used repositories:

```
root # zypper lr -e repositories.bak
```

Also create a file named `installed-software.bak` containing a list of all installed packages:

```
root # rpm -qa --queryformat '%{NAME}\n' > installed-software.bak
```

Back up both files. The repositories and installed packages can be restored with the following commands:

```
root # zypper ar repositories.bak
root # zypper install $(cat installed-software.bak)
```

Note: Amount of Packages Increases with an Update to a new Major Release

A system upgraded to a new major version (SLE *X+1*) may contain more packages than the initial system (SLE *X*). It will also contain more packages than a fresh installation of SLE *X+1* with the same pattern selection. Reasons for this are:

- Packages got split to allow a more fine-grained package selection. For example, 37 `texlive` packages on SLE 11 were split into 422 packages on SLE 12.

- When a package got split into other packages all new packages are installed in the upgrade case to retain the same functionality as with the previous version. However, the new default for a fresh installation of SLE *X+1* may be to not install all packages.

- Legacy packages from SLE *X* may be kept for compatibility reasons.

- Package dependencies and the scope of patterns may have changed.

18.3.4   Migrate your MySQL Database

As of SUSE Linux Enterprise 12, SUSE switched from MySQL to MariaDB. Before you start any upgrade, it is highly recommended to back up your database.

To perform the database migration, do the following:

1. Log in to your SUSE Linux Enterprise 11 machine.

2. Create a dump file:

   ```
   root # mysqldump -u root -p --all-databases > mysql_backup.sql
   ```

   By default, **mysqldump** does not dump the INFORMATION_SCHEMA or perfor-mance_schema database. For more details refer to https://dev.mysql.com/doc/ref-man/5.5/en/mysqldump.html ↗.

3. Store your dump file, the configuration file /etc/my.cnf, and the directory /etc/mysql/ for later investigation (*NOT* installation!) in a safe place.

4. Perform your upgrade. After the upgrade, your former configuration file /etc/my.cnf is still intact. You can find the new configuration in the file /etc/my.cnf.rpmnew.

5. Configure your MariaDB database to your needs. Do *NOT* use the former configuration file and directory, but use it as a reminder and adapt it.

6. Make sure you start the MariaDB server:

   ```
   root # systemctl start mysql
   ```

   If you want to start the MariaDB server on every boot, enable the service:

   ```
   root # systemctl enable mysql
   ```

7. Verify that MariaDB is running properly by connecting to the database:

   ```
   root # mysql -u root -p
   ```

18.3.5   Migrate your PostgreSQL Database

SLE11 SP3 and SLE12 GA get a newer version of the PostgreSQL database as a maintenance update. Because of the required migration work of the database, there is no automatic upgrade process. As such, the switch from one version to another needs to be done manually.

The migration process is conducted by the **pg_upgrade** command which is an alternative method of the classic dump and reload. In comparison with the "dump & reload" method, **pg_upgrade** makes the migration less time-consuming.

Each PostgreSQL version stores its files in different, version-dependent directories. After the update the directories will change to:

SLE11 SP3/SP4

`/usr/lib/postgresql91/` to `/usr/lib/postgresql94/`

SLE12 GA

`/usr/lib/postgresql93/` to `/usr/lib/postgresql94/`

To perform the database migration, do the following:

1. Make sure the following preconditions are fulfilled:

   - If not already done, upgrade any package of the old PostgreSQL version to the latest release through a maintenance update.

   - Create a backup of your existing database.

   - Install the packages of the new PostgreSQL major version. For SLE12 this means to install `postgresql94-server` and all the packages it depends on.

   - Install the package `postgresql94-contrib` which contains the command **pg_upgrade**.

   - Make sure you have enough free space in your PostgreSQL data area, which is `/var/lib/pgsql/data` by default. If space is tight, try to reduce size with the following SQL command on each database (can take very long!):

     ```
     VACUUM FULL
     ```

2. Stop the PostgreSQL server:

   ```
   root # /usr/sbin/rcpostgresql stop
   ```

3. Rename your old data directory:

   ```
   root # mv /var/lib/pgsql/data /var/lib/pgsql/data.old
   ```

4. Create a new data directory:

```
root # mkdir -p /var/lib/pgsql/data
```

5. If you have changed your configuration files in the old version, copy the files post-gresql.conf pg_hba.conf to your new data directory:

```
root # cp /var/lib/pgsql/data.old/*.conf \
    /var/lib/pgsql/data
```

6. Initialize your new database instance either manually with **initdb** or by starting and stopping PostgreSQL, which will do it automatically:

```
root # /usr/sbin/rcpostgresql start
root # /usr/sbin/rcpostgresql stop
```

7. Start the migration process and replace the *OLD* placeholder with the older version:

```
root # pg_upgrade \
    --old-datadir "/var/lib/pgsql/data.old" \
    --new-datadir "/var/lib/pgsql/data" \
    --old-bindir "/usr/lib/postgresqlOLD/bin/" \
    --new-bindir "/usr/lib/postgresql94/bin/"
```

8. Start your new database instance:

```
root # /usr/sbin/rcpostgresql start
```

9. Check if the migration was successful. There is no general tool to automate this step. It depends on your use case how much and what you want to test.

10. Remove any old PostgreSQL packages and your old data directory:

```
root # zypper search -s postgresqlOLD | xargs zypper rm -u
root # rm -rf /var/lib/pgsql/data.old
```

18.3.6 Create Non-MD5 Server Certificates for Java Applications

During the update from SP1 to SP2, MD5-based certificates were disabled as part of a security fix. If you have certificates created as MD5, re-create your certificates with the following steps:

1. Open a terminal and log in as root.

2. Create a private key:

```
root # openssl genrsa -out server.key 1024
```

If you want a stronger key, replace 1024 with a higher number, for example, 4096.

3. Create a certificate signing request (CSR):

```
root # openssl req -new -key server.key -out server.csr
```

4. Self-sign the certificate:

```
root # openssl x509 -req -days 365 -in server.csr -signkey server.key -out
  server.crt
```

5. Create the PEM file:

```
root # cat server.key server.crt > server.pem
```

6. Place the files server.crt, server.csr, server.key, and server.pem in the respective directories where the keys can be found. For Tomcat, for example, this directory is /etc/tomcat/ssl/.

18.3.7 Shut Down Virtual Machine Guests

If your machine serves as a VM Host Server for KVM or Xen, make sure to properly shut down all running VM Guests prior to the update. Otherwise you may not be able to access the guests after the update.

18.3.8 Check the clientSetup4SMT.sh Script on SMT Clients

If you are migrating your client OS that is registered against an SMT server, you need to check if the version of the clientSetup4SMT.sh script on your host is up to date. clientSetup4SMT.sh from older versions of SMT cannot manage SMT 12 clients. If you apply software patches regularly on your SMT server, you can always find the latest version of clientSetup4SMT.sh at <SMT_HOSTNAME>/repo/tools/clientSetup4SMT.sh.

18.3.9   Disk Space

Software tends to grow from version to version. Therefore, take a look at the available partition space before updating. If you suspect you are running short of disk space, back up your data before increasing the available space by resizing partitions, for example. There is no general rule regarding how much space each partition should have. Space requirements depend on your particular partitioning profile and the software selected.

 Note: Automatic Check for Enough Space in YaST

During the update procedure, YaST will check how much free disk space is available and display a warning to the user if the installation may exceed the available amount. In that case, performing the update may lead to an *unusable system*! Only if you know exactly what you are doing (by testing beforehand), you can skip the warning and continue the update.

18.3.9.1   Checking Disk Space on Non-Btrfs File Systems

Use the **df** command to list available disk space. For example, in *Example 18.1, "List with df -h"*, the root partition is /dev/sda3 (mounted as /).

EXAMPLE 18.1: LIST WITH df -h

```
Filesystem     Size  Used Avail Use% Mounted on
/dev/sda3       74G   22G   53G  29% /
tmpfs          506M     0  506M   0% /dev/shm
/dev/sda5      116G  5.8G  111G   5% /home
/dev/sda1       44G    4G   40G   9% /data
```

18.3.9.2   Checking Disk Space on Btrfs Root File Systems

If you use Btrfs as root file systems on your machine, make sure there is enough free space. In the worst case, an upgrade needs as much disk space as the current root file system (without /.snapshot) for a new snapshot. To display available disk space use the command:

```
root # df -h /
```

Check the available space on all other mounted partitions as well. The following recommendations have been proven:

- For all file systems including Btrfs you need enough free disk space to download and install big RPMs. The space of old RPMs are only freed after new RPMs are installed.

- For Btrfs with snapshots, you need at minimum as much free space as your current installation takes. We recommend to have twice as much free space as the current installation. If you do not have enough free space, you can try to delete old snapshots with **snapper**:

```
root # snapper list
root # snapper delete NUMBER
```

However, this may not help in all cases. Before migration, most snapshots occupy only little space.

18.3.10 Temporarily Disabling Kernel Multiversion Support

SUSE Linux Enterprise Server allows installing multiple kernel versions by enabling the respective settings in /etc/zypp/zypp.conf. Support for this feature needs to be temporarily disabled to upgrade to a service pack. When the update has successfully finished, multiversion support can be re-enabled. To disable multiversion support, comment the respective lines in /etc/zypp/zypp.conf. The result should look similar to:

```
#multiversion = provides:multiversion(kernel)
#multiversion.kernels = latest,running
```

To re-activate this feature after a successful update, remove the comment signs. For more information about multiversion support, refer to *Section 14.1, "Enabling and Configuring Multiversion Support"*.

18.4 Upgrading on IBM z Systems

Upgrading a SUSE Linux Enterprise installation on z Systems requires the **Upgrade=1** kernel parameter, for example via the parmfile. See *Section 4.3, "The parmfile—Automating the System Configuration"*.

18.5   IBM POWER: Starting an X Server

On SLES 12 for IBM POWER the display manager is configured not to start a local X Server by default. This setting was reversed on SLES 12 SP1—the display manager now starts an X Server.

To avoid problems during upgrade, the SUSE Linux Enterprise Server setting is not changed automatically. If you want the display manager to start an X Server after the upgrade, change the setting of `DISPLAYMANAGER_STARTS_XSERVER` in `/etc/sysconfig/displaymanager` as follows:

```
DISPLAYMANAGER_STARTS_XSERVER="yes"
```

19 Upgrading Offline

This chapter describes how to upgrade an existing SUSE Linux Enterprise installation using YaST which is booted from an installation medium. The YaST installer can, for example, be started from a DVD, over the network, or from the hard disk the system resides on.

19.1 Conceptual Overview

Before upgrading your system, read *Section 18.3, "Preparing the System"* first.

To upgrade your system, boot from an installation source, as you would do for a fresh installation. However, when the boot screen appears, you need to select *Upgrade* (instead of *Installation*). The upgrade can be started from:

- **Removable Media.** This includes media such as CDs, DVDs or USB mass storage devices. For more information, see *Section 19.2, "Starting the Upgrade from Installation Medium"*.

- **Network Resource.** You can either boot from the local medium and then select the respective network installation type, or boot via PXE. For more information, see *Section 19.3, "Starting Upgrade from Network Source"*.

- **Hard Disk.** You can copy the new kernel and initrd image from the ISO image to your hard disk containing the current SUSE Linux Enterprise installation and adjust the boot menu. For more information, see *Section 19.4, "Starting Upgrade from Hard Disk"*.

19.2 Starting the Upgrade from Installation Medium

The procedure below describes booting from a DVD, but you can also use another local installation medium like an ISO image on a USB mass storage device. The medium and boot method to select depends on the system architecture and on whether the machine has a traditional BIOS or UEFI.

PROCEDURE 19.1: MANUALLY UPGRADING FROM SLE 11 SP4 TO SLE 12 SP3

1. Select and prepare a boot medium, see *Section 6.2, "System Start-up for Installation"*.

2. Insert DVD 1 of the SUSE Linux Enterprise 12 SP3 installation medium and boot your machine. A *Welcome* screen is displayed, followed by the boot screen.

3. Start up the system by selecting *Upgrade* in the boot menu.

4. Proceed with the upgrade process as described in *Section 19.6, "Upgrading SUSE Linux Enterprise".*

19.3 Starting Upgrade from Network Source

To start an upgrade from a network installation source, make sure that the following requirements are met:

REQUIREMENTS FOR UPGRADING FROM A NETWORK INSTALLATION SOURCE

Network Installation Source

A network installation source is set up according to *Chapter 7, Setting Up the Server Holding the Installation Sources*.

Network Connection and Network Services

Both the installation server and the target machine must have a functioning network connection. Required network services are:

- Domain Name Service

- DHCP (only needed for booting via PXE, IP can be set manually during setup)

- OpenSLP (optional)

Boot Medium

You have a SUSE Linux Enterprise Server DVD 1 (or a local ISO image) at hand to boot the target system *or* a target system that is set up for booting via PXE according to *Section 8.5, "Preparing the Target System for PXE Boot"*. **Refer to** *Chapter 9, Remote Installation* **for in-depth** information on starting the upgrade from a remote server.

19.3.1 Manually Upgrading via Network Installation Source—Booting from DVD

This procedure describes booting from a DVD as an example, but you can also use another local installation medium like an ISO image on a USB mass storage device. The way to select the boot method and to start up the system from the medium depends on the system architecture and on whether the machine has a traditional BIOS or UEFI. For details, see the links below.

1. Insert DVD 1 of the SUSE Linux Enterprise 12 SP2 installation media and boot your machine. A *Welcome* screen is displayed, followed by the boot screen.

2. Select the type of network installation source you want to use (FTP, HTTP, NFS, SMB, or SLP). Usually you get this choice by pressing F4 , but in case your machine is equipped with UEFI instead of a traditional BIOS, you may need to manually adjust boot parameters. For details, see *Installing from a Network Server* in *Chapter 6, Installation with YaST*.

3. Proceed with the upgrade process as described in *Section 19.6, "Upgrading SUSE Linux Enterprise"*.

19.3.2 Manually Upgrading via Network Installation Source—Booting via PXE

To perform an upgrade from a network installation source using PXE boot, proceed as follows:

1. Adjust the setup of your DHCP server to provide the address information needed for booting via PXE. For details, see *Section 8.5, "Preparing the Target System for PXE Boot"*.

2. Set up a TFTP server to hold the boot image needed for booting via PXE. Use DVD 1 of your SUSE Linux Enterprise 12 SP2 installation media for this or follow the instructions in *Section 8.2, "Setting Up a TFTP Server"*.

3. Prepare PXE Boot and Wake-on-LAN on the target machine.

4. Initiate the boot of the target system and use VNC to remotely connect to the installation routine running on this machine. For more information, see *Section 9.3.1, "VNC Installation"*.

5. Proceed with the upgrade process as described in *Section 19.6, "Upgrading SUSE Linux Enterprise"*.

19.4   Starting Upgrade from Hard Disk

19.4.1   Automated Migration from SUSE Linux Enterprise 11 SP3 or SP4 to SUSE Linux Enterprise 12 SP2

1. Copy the installation kernel `linux` and the file `initrd` from `/boot/x86_64/loader/` from your first installation DVD to your system's `/boot` directory:

```
root # cp -vi DVDROOT/boot/x86_64/loader/linux /boot/linux.upgrade
root # cp -vi DVDROOT/boot/x86_64/loader/initrd /boot/initrd.upgrade
```

   DVDROOT denotes the path where your system mounts the DVD, usually `/run/media/$USER/$DVDNAME`.

2. Open the GRUB legacy configuration file `/boot/grub/menu.lst` and add another section. For other boot loaders, edit the respective configuration file(s). Adjust device names and the `root` parameter accordingly. For example:

```
title Linux Upgrade Kernel
kernel (hd0,0)/boot/linux.upgrade root=/dev/sda1 upgrade=1 autoupgrade=1
initrd (hd0,0)/boot/initrd.upgrade
```

3. The following steps either need the DVD in the drive or the ISO image has to be present on the local disk. If the computer has no DVD drive, either download the ISO and save it as `/install.iso` or copy it from the DVD.

```
root # dd if=/dev/cdrom of=/install.iso
```

   If you copied the ISO to your hard disk, you need to add a parameter to the previously edited `/boot/grub/menu.lst`. To the line beginning with `kernel` add the option

```
install=hd:/install.iso
```

4. Reboot your machine and select the newly added section from the boot menu (here: *Linux Upgrade Kernel*). You can use **grubonce** to preselect the newly created GRUB entry for an unattended automatic reboot into the newly created entry. You can also use **reboot** to initiate the reboot from the command line.

5. Proceed with the upgrade process as described in *Section 19.6, "Upgrading SUSE Linux Enterprise"*.

6. After the upgrade process was finished successfully, remove the installation kernel and initrd files (`/boot/linux.upgrade` and `/boot/initrd.upgrade`). They are not needed anymore.

19.5 Enabling Automatic Upgrade

The upgrade process can be executed automatically. To enable the automatic update, the kernel parameter `autoupgrade=1` must be set. The parameter can be set on boot in the `Boot Options` field. For details, see https://www.suse.com/documentation/sles-12/book_autoyast/data/introduction.html ↗.

19.6 Upgrading SUSE Linux Enterprise

Before you upgrade your system, read *Section 18.3, "Preparing the System"* first. To perform an automated migration, proceed as follows:

1. After you have booted (either from an installation medium or the network), select the *Upgrade* entry on the boot screen. If you want to do the upgrade as described in the next steps manually, you need to disable the automatic upgrade process. Refer to *Section 19.5, "Enabling Automatic Upgrade"*.

    Warning: Wrong Choice May Lead to Data Loss

   If you select *Installation* instead of *Upgrade*, data may be lost later. You need to be extra careful not to destroy your data partitions by doing a fresh installation.

   Make sure to select *Upgrade* here.

   YaST starts the installation system.

2. On the *Welcome* screen, choose *Language* and *Keyboard* and accept the license agreement. Proceed with *Next*.

   YaST checks your partitions for already installed SUSE Linux Enterprise systems.

3. On the *Select for Upgrade* screen, select the partition to upgrade and click *Next*. YaST mounts the selected partition and displays all repositories that have been found on the partition that you want to upgrade.

4. On the *Previously Used Repositories* screen, adjust the status of the repositories: enable those you want to include in the upgrade process and disable any repositories that are no longer needed. Proceed with *Next*.

5. On the *Registration* screen, select whether to register the upgraded system now (by entering your registration data and clicking *Next*) or if to *Skip Registration*. For details on registering your system, see *Section 19.9, "Registering Your System"*.

6. Review the *Installation Settings* for the upgrade, especially the *Update Options*. Choose between the following options:

   - *Only Update Installed Packages*, in which case you might miss new features shipped with the latest SUSE Linux Enterprise version.

   - *Update with Installation of New Software and Features*. Click *Select Patterns* if you want to enable or disable patterns and packages according to your wishes.

    ### Note: Choice of Desktop

   If you used KDE before upgrading to SUSE Linux Enterprise 12 (`DEFAULT_WM` in `/etc/sysconfig/windowmanager` was set to `kde*`), your desktop environment will automatically be replaced with GNOME after the upgrade. By default, the KDM display manager will be replaced with GDM.

   To change the choice of desktop environment or window manager, adjust the software selection by clicking *Select Patterns*.

7. If all settings are according to your wishes, start the installation and removal procedure by clicking *Update*.

8. After the upgrade process was finished successfully, check for any "orphaned packages". Orphaned packages are packages which belong to no active repository anymore. The following command gives you a list of these:

```
zypper packages --orphaned
```

With this list, you can decide if a package is still needed or can be uninstalled safely.

19.7 Updating via SUSE Manager

SUSE Manager is a server solution for providing updates, patches, and security fixes for SUSE Linux Enterprise clients. It comes with a set of tools and a Web-based user interface for management tasks. See https://www.suse.com/products/suse-manager/ ↗ for more information about SUSE Manager.

SUSE Manager can support you with SP Migration or a full system upgrade.

SP Migration

SP Migration allows migrating from one Service Pack (SP) to another within one major version (for example, from SLES 12 SP1 to 12 SP2). For more information, see the *SUSE Manager Best Practices*, chapter "Client Migration", section "Migrating SUSE Linux Enterprise Server 12 or later to version 12 SP2":

https://www.suse.com/documentation/suse-manager/ ↗, version 3.1.

System Upgrade

With SUSE Manager you can perform a system upgrade. With the integrated AutoYaST technology, upgrades from one major version to the next are possible (for example, from SLES 11 SP3 to 12 SP2). For more information, see the *SUSE Manager Best Practices*, chapter "Client Migration", section "Migrating SUSE Linux Enterprise 11 SP3 to version 12 SP2":

https://www.suse.com/documentation/suse-manager/ ↗, version 3.1.

19.8 Updating Registration Status after Rollback

When performing a service pack upgrade, it is necessary to change the configuration on the registration server to provide access to the new repositories. If the upgrade process is interrupted or reverted (via restoring from a backup or snapshot), the information on the registration server is inconsistent with the status of the system. This may lead to you being prevented from accessing update repositories or to wrong repositories being used on the client.

When a rollback is done via Snapper, the system will notify the registration server to ensure access to the correct repositories is set up during the boot process. If the system was restored any other way or the communication with the registration server failed for any reason (for example, because the server was not accessible because of network issues), trigger the rollback on the client manually by calling:

```
snapper rollback
```

We suggest always checking that the correct repositories are set up on the system, especially after refreshing the service using:

```
zypper ref -s
```

This functionality is available in the `rollback-helper` package.

19.9 Registering Your System

If you skipped the registration step during the installation, you can register your system at any time using the *Product Registration* module in YaST.

Registering your systems has these advantages:

- Eligibility for support
- Availability of security updates and bug fixes
- Access to SUSE Customer Center

1. Start YaST and select *Software* > *Product Registration* to open the *Registration* dialog.

2. Provide the *E-mail* address associated with the SUSE account you or your organization uses to manage subscriptions. In case you do not have a SUSE account yet, go to the SUSE Customer Center home page (https://scc.suse.com/ ↗) to create one.

3. Enter the *Registration Code* you received with your copy of SUSE Linux Enterprise Server.

4. To start the registration, proceed with *Next*. If one or more local registration servers are available on your network, you can choose one of them from a list. Alternatively, to ignore the local registration servers and register with the default SUSE registration server, choose *Cancel*.

   During the registration, the online update repositories will be added to your upgrade setup. When finished, you can choose whether to install the latest available package versions from the update repositories. This provides a clean upgrade path for all packages and ensures that SUSE Linux Enterprise Server is upgraded with the latest security updates available. If you choose *No*, all packages will be installed from the installation media. Proceed with *Next*.

   After successful registration, YaST lists extensions, add-ons, and modules that are available for your system. To select and install them, proceed with *Section 13.1, "Installing Modules and Extensions from Online Channels"*.

20 Upgrading Online

SUSE offers an intuitive graphical and a simple command line tool to upgrade a running system to a new service pack. They provide support for "rollback" of service packs and more. This chapter explains how to do a service pack upgrade step by step with these tools.

20.1 Conceptual Overview

SUSE releases new service packs for the SUSE Linux Enterprise family at regular intervals. To make it easy for customers to migrate to a new service pack and minimize downtime, SUSE supports migrating online while the system is running.

Starting with SLE 12, YaST Wagon has been replaced by YaST migration (GUI) and Zypper migration (command line). The following features are supported:

- System always in a defined state until the first RPM is updated

- Canceling is possible until the first RPM is updated

- Simple recovery, if there is an error

- "Rollback" via system tools; no backup/restore needed

- Use of all active repositories

- The ability to skip a service pack

20.2 Service Pack Migration Workflow

A service pack migration can be executed by either YaST, **zypper**, or AutoYaST.

Before you can start a service pack migration, your system must be registered at the SUSE Customer Center or a local SMT server. SUSE Manager can also be used.

Regardless of the method, a service pack migration consists of the following steps:

1. Find possible migration targets on your registered systems.

2. Select one migration target.

3. Request and enable new repositories.

4. Run the migration.

The list of migration targets depends on the products you have installed and registered. If you have an extension installed for which the new SP is not yet available, it could be that no migration target is offered to you.

The list of migration targets available for your host will always be retrieved from the SUSE Customer Center and depend on products or extensions installed.

20.3 Canceling Service Pack Migration

A service pack migration can only be cancelled at specific stages during the migration process:

1. Until the package upgrade starts, there are only minimal changes on the system, like for services and repositories. Restore `/etc/zypp/repos.d/*` to revert to the former state.

2. After the package upgrade starts, you can revert to the former state by using a Snapper snapshot (see *Book "Administration Guide", Chapter 7 "System Recovery and Snapshot Management with Snapper"*).

3. After the migration target was selected, SUSE Customer Center changes the repository data. To revert this state manually, use **SUSEConnect** `--rollback`.

20.4 Upgrading with the Online Migration Tool (YaST)

To perform a service pack migration with YaST, use the *Online Migration* tool. By default, YaST does not install any packages from a third-party repository. If a package was installed from a third-party repository, YaST prevents packages from being replaced with the same package coming from SUSE.

 Note: Reduce Installation Size

When performing the SP migration, YaST will install all recommended packages. Especially in the case of custom minimal installations, this may increase the installation size of the system significantly.

To change this default behavior and allow only required packages, adjust `/etc/zypp/zypp.conf` and set the following variable:

```
solver.onlyRequires = true
installRecommends=false # or commented
```

This changes the behavior of all package operations, such as the installation of patches or new packages.

To start the service pack migration, do the following:

1. Deactivate all unused extensions on your registration server to avoid future dependency conflicts. In case you forget an extension, YaST will later detect unused extension repositories and deactivate them.

2. If you are logged in to a GNOME session running on the machine you are going to update, switch to a text console. Running the update from within a GNOME session is not recommended. Note that this does not apply when being logged in from a remote machine (unless you are running a VNC session with GNOME).

3. If you are an LTSS subscriber, make sure that the LTSS extension repository is active.

4. Run YaST online update to get the latest package updates for your system.

5. Install the package `yast2-migration` and its dependencies (in YaST under *Software > Software Management*).

6. Restart YaST, otherwise the newly installed module will not be shown in the control center.

7. Start in YaST *System > Online Migration*. YaST will show possible migration targets and a summary. If more than one migration target is available for your system, select one from the list.

8. Select one migration target from the list and proceed with *Next*.

9. In case the migration tool offers update repositories, it is recommended to proceed with *Yes*.

10. If the Online Migration tool finds obsolete repositories coming from DVD or a local server, it is highly recommended to disable them. Obsolete repositories are from a previous SP. Any old repositories from SCC or SMT are removed automatically.

11. Check the summary and proceed with the migration by clicking *Next*. Confirm with *Start Update*.

12. After the successful migration restart your system.

20.5 Upgrading with Zypper

To perform a service pack migration with Zypper, use the command line tool **zypper** `migration` from the package `zypper-migration-plugin`.

 Note: Reduce Installation Size

> When performing the SP migration, YaST will install all recommended packages. Especially in the case of custom minimal installations, this may increase the installation size of the system significantly.
>
> To change this default behavior and allow only required packages, adjust `/etc/zypp/zypp.conf` and set the following variable:
>
> ```
> solver.onlyRequires = true
> installRecommends=false # or commented
> ```

This changes the behavior of all package operations, such as the installation of patches or new packages. To change the behavior of Zypper for a single invocation, add the parameter `--no-recommends` to your command line.

To start the service pack migration, do the following:

1. If you are logged in to a GNOME session running on the machine you are going to update, switch to a text console. Running the update from within a GNOME session is not recommended. Note that this does not apply when being logged in from a remote machine (unless you are running a VNC session with GNOME).

2. Register your SUSE Linux Enterprise machine if you have not done so:

   ```
   sudo SUSEConnect --regcode YOUR_REGISTRATION_CODE
   ```

3. If you are an LTSS subscriber, make sure that the LTSS extension repository is active.

4. Install the latest updates:

```
sudo zypper patch
```

5. Install the `zypper-migration-plugin` package and its dependencies:

```
sudo zypper in zypper-migration-plugin
```

6. Run **zypper** `migration`:

```
tux > sudo zypper migration
Executing 'zypper  patch-check'

Refreshing service 'SUSE_Linux_Enterprise_Server_12_x86_64'.
Loading repository data...
Reading installed packages...
0 patches needed (0 security patches)

Available migrations:

    1 | SUSE Linux Enterprise Server 12 SP1 x86_64
    2 | SUSE Linux Enterprise Server 12 SP2 x86_64
```

Some notes about the migration process:

- If more than one migration target is available for your system, Zypper allows you to select one SP from the list. This is the same as skipping one or more SPs. Keep in mind, online migration for base products (SLES, SLED) remains available only between the SPs of a major version.

- By default, Zypper uses the option `--no-allow-vendor-change` which is passed to **zypper** `dup`. If a package was installed from a third-party repository, this option prevents packages from being replaced with the same package coming from SUSE.

- If Zypper finds obsolete repositories coming from DVD or a local server, it is highly recommended to disable them. Old SCC or SMT repositories are removed automatically.

7. Review all the changes, especially the packages that are going to be removed. Proceed by typing y (the exact number of packages to upgrade can vary on your system):

```
266 packages to upgrade, 54 to downgrade, 17 new, 8 to reinstall, 5 to remove, 1 to
 change arch.
```

```
Overall download size: 285.1 MiB. Already cached: 0 B  After the operation,
 additional 139.8 MiB will be used.
Continue? [y/n/? shows all options] (y):
```

Use the Shift - Page ↑ or Shift - Page ↓ keys to scroll in your shell.

8. After successful migration restart your system.

20.6 Upgrading with Plain Zypper

If you cannot use YaST migration or the Zypper migration, you can still migrate with plain Zypper and some manual interactions. To start a service pack migration, do the following:

1. If you are logged in to a GNOME session running on the machine you are going to update, switch to a text console. Running the update from within a GNOME session is not recommended. Note that this does not apply when being logged in from a remote machine (unless you are running a VNC session with GNOME).

2. Update the package management tools with the old SUSE Linux Enterprise repositories:

   ```
   sudo zypper patch --updatestack-only
   ```

3. If the system is registered, it needs to be deregistered:

   ```
   sudo SUSEConnect --de-register
   ```

4. Remove the old installation sources and repositories and adjust the third-party repositories.

5. Add the new installation sources, be it local or remote sources (for the placeholder *RE-POSITORY*, refer to *Section 17.6, "Repository Model"*):

   ```
   sudo zypper addrepo REPOSITORY
   ```

   You can also use SUSE Customer Center or Subscription Management Tool. The command for SUSE Linux Enterprise 12 SP1 on x86-64 is:

   ```
   sudo SUSEConnect -p SLES/12.2/x86_64 OPTIONS
   ```

   Keep in mind, cross-architecture upgrades are not supported.

   Zypper will display a conflict between the old and new kernel. Choose Solution 1 to continue.

```
Problem: product:SLES-12.2-0.x86_64 conflicts with kernel < 4.4 provided by kernel-
default-VERSION
 Solution 1: Following actions will be done:
  replacement of kernel-default-VERSION with kernel-default-VERSION
  deinstallation of kernel-default-VERSION
 Solution 2: do not install product:SLES-12.2-0.x86_64
```

6. Finalize the migration:

```
sudo zypper ref -f -s
sudo zypper dup --no-allow-vendor-change --no-recommends
```

The first command will update all services and repositories. The second command performs a distribution upgrade. Here, the last two options are important: -no-allow-vendor-change ensures that third-party RPMs will not overwrite RPMs from the base system. The option --no-recommends ensures that packages deselected during initial installation will not be added again.

20.7   Rolling Back a Service Pack

If a service pack does not work for you, SUSE Linux Enterprise supports reverting the system to the state before the service pack migration was started. Prerequisite is a Btrfs root partition with snapshots enabled (this is the default when installing SLES 12). See *Book "Administration Guide", Chapter 7 "System Recovery and Snapshot Management with Snapper"* for details.

1. Get a list of all Snapper snapshots:

```
sudo snapper list
```

Review the output to locate the snapshot that was created immediately before the service pack migration was started. The column *Description* contains a corresponding statement and the snapshot is marked as important in the column *Userdata*. Memorize the snapshot number from the column # and its date from the column *Date*.

2. Reboot the system. From the boot menu, select *Start boot loader from a read-only snapshot* and then choose the snapshot with the date and number you memorized in the previous step. A second boot menu (the one from the snapshot) is loaded. Select the entry starting with SLES 12 and boot it.

3. The system boots into the previous state with the system partition mounted read-only. Log in as <u>root</u> and check whether you have chosen the correct snapshot. Also make sure everything works as expected. Note that since the root file system is mounted read-only, restrictions in functionality may apply.

In case of problems or if you have booted the wrong snapshot, reboot and choose a different snapshot to boot from—up to this point no permanent changes have been made. If the snapshot is correct and works as expected, make the change permanent by running the following command:

```
snapper rollback
```

Reboot afterward. On the boot screen, choose the default boot entry to reboot into the reinstated system.

4. Check if the repository configuration has been properly reset. Furthermore, check if all products are properly registered. If either one is not the case, updating the system at a later point in time may no longer work, or the system may be updated using the wrong package repositories.

Make sure the system can access the Internet before starting this procedure.

a. Refresh services and repositories by running

```
sudo zypper ref -fs
```

b. Get a list of active repositories by running

```
sudo zypper lr
```

Carefully check the output of this command. No services and repositories that were added for the update should be listed. If you, for example, are rolling back from a service pack migration from SLES 12 SP1 to SLES 12 SP2, the list must *not* contain the repositories `SLES12-SP2-Pool` and `SLES12-SP2-Updates`, but rather the `SP1` versions.

If wrong repositories are listed, delete them and, if necessary, replace them with the versions matching your product or service pack version. For a list of repositories for the supported migration paths refer to *Section 17.6, "Repository Model"*.

c. Last, check the registration status for all products installed by running

```
SUSEConnect --status
```

All products should be reported as being `Registered`. If this is not the case, repair the registration by running

```
SUSEConnect --rollback
```

Now you have successfully reverted the system to the state that was captured immediately before the service pack migration was started.

21 Backporting Source Code

SUSE extensively uses backports, for example for the migration of current software fixes and features into released SUSE Linux Enterprise packages. The information in this chapter explains why it can be misleading to compare version numbers to judge the capabilities and the security of SUSE Linux Enterprise software packages. This chapter also explains how SUSE keeps the system software secure and current while maintaining compatibility for your application software on top of SUSE Linux Enterprise products. You will also learn how to check which public security issues actually are addressed in your SUSE Linux Enterprise system software, and the current status of your software.

21.1 Reasons for Backporting

Upstream developers are primarily concerned with advancing the software they develop. Often they combine fixing bugs with introducing new features which have not yet received extensive testing and which may introduce new bugs.

For distribution developers, it is important to distinguish between:

* bugfixes with a limited potential for disrupting functionality; and

* changes that may disrupt existing functionality.

Usually, distribution developers do not follow all upstream changes when a package has become part of a released distribution. Usually they stick instead with the upstream version that they initially released and create patches based on upstream changes to fix bugs. This practice is known as *backporting*.

Distribution developers generally will only introduce a newer version of software in two cases:

* when the changes between their packages and the upstream versions have become so large that backporting is no longer feasible, or

* for software that inherently ages badly, like anti-malware software.

SUSE uses backports extensively as we strike a good balance between several concerns for enterprise software. The most important of them are:

- Having stable interfaces (APIs) that software vendors can rely on when building products for use on SUSE's enterprise products.

- Ensuring that packages used in the release of SUSE's enterprise products are of the highest quality and have been thoroughly tested, both in themselves and as part of the whole enterprise product.

- Maintaining the various certifications of SUSE's enterprise products by other vendors, like certifications for Oracle or SAP products.

- Allowing SUSE's developers to focus on making the next version of the product as good as they can make it, rather than them having to spread their focus thinly across a wide range of releases.

- Keeping a clear view of what is in a particular enterprise release, so that our support can provide accurate and timely information about it.

21.2   Reasons against Backports

It is a general policy rule that no new upstream versions of a package are introduced into our enterprise products. This rule is not an absolute rule however. For certain types of packages, in particular anti-virus software, security concerns weigh heavier than the conservative approach that is preferable from the perspective of quality assurance. For packages in that class, occasionally newer versions are introduced into a released version of an enterprise product line.

Sometimes also for other types of packages the choice is made to introduce a new version rather than a backport. This is done when producing a backport is not economically feasible or when there is a very relevant technical reason to introduce the newer version.

21.3   The Implications of Backports for Interpreting Version Numbers

Because of the practice of backporting, one cannot simply compare version numbers to determine whether a SUSE package contains a fix for a particular issue or has had a particular feature added to it. With backporting, the upstream part of a SUSE package's version number merely indicates what upstream version the SUSE package is based on. It may contain bug fixes and features that are not in the corresponding upstream release, but that have been backported into the SUSE package.

One particular area where this limited value of version numbers when backporting is involved can cause problems is with security scanning tools. Some security vulnerability scanning tools (or particular tests in such tools) operate solely on version information. These tools and tests are therefore prone to generating "false positives" (when a piece of software is incorrectly identified as vulnerable) when backports are involved. When evaluating reports from security scanning tools, always check whether an entry is based on a version number or on an actual vulnerability test.

21.4 How to Check Which Bugs are Fixed and Which Features are Backported and Available

There are several locations where information regarding backported bug fixes and features are stored:

- The package's changelog:

```
rpm -q --changelog name-of-installed-package
rpm -qp --changelog packagefile.rpm
```

  The output briefly documents the change history of the package.

- The package changelog may contain entries like bsc#1234 ("Bugzilla Suse.Com") that refer to bugs in SUSE's Bugzilla tracking system or links to other bugtracking systems. Because of confidentiality policies, not all such information may be accessible to you.

- A package may contain a /usr/share/doc/PACKAGENAME/README.SUSE file which contains general, high-level information specific to the SUSE package.

- The RPM source package contains the patches that were applied during the building of the regular binary RPMs as separate files that can be interpreted if you are familiar with reading source code. See Book "Administration Guide", Chapter 6 "Managing Software with Command Line Tools", Section 6.1.2.5 "Installing or Downloading Source Packages" for installing sources of SUSE Linux Enterprise software, see Book "Administration Guide", Chapter 6 "Managing Software with Command Line Tools", Section 6.2.5 "Installing and Compiling Source Packages" for building packages on SUSE Linux Enterprise and see the Maximum RPM (http://www.rpm.org/max-rpm/)↗ book for the inner workings of SUSE Linux Enterprise software package builds.

- For security bug fixes, consult the SUSE security announcements (http://www.suse.com/support/security/#1)↗. These often refer to bugs through standardized names like CAN-2005-2495 which are maintained by the Common Vulnerabilities and Exposures (CVE) (http://cve.mitre.org)↗ project.

A Documentation Updates

This chapter lists content changes for this document.

This manual was updated on the following dates:

A.1 September 2017 (Initial Release of SUSE Linux Enterprise Server 12 SP3)

General

- Numerous small fixes and additions to the documentation, based on technical feedback.

- Removed all references to the `faillog` package, which is no longer shipped (https://bugzilla.suse.com/show_bug.cgi?id=710788).

Chapter 6, Installation with YaST

In *Section 6.6, "IBM z Systems: Disk Activation"*, adjusted a link to point to a more appropriate section in the *Storage Administration Guide* (https://bugzilla.suse.com/show_bug.cgi?id=1042060).

- Removed all documentation about connecting to a VNC server with a Java-capable browser. Java is no longer supported by most browsers for security reasons.

- Modified PXE boot to accommodate UEFI (https://bugzilla.suse.com/show_bug.cgi?id=1006558 ↗).

- Added *Section 8.9, "Booting from CD or USB Drive Instead of PXE"*.

Chapter 13, Installing Modules, Extensions, and Third Party Add-On Products

- Moved *Section 13.4, "SUSE Package Hub"* from the chapter *Chapter 6, Installation with YaST* to this chapter.

- In *Section 13.3, "SUSE Software Development Kit (SDK) 12 SP3"*, added information about the support status of the SDK.

- In *Procedure 13.1, "Installing Add-ons and Extensions from Online Channels with YaST"*, mentioned new entry in YaST to directly install extensions and modules (Fate #321044).

Chapter 17, Life Cycle and Support

- In *Section 17.6, "Repository Model"*, updated repository model with SLE 12 SP3.

- Added *Section 17.4, "Generating Periodic Life Cycle Report"* (Fate #322059).

- In *Section 17.6.3, "Module-Specific Repositories for SUSE Linux Enterprise Server"*, mentioned that a certain module is not available on POWER (https://bugzilla.suse.com/show_bug.cgi?id=1048670 ↗).

- In *Section 17.6.6, "Origin of Packages"*, rephrased a sentence (https://bugzilla.suse.com/show_bug.cgi?id=1048672 ↗).

Chapter 18, Upgrading SUSE Linux Enterprise

- Updated *Figure 18.1, "Overview of Shortest Upgrade Paths"*.

- Added information about offline and online upgrading methods to *Section 18.2, "Online and Offline Upgrade"*.

- Added backup of package and repository list to *Section 18.3.3.1, "Listing Installed Packages and Repositories"*.

- Mentioned zypper and YaST as the suggested methods for Service Pack migration in *Section 18.2, "Online and Offline Upgrade"*.

- **Added** *Note: Amount of Packages Increases with an Update to a new Major Release* (https://bugzilla.suse.com/show_bug.cgi?id=1045649 ↗).

- Corrected terminology in the introduction to the chapter (https://bugzilla.suse.com/show_bug.cgi?id=1048680 ↗).

- **In** *Section 18.1, "Supported Upgrade Paths to SLE 12 SP3"*, **added missing version numbers** (https://bugzilla.suse.com/show_bug.cgi?id=1048675 ↗).

- **Added** *Section 18.3.1, "Make Sure the Current System is Up-To-Date"* (https://bugzilla.suse.com/show_bug.cgi?id=1051670 ↗).

Chapter 19, Upgrading Offline

- Added information about migration options with SUSE Manager, see *Section 19.7, "Updating via SUSE Manager"* (https://bugzilla.suse.com/show_bug.cgi?id=1035716 ↗).

- **In** *Section 19.4.1, "Automated Migration from SUSE Linux Enterprise 11 SP3 or SP4 to SUSE Linux Enterprise 12 SP2"*, **mentioned that DVD or ISO are needed.**

Chapter 20, Upgrading Online

- When upgrading with plain zypper, a solution for a kernel version conflict needs to be picked, see *Section 20.6, "Upgrading with Plain Zypper"* (https://bugzilla.suse.com/show_bug.cgi?id=1032595 ↗).

- Automatic LUN scanning on z Systems only works with NPIV enabled, see *Section 6.6.2, "Configuring zFCP Disks"*.

- SCC, SMT and SUMA repositories can be used for online migration, see *Section 20.2, "Service Pack Migration Workflow"* **(Doc Comment #32436).**

Bugfixes

- In *Section 6.2.2.2, "The Boot Screen on Machines Equipped with UEFI"*, fixed a typo in an installation entry example (https://bugzilla.suse.com/show_bug.cgi?id=1051387 ↗).

A.2 April 2017 (Maintenance Release of SUSE Linux Enterprise Server 12 SP2)

Chapter 4, Installation on IBM z Systems

- Mentioned possibility of using `susehmc.ins` (https://bugzilla.suse.com/show_bug.cgi?id=1009081 ↗).

Section 17.3, "Module Life Cycles"

- Added link to Module Life Cycles Web site (https://bugzilla.suse.com/show_bug.cgi?id=1014266 ↗).

Bugfixes

- Explicitly advised not to specify other repositories with the self-update parameter than the installer self-update one. In addition, specified how to enable such repository in SMT (https://bugzilla.suse.com/show_bug.cgi?id=1015481 ↗).

A.3 November 2016 (Initial Release of SUSE Linux Enterprise Server 12 SP2)

General

- The e-mail address for documentation feedback has changed to `doc-team@suse.com`.

- The documentation for Docker has been enhanced and renamed to *Docker Guide*.

General Changes to this Guide

- The complete guide has been revised, restructured, and flattened (Fate #319115).

- *Chapter 5, Installation on ARM AArch64* has been added (Fate #318444).

- Updates and corrections on installation with Kimchi (https://bugzil-la.suse.com/show_bug.cgi?id=979054 ↗).

- linuxrc now suggests default values (Fate #318453).

- Added documentation for installing KVM guests on IBM z Systems (https://bugzil-la.suse.com/show_bug.cgi?id=958733 ↗).

Chapter 4, Installation on IBM z Systems

- linuxrc no longer asks for a portname (Fate #320112).

- linuxrc now suggests default values (Fate #318453).

- Added documentation for installing KVM guests on IBM z Systems (https://bugzil-la.suse.com/show_bug.cgi?id=958733 ↗).

Chapter 6, Installation with YaST

- Added a tip on how to access network storage to *Section 6.7, "Network Settings"*.

- Dialog options for creating an encrypted LVM file system (*Section 6.11, "Suggested Partitioning"*) have changed (Fate #320418).

- Added a note on `cio_ignore` to *Section 6.16.1, "IBM z Systems: IPLing the Installed System"*.

- The *Receive System Mail* has been removed from the *Add User* dialog (Fate #320448).

- Added *Section 6.2.3.6, "Enabling the Installer Self-Update"*.

- zKVM machines are shut down at the end of the installation (https://bugzil-la.suse.com/show_bug.cgi?id=992081 ↗).

- Updated list of modules, see *Section 17.6, "Repository Model"* (Fate #320579).

Chapter 20, Upgrading Online

- Added *Section 18.3.6, "Create Non-MD5 Server Certificates for Java Applications"* (https://bugzilla.suse.com/show_bug.cgi?id=970153 ↗).

- Added a conceptual overview and mentioned additional migration strategies (https://bugzilla.suse.com/show_bug.cgi?id=968195 ↗).

- Added *Section 19.8, "Updating Registration Status after Rollback"* (Fate #319118).

- Added *Section 18.3.8, "Check the* `clientSetup4SMT.sh` *Script on SMT Clients"* (https://bugzilla.suse.com/show_bug.cgi?id=944342 ↗).

- Implemented a notice to make sure a service pack migration is not performed with insufficient disk space (Fate #317784, see *Section 18.3.9, "Disk Space"*).

- Mentioned that during installation, an installation resource is added and removed afterward (Fate #320494).

Bugfixes

- Removed link (https://bugzilla.suse.com/show_bug.cgi?id=972355 ↗).

- Added documentation for installing KVM guests on IBM z Systems (https://bugzilla.suse.com/show_bug.cgi?id=958733 ↗).

- Added note about where to place `/boot` for an LVM root file system (https://bugzilla.suse.com/show_bug.cgi?id=1000631 ↗).

- Added more information about rolling back a service pack (https://bugzilla.suse.com/show_bug.cgi?id=1001070 ↗).

- Added recommendations for the case of running an update from within a GNOME session (https://bugzilla.suse.com/show_bug.cgi?id=1001684 ↗).

A.4 March 2016 (Maintenance Release of SUSE Linux Enterprise Server 12 SP1)

Chapter 4, Installation on IBM z Systems

- Mentioned requirement for a local X server and instructions for Microsoft Windows (https://bugzilla.suse.com/show_bug.cgi?id=956059 ↗).

- Renamed `zpxe.exec` to `zpxe.rexx` and rephrased sentence regarding correct place (https://bugzilla.suse.com/show_bug.cgi?id=867809 ↗).

- Added note about z/VM 6.3 regarding installation of APAR VM65419 (https://bugzilla.suse.com/show_bug.cgi?id=958054 ↗).

Chapter 11, Advanced Disk Setup

- Distinguished between remote and local repository more clearly (https://bugzilla.suse.com/show_bug.cgi?id=956058 ↗).

- Added note about reformatting partitions with `mkswap`, because initrd image cannot boot up when swap partition has changed (https://bugzilla.suse.com/show_bug.cgi?id=955822 ↗).

A.5 December 2015 (Initial Release of SUSE Linux Enterprise Server 12 SP1)

General

- *Book "Subscription Management Tool for SLES 12 SP3"* is now part of the documentation for SUSE Linux Enterprise Server.

- Add-ons provided by SUSE have been renamed as modules and extensions. The manuals have been updated to reflect this change.

- Numerous small fixes and additions to the documentation, based on technical feedback.

- The registration service has been changed from Novell Customer Center to SUSE Customer Center.

- In YaST, you will now reach *Network Settings* via the *System* group. *Network Devices* is gone (https://bugzilla.suse.com/show_bug.cgi?id=867809 ↗).

Chapter 2, Installation on AMD64 and Intel 64

- Removed pointers to the *Failsafe* boot option, which has been removed (Fate #317016).

Chapter 4, Installation on IBM z Systems

- Added installation instruction for KVM guests (Fate #319264).

- **Added** *Section 4.2.7, "The SUSE Linux Enterprise Server Boot Procedure on IBM z Systems".*

Chapter 6, Installation with YaST

- **Added** *Section 6.2.3.4, "Using a Proxy During the Installation"* (Fate #318488).

- Added a warning on using unsigned drivers in secure boot mode to *Section 6.2.2.2, "The Boot Screen on Machines Equipped with UEFI"* (Fate #317593).

- Added *Section 12.2.4.1, "Handling of Package Recommendations"* (Fate #318099).

Chapter 13, Installing Modules, Extensions, and Third Party Add-On Products

- Updated chapter to reflect the software changes to the former YaST *SUSE Customer Center Configuration* dialog (now called *Product Registration*) and the YaST *Add-On Products* module (Fate #318800).

Chapter 11, Advanced Disk Setup

- Mentioned that subvolumes for `/var/lib/mariadb`, `/var/lib/pgsql`, and `/var/lib/libvirt/images` are created with the option `no copy on write` by default to avoid extensive fragmenting with Btrfs.

Subscription Management

- The chapter about registering clients at a Subscription Management Tool server has been replaced by *Book "Subscription Management Tool for SLES 12 SP3", Chapter 8 "Configuring Clients to Use SMT"*.

Part VI, "Updating and Upgrading SUSE Linux Enterprise"

- Split former update chapter into several independent chapters and combined them under this new part.

- Removed YaST Wagon chapter, as YaST Wagon is unsupported for SUSE Linux Enterprise Server 12 SP3.

- Added new chapter: *Chapter 20, Upgrading Online*.

- Added *Section 18.3.4, "Migrate your MySQL Database"* and *Section 18.3.5, "Migrate your PostgreSQL Database"*.

- Integrated various new features: Fate #315161, Fate #318636, Fate #319128, Fate #319129, Fate #319138, Fate #319140.

Bugfixes

- Fixed path to `zpxe.exec` (https://bugzilla.suse.com/show_bug.cgi?id=937511 ↗).

- Added the `https` protocol to *Section 4.3.3, "Specifying the Installation Source and YaST Interface"* (https://bugzilla.suse.com/show_bug.cgi?id=951421 ↗).

- Consistent use of `yast`, `yast2.ssh`, `yast.ssh` for SSH based installation (https://bugzilla.suse.com/show_bug.cgi?id=956060 ⁊).

- Consistent spelling of boot parameters (https://bugzilla.suse.com/show_bug.cgi?id=956054 ⁊).

- PowerKVM: virt-install does not know about SLES12 (https://bugzilla.suse.com/show_bug.cgi?id=880918 ⁊).

- IBM POWER: Starting an X-Server after an Upgrade (https://bugzilla.suse.com/show_bug.cgi?id=948980 ⁊).

- Added documentation on the boot process for IBM z Systems (https://bugzilla.suse.com/show_bug.cgi?id=942772 ⁊).

- Description of encrypted / and /boot on Btrfs was missing. Added an important note in *Section 6.11, "Suggested Partitioning"* and *Section 11.1.2.1, "Btrfs Partitioning"* (https://bugzilla.suse.com/show_bug.cgi?id=926951 ⁊).

- Zypper multiversion kernels should be mentioned for SP2 Update (https://bugzilla.suse.com/show_bug.cgi?id=753809 ⁊).

- SLES 12 Deployment Guide errors for zPXE installations (https://bugzilla.suse.com/show_bug.cgi?id=944384 ⁊).

- AutoYaST hangs at "Configuring Bootloader ... 50%" with 512RAM (https://bugzilla.suse.com/show_bug.cgi?id=927237 ⁊).

- Netsetup Parameters Wrong (https://bugzilla.suse.com/show_bug.cgi?id=928792 ⁊).

- Documentation on not creating /usr as separate partition is missing (https://bugzilla.suse.com/show_bug.cgi?id=930267 ⁊).

- Document how to enable SELinux during install (https://bugzilla.suse.com/show_bug.cgi?id=928153 ⁊).

- YaST boot loader: supported scenarios needs updating clarification (https://bugzilla.suse.com/show_bug.cgi?id=939197 ⁊).

A.6 February 2015 (Documentation Maintenance Update)

Section 6.12, "Clock and Time Zone"

With NTP disabled it is recommended to avoid writing system time to the hardware clock. Thus set `SYSTOHC=no`.

Bugfixes

* Adjustments for SMT because of the switch from SUSE Customer Center to SUSE Customer Center (https://bugzilla.suse.com/show_bug.cgi?id=857639 ⌐).

* *Section 15.3.2, "Enforcing Password Policies"*: Password Settings, Expiration Date is expiring user accounts in YaST Users module (https://bugzilla.suse.com/show_bug.cgi?id=743874 ⌐).

* Various bugfixes for *Chapter 18, Upgrading SUSE Linux Enterprise*:

  * The named upgrade path does not work, there is no working upgrade path from SLES 11 SP3 to SLES 12 on Linux for System z (https://bugzilla.suse.com/show_bug.cgi?id=907648 ⌐).

  * The Atomic Update (https://bugzilla.suse.com/show_bug.cgi?id=905330 ⌐).

  * Upgrading to SLE 12 (https://bugzilla.suse.com/show_bug.cgi?id=904188 ⌐).

  * Intermediate step: Updating SLE 11 SP2 to SLE 11 SP3 (https://bugzilla.suse.com/show_bug.cgi?id=904186 ⌐).

  * Supported Upgrade Paths to SLE (https://bugzilla.suse.com/show_bug.cgi?id=904182 ⌐).

  * Potentially misleading info around the 6-month overlap in support (https://bugzilla.suse.com/show_bug.cgi?id=902463 ⌐).

A.7 October 2014 (Initial Release of SUSE Linux Enterprise Server 12)

General

- Removed all KDE documentation and references because KDE is no longer shipped.

- Removed all references to SuSEconfig, which is no longer supported (Fate #100011).

- Move from System V init to systemd (Fate #310421). Updated affected parts of the documentation.

- YaST Runlevel Editor has changed to Services Manager (Fate #312568). Updated affected parts of the documentation.

- Removed all references to ISDN support, as ISDN support has been removed (Fate #314594).

- Removed all references to the YaST DSL module as it is no longer shipped (Fate #316264).

- Removed all references to the YaST Modem module as it is no longer shipped (Fate #316264).

- Btrfs has become the default file system for the root partition (Fate #315901). Updated affected parts of the documentation.

- The **dmesg** now provides human-readable time stamps in `ctime()` -like format (Fate #316056). Updated affected parts of the documentation.

- syslog and syslog-ng have been replaced by rsyslog (Fate #316175). Updated affected parts of the documentation.

- MariaDB is now shipped as the relational database instead of MySQL (Fate #313595). Updated affected parts of the documentation.

- SUSE-related products are no longer available from http://download.novell.com ↗ but from http://download.suse.com ↗. Adjusted links accordingly.

- Novell Customer Center has been replaced with SUSE Customer Center. Updated affected parts of the documentation.

- /var/run is mounted as tmpfs (Fate #303793). Updated affected parts of the documentation.

- The following architectures are no longer supported: IA64 and x86. Updated affected parts of the documentation.

- The traditional method for setting up the network with `ifconfig` has been replaced by `wicked`. Updated affected parts of the documentation.

- A lot of networking commands are deprecated and have been replaced by newer commands (usually **ip**). Updated affected parts of the documentation.

  `arp`: **ip neighbor**
  `ifconfig`: **ip addr**, **ip link**
  `iptunnel`: **ip tunnel**
  `iwconfig`: **iw**
  `nameif`: **ip link**, **ifrename**
  `netstat`: **ss**, **ip route**, **ip -s link**, **ip maddr**
  `route`: **ip route**

- Numerous small fixes and additions to the documentation, based on technical feedback.

Chapter 2, Installation on AMD64 and Intel 64

- Updated system requirements.

Chapter 3, Installation on IBM POWER

- Added POWER8 to the list of supported hardware (Fate #315272).

- SUSE Linux Enterprise Server 12 for POWER has moved to Little Endian. Updated affected parts of the documentation.

Chapter 4, Installation on IBM z Systems

- Updated the list of supported platforms: Removed IBM Series z9 and z10 machines and added IBM zEnterprise BC12.

- Updated the memory and disk space requirements.

- Removed instructions on how to IPL from tape—this is no longer supported.

- Rewrote large parts of *Section 4.2.5, "Network Configuration"* to remove redundant information and make it more concise.

- Removed references to Token Ring, which is no longer supported (Fate #313154).

Chapter 6, Installation with YaST

- Completely rewrote the chapter because of the new installation workflow.

- The installation routine now supports setting up multiple network devices during the installation (Fate #315680): *Section 6.7, "Network Settings"*.

- The installation proposal contains a separate `/home` partition formatted with XFS (Fate #316637 and Fate #316624): *Section 6.11, "Suggested Partitioning"*.

- Removed occurrences of the YaST Repair module which has been dropped (Fate #308670).

- Update repositories are added after having registered with SUSE Customer Center and can be used during installation (Fate #312012): *Section 6.9, "Extension Selection"*.

- Extensions and modules can be added to the system during the installation (Fate #316548): *Section 6.8, "SUSE Customer Center Registration"*.

- SUSE Linux Enterprise Desktop can be installed as an add-on on top of SUSE Linux Enterprise Server (Fate #316436): *Section 6.9, "Extension Selection"*.

- The HW crypto stack for IBM z Systems can be selected for installation via a pattern (Fate #316143): *Section 6.15.1, "Software"*.

- Automatically importing SSH keys from a previous installation can be disabled (Fate #314982).

Chapter 18, Upgrading SUSE Linux Enterprise

- Added new section: *Section 18.2, "Online and Offline Upgrade"*.

Chapter 10, Setting Up Hardware Components with YaST

- Removed the following sections as the respective YaST modules are no longer included: *Hardware Information, Setting Up Graphics Card and Monitor, Mouse Model,* and *Setting Up a Scanner.*

- Removed content about mouse setup and adjusted *Section 10.1, "Setting Up Your System Keyboard Layout"*.

- Completely rewrote *Section 12.4, "Keeping the System Up-to-date"* because of changes in the GNOME software updater.

- Installing add-on products or software extensions is now also possible without access to physical media. Added the following new sections: *Section 19.9, "Registering Your System"* and *Section 13.1, "Installing Modules and Extensions from Online Channels"*. Modified *Section 13.2, "Installing Extensions and Third Party Add-On Products from Media"* accordingly.

Subscription Management

- For registering clients against an SMT server, **suse_register** has been replaced with **SUSEConnect** (Fate #316585).

Bugfixes

- Updated section *Section 12.4, "Keeping the System Up-to-date"* according to http://bugzilla.suse.com/show_bug.cgi?id=839692 ↗.

- Removed section *Using Fingerprint Authentication.* Further minor corrections and additions (http://bugzilla.suse.com/show_bug.cgi?id=857680 ↗).

- Removed obsolete parameter OsaMedium from parmfile and Cobbler examples (http://bugzilla.suse.com/show_bug.cgi?id=860404 ↗).

- Added instructions on how to add secondary languages during installation (http://bugzilla.suse.com/show_bug.cgi?id=870482 ↗).

- Multiversion feature (more than one kernel installed) is enabled by default (http://bugzilla.suse.com/show_bug.cgi?id=891805 ↗).

- Warn about incompatible Kernel Module Packages (KPMs) (http://bugzilla.suse.com/show_bug.cgi?id=891805 ↗).

B GNU Licenses

This appendix contains the GNU Free Documentation License version 1.2.

GNU Free Documentation License

Copyright (C) 2000, 2001, 2002 Free Software Foundation, Inc. 51 Franklin St, Fifth Floor, Boston, MA 02110-1301 USA. Everyone is permitted to copy and distribute verbatim copies of this license document, but changing it is not allowed.

0. PREAMBLE

The purpose of this License is to make a manual, textbook, or other functional and useful document "free" in the sense of freedom: to assure everyone the effective freedom to copy and redistribute it, with or without modifying it, either commercially or non-commercially. Secondarily, this License preserves for the author and publisher a way to get credit for their work, while not being considered responsible for modifications made by others.

This License is a kind of "copyleft", which means that derivative works of the document must themselves be free in the same sense. It complements the GNU General Public License, which is a copyleft license designed for free software.

We have designed this License to use it for manuals for free software, because free software needs free documentation: a free program should come with manuals providing the same freedoms that the software does. But this License is not limited to software manuals; it can be used for any textual work, regardless of subject matter or whether it is published as a printed book. We recommend this License principally for works whose purpose is instruction or reference.

1. APPLICABILITY AND DEFINITIONS

This License applies to any manual or other work, in any medium, that contains a notice placed by the copyright holder saying it can be distributed under the terms of this License. Such a notice grants a world-wide, royalty-free license, unlimited in duration, to use that work under the conditions stated herein. The "Document", below, refers to any such manual or work. Any member of the public is a licensee, and is addressed as "you". You accept the license if you copy, modify or distribute the work in a way requiring permission under copyright law.

A "Modified Version" of the Document means any work containing the Document or a portion of it, either copied verbatim, or with modifications and/or translated into another language.

A "Secondary Section" is a named appendix or a front-matter section of the Document that deals exclusively with the relationship of the publishers or authors of the Document to the Document's overall subject (or to related matters) and contains nothing that could fall directly within that overall subject. (Thus, if the Document is in part a textbook of mathematics, a Secondary Section may not explain any mathematics.) The relationship could be a matter of historical connection with the subject or with related matters, or of legal, commercial, philosophical, ethical or political position regarding them.

The "Invariant Sections" are certain Secondary Sections whose titles are designated, as being those of Invariant Sections, in the notice that says that the Document is released under this License. If a section does not fit the above definition of Secondary then it is not allowed to be designated as Invariant. The Document may contain zero Invariant Sections. If the Document does not identify any Invariant Sections then there are none.

The "Cover Texts" are certain short passages of text that are listed, as Front-Cover Texts or Back-Cover Texts, in the notice that says that the Document is released under this License. A Front-Cover Text may be at most 5 words, and a Back-Cover Text may be at most 25 words.

A "Transparent" copy of the Document means a machine-readable copy, represented in a format whose specification is available to the general public, that is suitable for revising the document straightforwardly with generic text editors or (for images composed of pixels) generic paint programs or (for drawings) some widely available drawing editor, and that is suitable for input to text formatters or for automatic translation to a variety of formats suitable for input to text formatters. A copy made in an otherwise Transparent file format whose markup, or absence of markup, has been arranged to thwart or discourage subsequent modification by readers is not Transparent. An image format is not Transparent if used for any substantial amount of text. A copy that is not "Transparent" is called "Opaque".

Examples of suitable formats for Transparent copies include plain ASCII without markup, Texinfo input format, LaTeX input format, SGML or XML using a publicly available DTD, and standard-conforming simple HTML, PostScript or PDF designed for human modification. Examples of transparent image formats include PNG, XCF and JPG. Opaque formats include proprietary formats that can be read and edited only by proprietary word processors, SGML or XML for which the DTD and/or processing tools are not generally available, and the machine-generated HTML, PostScript or PDF produced by some word processors for output purposes only.

The "Title Page" means, for a printed book, the title page itself, plus such following pages as are needed to hold, legibly, the material this License requires to appear in the title page. For works in formats which do not have any title page as such, "Title Page" means the text near the most prominent appearance of the work's title, preceding the beginning of the body of the text.

A section "Entitled XYZ" means a named subunit of the Document whose title either is precisely XYZ or contains XYZ in parentheses following text that translates XYZ in another language. (Here XYZ stands for a specific section name mentioned below, such as "Acknowledgements", "Dedications", "Endorsements", or "History".) To "Preserve the Title" of such a section when you modify the Document means that it remains a section "Entitled XYZ" according to this definition.

The Document may include Warranty Disclaimers next to the notice which states that this License applies to the Document. These Warranty Disclaimers are considered to be included by reference in this License, but only as regards disclaiming warranties: any other implication that these Warranty Disclaimers may have is void and has no effect on the meaning of this License.

2. VERBATIM COPYING

You may copy and distribute the Document in any medium, either commercially or non-commercially, provided that this License, the copyright notices, and the license notice saying this License applies to the Document are reproduced in all copies, and that you add no other conditions whatsoever to those of this License. You may not use technical measures to obstruct or control the reading or further copying of the copies you make or distribute. However, you may accept compensation in exchange for copies. If you distribute a large enough number of copies you must also follow the conditions in section 3.

You may also lend copies, under the same conditions stated above, and you may publicly display copies.

3. COPYING IN QUANTITY

If you publish printed copies (or copies in media that commonly have printed covers) of the Document, numbering more than 100, and the Document's license notice requires Cover Texts, you must enclose the copies in covers that carry, clearly and legibly, all these Cover Texts: Front-Cover Texts on the front cover, and Back-Cover Texts on the back cover. Both covers must also clearly and legibly identify you as the publisher of these copies. The front cover must present the full title with all words of the title equally prominent and visible. You may add other material on the covers in addition. Copying with changes limited to the covers, as long as they preserve the title of the Document and satisfy these conditions, can be treated as verbatim copying in other respects.

If the required texts for either cover are too voluminous to fit legibly, you should put the first ones listed (as many as fit reasonably) on the actual cover, and continue the rest onto adjacent pages.

If you publish or distribute Opaque copies of the Document numbering more than 100, you must either include a machine-readable Transparent copy along with each Opaque copy, or state in or with each Opaque copy a computer-network location from which the general network-using public has access to download using public-standard network protocols a complete Transparent copy of the Document, free of added material. If you use the latter option, you must take reasonably prudent steps, when you begin distribution of Opaque copies in quantity, to ensure that this Transparent copy will remain thus accessible at the stated location until at least one year after the last time you distribute an Opaque copy (directly or through your agents or retailers) of that edition to the public.

It is requested, but not required, that you contact the authors of the Document well before redistributing any large number of copies, to give them a chance to provide you with an updated version of the Document.

4. MODIFICATIONS

You may copy and distribute a Modified Version of the Document under the conditions of sections 2 and 3 above, provided that you release the Modified Version under precisely this License, with the Modified Version filling the role of the Document, thus licensing distribution and modification of the Modified Version to whoever possesses a copy of it. In addition, you must do these things in the Modified Version:

A. Use in the Title Page (and on the covers, if any) a title distinct from that of the Document, and from those of previous versions (which should, if there were any, be listed in the History section of the Document). You may use the same title as a previous version if the original publisher of that version gives permission.

B. List on the Title Page, as authors, one or more persons or entities responsible for authorship of the modifications in the Modified Version, together with at least five of the principal authors of the Document (all of its principal authors, if it has fewer than five), unless they release you from this requirement.

C. State on the Title page the name of the publisher of the Modified Version, as the publisher.

D. Preserve all the copyright notices of the Document.

E. Add an appropriate copyright notice for your modifications adjacent to the other copyright notices.

F. Include, immediately after the copyright notices, a license notice giving the public permission to use the Modified Version under the terms of this License, in the form shown in the Addendum below.

G. Preserve in that license notice the full lists of Invariant Sections and required Cover Texts given in the Document's license notice.

H. Include an unaltered copy of this License.

I. Preserve the section Entitled "History", Preserve its Title, and add to it an item stating at least the title, year, new authors, and publisher of the Modified Version as given on the Title Page. If there is no section Entitled "History" in the Document, create one stating the title, year, authors, and publisher of the Document as given on its Title Page, then add an item describing the Modified Version as stated in the previous sentence.

J. Preserve the network location, if any, given in the Document for public access to a Transparent copy of the Document, and likewise the network locations given in the Document for previous versions it was based on. These may be placed in the "History" section. You may omit a network location for a work that was published at least four years before the Document itself, or if the original publisher of the version it refers to gives permission.

K. For any section Entitled "Acknowledgements" or "Dedications", Preserve the Title of the section, and preserve in the section all the substance and tone of each of the contributor acknowledgements and/or dedications given therein.

L. Preserve all the Invariant Sections of the Document, unaltered in their text and in their titles. Section numbers or the equivalent are not considered part of the section titles.

M. Delete any section Entitled "Endorsements". Such a section may not be included in the Modified Version.

N. Do not retitle any existing section to be Entitled "Endorsements" or to conflict in title with any Invariant Section.

O. Preserve any Warranty Disclaimers.

If the Modified Version includes new front-matter sections or appendices that qualify as Secondary Sections and contain no material copied from the Document, you may at your option designate some or all of these sections as invariant. To do this, add their titles to the list of Invariant Sections in the Modified Version's license notice. These titles must be distinct from any other section titles.

You may add a section Entitled "Endorsements", provided it contains nothing but endorsements of your Modified Version by various parties--for example, statements of peer review or that the text has been approved by an organization as the authoritative definition of a standard.

You may add a passage of up to five words as a Front-Cover Text, and a passage of up to 25 words as a Back-Cover Text, to the end of the list of Cover Texts in the Modified Version. Only one passage of Front-Cover Text and one of Back-Cover Text may be added by (or through arrangements made by) any one entity. If the Document already includes a cover text for the same cover, previously added by you or by arrangement made by the same entity you are acting on behalf of, you may not add another; but you may replace the old one, on explicit permission from the previous publisher that added the old one.

The author(s) and publisher(s) of the Document do not by this License give permission to use their names for publicity for or to assert or imply endorsement of any Modified Version.

5. COMBINING DOCUMENTS

You may combine the Document with other documents released under this License, under the terms defined in section 4 above for modified versions, provided that you include in the combination all of the Invariant Sections of all of the original documents, unmodified, and list them all as Invariant Sections of your combined work in its license notice, and that you preserve all their Warranty Disclaimers.

The combined work need only contain one copy of this License, and multiple identical Invariant Sections may be replaced with a single copy. If there are multiple Invariant Sections with the same name but different contents, make the title of each such section unique by adding at the end of it, in parentheses, the name of the original author or publisher of that section if known, or else a unique number. Make the same adjustment to the section titles in the list of Invariant Sections in the license notice of the combined work.

In the combination, you must combine any sections Entitled "History" in the various original documents, forming one section Entitled "History"; likewise combine any sections Entitled "Acknowledgements", and any sections Entitled "Dedications". You must delete all sections Entitled "Endorsements".

6. COLLECTIONS OF DOCUMENTS

You may make a collection consisting of the Document and other documents released under this License, and replace the individual copies of this License in the various documents with a single copy that is included in the collection, provided that you follow the rules of this License for verbatim copying of each of the documents in all other respects.

You may extract a single document from such a collection, and distribute it individually under this License, provided you insert a copy of this License into the extracted document, and follow this License in all other respects regarding verbatim copying of that document.

7. AGGREGATION WITH INDEPENDENT WORKS

A compilation of the Document or its derivatives with other separate and independent documents or works, in or on a volume of a storage or distribution medium, is called an "aggregate" if the copyright resulting from the compilation is not used to limit the legal rights of the compilation's users beyond what the individual works permit. When the Document is included in an aggregate, this License does not apply to the other works in the aggregate which are not themselves derivative works of the Document.

If the Cover Text requirement of section 3 is applicable to these copies of the Document, then if the Document is less than one half of the entire aggregate, the Document's Cover Texts may be placed on covers that bracket the Document within the aggregate, or the electronic equivalent of covers if the Document is in electronic form. Otherwise they must appear on printed covers that bracket the whole aggregate.

8. TRANSLATION

Translation is considered a kind of modification, so you may distribute translations of the Document under the terms of section 4. Replacing Invariant Sections with translations requires special permission from their copyright holders, but you may include translations of some or all Invariant Sections in addition to the original versions of these Invariant Sections. You may include a translation of this License, and all the license notices in the Document, and any Warranty Disclaimers, provided that you also include the original English version of this License and the original versions of those notices and disclaimers. In case of a disagreement between the translation and the original version of this License or a notice or disclaimer, the original version will prevail.

If a section in the Document is Entitled "Acknowledgements", "Dedications", or "History", the requirement (section 4) to Preserve its Title (section 1) will typically require changing the actual title.

9. TERMINATION

You may not copy, modify, sublicense, or distribute the Document except as expressly provided for under this License. Any other attempt to copy, modify, sublicense or distribute the Document is void, and will automatically terminate your rights under this License. However, parties who have received copies, or rights, from you under this License will not have their licenses terminated so long as such parties remain in full compliance.

10. FUTURE REVISIONS OF THIS LICENSE

The Free Software Foundation may publish new, revised versions of the GNU Free Documentation License from time to time. Such new versions will be similar in spirit to the present version, but may differ in detail to address new problems or concerns. See http://www.gnu.org/copyleft/ ↗.

Each version of the License is given a distinguishing version number. If the Document specifies that a particular numbered version of this License "or any later version" applies to it, you have the option of following the terms and conditions either of that specified version or of any later version that has been published (not as a draft) by the Free Software Foundation. If the Document does not specify a version number of this License, you may choose any version ever published (not as a draft) by the Free Software Foundation.

ADDENDUM: How to use this License for your documents

```
Copyright (c) YEAR YOUR NAME.
Permission is granted to copy, distribute and/or modify this document
under the terms of the GNU Free Documentation License, Version 1.2
or any later version published by the Free Software Foundation;
with no Invariant Sections, no Front-Cover Texts, and no Back-Cover Texts.
A copy of the license is included in the section entitled "GNU
Free Documentation License".
```

If you have Invariant Sections, Front-Cover Texts and Back-Cover Texts, replace the "with...Texts." line with this:

```
with the Invariant Sections being LIST THEIR TITLES, with the
Front-Cover Texts being LIST, and with the Back-Cover Texts being LIST.
```

If you have Invariant Sections without Cover Texts, or some other combination of the three, merge those two alternatives to suit the situation.

If your document contains nontrivial examples of program code, we recommend releasing these examples in parallel under your choice of free software license, such as the GNU General Public License, to permit their use in free software.